A Way of Seeing

By *Francis and Edith Schaeffer*

EVERYBODY CAN KNOW

By *Edith Schaeffer*

L'ABRI
HIDDEN ART
CHRISTIANITY IS JEWISH
WHAT IS A FAMILY?
A WAY OF SEEING

Edith Schaeffer

A Way of Seeing

FLEMING H. REVELL COMPANY
OLD TAPPAN, NEW JERSEY

Scripture quotations in this book are based on the King James Version of the Bible.

Excerpts from *TM: Discovering Inner Energy and Overcoming Stress* by Harold H. Bloomfield, Michael Peter Cain, and Dennis T. Jaffe. Copyright © 1975 by Harold H. Bloomfield, Michael Peter Cain, Dennis T. Jaffe. Reprinted by permission of DELACORTE PRESS.

The material in this book was originally published by *Christianity Today* in edited form. This text has been edited and revised by Mrs. Schaeffer.

Library of Congress Cataloging in Publication Data

Schaeffer, Edith.
   A way of seeing.

   1.   Christian life—1960–   —Addresses,
essays, lectures.   I.   Title.
BV4501.2.S293   248′.4   77-4945
ISBN 0-8007-0871-7

Dedicated to my sister Elsa
who has led a life of caring

Contents

8   Contents

An Author's Apology

Anyone who knows me knows that "condensation" does not come naturally to me, nor is "being brief" my talent. When I was asked by *Christianity Today* to write pieces of a limited length, it was a curiously strong challenge. It became a matter of actual excitement to discover how much could be developed in a short space. The discipline of limiting this development to a bare framework became a kind of freedom, rather than a harsh matter of rigid boundaries. At times I felt like flying, as the lightness of having found a new kind of communication became so exhilarating. I had said something I wanted very much to put into understandable communication—and it was short!

Often people ask me, "How can you keep on going so many hours a day?" And *one* area of the "how" is the taking of a variety of little breaks. One special kind of refreshment is to take a glass of milk or a cup of tea to a favorite spot in the house—the chaise lounge in our bedroom—to put myself in a horizontal position, to feel the cared-for feeling, even though no one is waiting on me, to sip my drink, and to read. The danger of doing this with a book which has no stopping place is finding that the allotted twelve minutes has turned into such a long time, that it simply can't be done again—it has spoiled the day's schedule too much. I found that books like James Herriot's not only took me into another area of thought—the vet's world of lambing and cows giving birth, and so on—but also that the chapters were so short that I could count on being able to stop at the end of about twelve minutes.

This book is prepared to give you sixty short breaks. You can take it with you along with a cup of your favorite pickup drink for your low-blood-sugar moments, and put your feet up on your couch, a park bench, a chair in the lunchroom at work, a stool in the empty office nearest you, somewhere on the nearest patch of grass, or even in the washroom. Go to a spot where you can be uninterrupted for a few minutes—and completely change your position, your atmosphere, and your line of thought. The relaxation of a short moment of changed pace and a bit of physical food can be a deeper relaxation with some mental or spiritual food added. You can then go back to your long line of figures to add up, your rows of vegetables to hoe, your tall pile of dishes to wash, your list of phone calls to make, your waiting line of patients to see, your filled room of students to teach, your large number of houses to inspect, your stack of patterns to cut out, your crying baby to feed— whatever your next "thing" is—with a feeling of refreshment and a new train of thought.

The material in these chapters is really in embryo form. It is to be developed in your own thinking and followed through. It is really a book full of seeds for you to plant and watch grow in your own mind. It may sound old-fashioned to say such things as "As a man thinketh, so is he," or "What is in the well of your heart comes up in the bucket of your mouth," but it is very true that what is going on inside in our thoughts and feelings is affecting our conversation and action, as well as making us "who we are becoming." It could be helpful to start the dinner-table conversation with the reading aloud of one of these pieces while others are eating their grapefruit or soup. Another way to use them would be to read one at the end of the meal—as "family devotions" to send everyone off with something to think about and pray about as the family scatters to do the next thing. The Bible's injunction to us concerning the need to "edify one another" deserves some attention and preparation if it is ever to be a practical reality in our times of being together. It is too easy to have all our times of conversation slip by, with no place given to any thought of even trying to steer the communication into channels which would be edifying in any sense of the word. To read aloud something that can be developed in conversation is as important as reading alone and steering one's own thinking into channels of fresh understanding and exploring the practical applications of the Word of God, as well as the worship of God.

However, these chapters are not simply to steer our thinking, impor- tant as our thinking is. Throughout the Word of God there runs the thread which James puts clearly, "But be ye doers of the word, and not hearers only, deceiving your own selves" (James 1:22). James goes on to say that those who only listen and show no change in practical action or "doing" are like one who looks in a mirror and then walks away, forgetting what sort of face was seen there. As we look in a mirror, if we see a face that needs washing, or a dour look that needs a smile so as not to cast gloom on everyone who sees it, we are supposed to do something about it. In verse 25, James goes on to warn us not to be "a forgetful hearer," but "a doer of the work." The deeds that spring forth from examining ourselves in the mirror or the light of the Word of God— which are therefore deeds that come from an attempt to have our actions in line with His teaching—are promised a blessing, as in the last phrase of the verse: ". . . this man shall be blessed in his deed."

These chapters are a weaving of some of the rich threads from God's Word into simple, day-by-day, real-life illustrations. The wide variety of readers—pastors, professors, journalists, teachers, students, secretaries, mothers, fathers, scientists, farmers, and so on—who have written to tell me what the columns in *Christianity Today* have meant to them have shown that people, in asking that these be made into a book to share with friends, have asked for it on the basis of some practical experience in their own lives and of finding a reality of help.

So here it is, in book form, to be carried around and used easily—put by the bed or couch to finish the day with, kept in the dining room for the gathered family, given as a gift to the friend in the hospital who needs short chapters, packed in the luggage for vacation reading in the woods or at the shore, or put along with the schoolbooks for the return to college. Here, in book form, is the kind of thing I stop to share with students who are asking questions while working with me in the garden or kitchen—brief moments while standing on one foot or squatting among the spinach weeding.

The marvel of printing thirty-two pages at once on huge sheets of paper, as modern presses do, is a feat of multiplication which makes me feel the limitations of finite conversation with one person at a time, and is akin to baskets of bread and fish made suddenly available to the five thousand. Since people no longer have to sit and painfully copy books on parchment and hand them about for times of sharing, there needs to be no limit of copies!

Preface

~~~

A Way of Seeing is the most descriptive title possible for this collection of pieces. What has really been collected here is a glimpse of what can go on inside one's head in the very middle of the noise and confusion of life. Day-by-day illustrations float around us like autumn leaves falling in drifts on a clear, breezy day in October. We are apt to see just a blur of leaves and to neglect picking one up and examining it carefully for color, texture, vein tracings, and the individuality which make it different from every other leaf. Events, experiences, happenings, news reports, weather, sickness, the daily grind, vacations, annoyances, interruptions, eating, drinking, washing, sleeping, loneliness, overwhelming numbers of people, things to do, human relationships—day by day fall around us like drifts of falling leaves, brushing us, but with fresh meaning apt to go unnoticed if we have "no eyes to see." We are told, "He that hath eyes to see, let him see," and we need to be praying that we might be "seeing-people" moment by moment in life, rather than "blind-people."

Over a two-and-a-half-year period I have deadlines to meet each two weeks, and the pieces have been written at some very strange times in a great variety of places at whatever moment they had to be written! These are not "ivory tower" selections written from imaginary flights of fancy as to what might be helpful to other people, but have been written from exactly where I myself was at the time. In a way this book is a diary, written during travels and work, in sickness and in health, in eight countries, on a great variety of other people's typewriters, at odd hours in diverse places. Not only have they been written from where I was geographically, but from the reality of where my thinking and feelings were. They are often a record of how the Lord led my thinking and brought to my mind portions of Scripture in combinations which gave me a way of seeing something quite differently, with a fresh comprehension.

"When do you have time to write?" is a frequent question, and to answer it I will simply relate to you when I actually wrote some of the pieces in this book. The one on earthquakes was written between two and four A.M. before leaving at seven for the airport to fly to Canada to speak in Waterloo. I had packed and said proudly to my husband, "Everything is finished and I can actually go to bed now. Two A.M. isn't so bad, is it?" Suddenly I clapped my hand over my mouth to stop a squeal. "Oh, I can't believe it; I have an article due." So I carried my typewriter and paper to the kitchen table and sat in the silence of the night, having just heard the radio's frantic report of the latest news from the Italian earthquake, and began to think through the Bible's way of seeing earthquakes.

Many of these pieces were written during the time when my husband was working on the manuscript for his film series and book *How Should We Then Live?* We were "hidden away" in a quiet hotel, and I wrote the book *What Is a Family?* in another room in between my times of being with Fran to fix lunch, prepare a tea break, take a walk, or just to give him someone with whom he could talk things over. In between writing chapters of my book, came deadline moments for the articles which invariably were remembered at strange hours. My husband always stopped to read each article and check it for me before sending it off—so sometimes they contained what I wanted to share with him very specifically. The one titled "The Security of Insecurity" was written my first day out of bed after a severe accident. I had tripped on a piece of iron grillwork on the sidewalk and had fallen straight onto my rib cage on a very hard sidewalk. Not only did I faint as the air was squashed out, but I had a rib concussion which took a long time to heal. The first three days were spent in bed. Then an article was due, and my mind started with the "security" of my position a moment before the fall, and the sudden change in that one second of time, and went on to the great succession of sudden changes possible. The comfort of God's Word in this area was an excitement to me—even while my ribs were hurting with the movement of typing.

"One God—One People" was written after we had traveled from Canada, expecting to stop for a very short time in Pittsburgh for a gathering of Presbyterian Synods. It was written in a hospital bed from midnight to about three A.M., after my blood tests and so on had been taken, and I had been "prepared" for the night preceding an emergency operation on my knee. I felt quite fit, and the article was due, and I didn't know what I'd feel like *after* the operation, so I wrote what had been in my thoughts as we flew away from Canada. I must say that the nurse who stuck her head in my door to see what I was doing was a bit surprised, but she kindly accepted the fact that I really had to prepare this for the morning mail! As my Bible was open on the bed table beside the borrowed typewriter, a "door" was opened to a conversation in answer to the nurse's questions.

The ride to the hospital had given me a moment of "seeing" the Holy Spirit's place in us in a vividly new way, when we passed the United States Steel building, "The Steel Triangle." As I stuck my head out of the car to gaze up at this impressive building, the explanation was given to me, which you will read in "Poured-In Protection," by a friend who was driving me to the hospital, who had formerly been in that building at the top! Later, on their borrowed typewriter, as I was recuperating from my operation in their home, that article was written where the accuracy of the details could be checked.

"Walled In or Walled Out?" was written right after we had been filming in Pompeii, with the memory of Berlin still fresh in my memory. It was written in Naples where it would have been easy to think of the cruelty of man to man as something in past history, which only the ruined crumbling walls could recall, and yet where the Berlin Wall could not be forgotten as *today's* picture of man. My only relief came in following into the future with the whole thought of walls, with a forward look at the city whose Builder and Maker is God. I sat at the desk of the hotel in Naples, batting away at the typewriter, longing to do something more to help more people be on the right side of the future wall, which I could see so truly in my imagination, in spite of being surrounded simply by four drab and very ordinary hotel-room walls.

We had been driving through marvelous Italian countryside in October's golden sun, with grapevine leaves yellow and red, as well as tree leaves changed into orange, red, and all shades of yellow, mixed in with the dark green of evergreens. As I bumped along in the back of a car, surrounded by filming equipment, I suddenly thought of how "one track" our minds usually are in thinking of harvesttime or Thanksgiving—with all the warm, lovely memories of that time of year. When I actually wrote the piece "What Harvest?" it was the next day. By this time I had developed a fever and flu, and I was "staying in" while the others went to do the day's filming. "In" consisted of a dark room with a tiny window looking out on the back of a building, and the hotel service bell brought only the information that the kitchen was closed on Wednesdays, and there could be no tea, let alone a meal. Pulling a twenty-five-watt lamp over from the bed to shine its dull light on the typewriter, I tried to develop the idea I had had while riding through the wonderful countryside on the way to Aosta. My misery and discomfort were soon pushed out of my thoughts as the Lord gave me a succession of "seeing" a lot that applied to me, as well as to others, in the whole idea of "sowing," and I realized that my sowing that day was to simply stick with it and not give up. Sowing is not a glamorous job at times. It doesn't take place in ideal conditions in any sense of the word, if it is to be done during the "right season."

The day we were in Ghent, Belgium, we had the amazing privilege of looking at van Eyck's *Adoration of the Lamb,* part of which is on the jacket of *How Should We Then Live?*, for over four hours, first as we waited for tourists to go, and then during the filming. It was an unusual opportunity to discover as well as enjoy and fix in one's memory the wonder of that painting, and to marvel over the genius of the man van Eyck way back in 1432! However, there was no place to go to write that day, and even supper was impossible to have until late at night, after which there had to be a fairly long drive to the Dutch location we were to film in the next day. So it was that the piece "God's Greatest Creation" was written in the wee hours of the morning, after packing again to move on. The darkness of that hour, the temporariness of the location, gave an urgency to writing, as if each key were a note on the trumpet! It was almost as if the circus-moves-on kind of life put everything into a more proper perspective than the cosy settled-in-one-place type of living. Isaiah's word in chapter 29 kept going over and over in my mind—connected with the artworks, and then with the Maker of the makers of the artworks. "Surely your turning of things upside down shall be esteemed as the potter's clay: for shall the work say of him that made it, He made me not? or shall the thing framed say of him that framed it, He had no understanding?" (v. 16). I had been growing in appreciation of the greatness of the skill and personaity of Masaccio, Leonardo da Vinci, van Eyck, and others, but I had also been growing in awe of the God who is the Creator. How furious I would be at the slashing scorn of any who would wrongfully attribute one artist's work to another—and I came, on that cold, gray Dutch morning, with the elevator's bang as the only noise, to feel a fury I wanted to blow forth through the meager trumpet of my typewriter against Satan's accusation concerning God's Creation. God made man in His image, God tells us. Satan's sneering voice continues to deny this as thoroughly as he denied God's statement to Adam and Eve. Words tumble out, trumpet notes spill forth, and then . . . . If there has been no hearing, no seeing, a flatness of silence follows. Bags were collected, the elevator's bang was for us, the day had started, cars followed the truck, and my strong emotions were simply folded papers in an envelope. "Where is the nearest post office?"

My husband had started a severe attack of sciatica by carrying a heavy bag in the London airport, and he landed in Paris with a rapidly worsening condition. The next hours on my part were spent in trying to find a doctor and a variety of remedies, as well as food to prepare in the room, and so on. For a time it seemed impossible that my husband would be able to get up and move at all for many days. However, the Deux Magots café had been arranged for, and no more postponing was possible. "If I get an ambulance," said Franky on the second day, "do you think you could go—and just come into the café when it was time for you to speak?" And so my husband attempted it, and the scene is in the film, without anyone knowing what had taken place "behind scenes." I spent the two days that we were in that ambulance, watching that busy corner of Paris and scribbling a description of the people walking by, on the backs of envelopes that were in my bag. Out of it came "Conformed Nonconformists or Transformed Conformists?" written on a desk in that hotel room with its dormer window and sloping ceiling, with me repeatedly hitting my head on the ceiling (for the first time in my life) which had a corner just above me which I could never remember! An ideal writing spot? Not exactly. And it had to double as a "kitchen tale" as I prepared meals for my husband to eat in bed. Several times I wished someone who had asked, "When do you write?" could have peered in just at that time.

January at home in the Swiss Alps is usually a month of snow, cold, and sometimes sun and sparkling peaks against blue skies. Writing at a table in a motel in San Jose in January, the "unusual heat spell"—which was hotter than most of our July days in the Alps—gave time itself an unreality. Not only the confusion of "Where am I?" but the confusion of "What month is it?" tended to blur life during that period. Writing in the hot sunshine which seemed to burn through the sealed windows of our ninth-floor room as if from a desert, I hurried to meet another deadline, perspiring away to finish, yet also full of what to me had been an exciting new "way of seeing" the night before, as we crossed the Golden Gate Bridge. "Illusion or Reality?" was the result of the clarification of certainty as we take it from the only One who can give a promise He can also fulfill, rather than from our own observation.

A few air flights later, in cold Michigan with the view of a half-snow-filled swimming pool from my window, and a wind whipping bits of ice against the window, I again "stayed in" to write. "Trustworthy Analyzing" had been conceived during an air flight as I read a long article on TM and also the review of a book on this subject. We had just a few hours before been in the electronic plant I describe, and the comparative quiet of the lonely time in that place of sudden change, where we had exchanged unseasonal summer weather for unusually cold winter weather, brought together the factors that caused the seed to continue to grow. What a terrific need there is for the *right* device to help us to analyze that which we take into our systems, and how much more dangerous is the poison which can destroy far more than the physical body. It is no wonder that Satan wants to get people to stop using the Bible as a base from which to judge other ideas, and rather to judge the Bible from the base of other ideas! If only someone had been able to quickly analyze the air the Legionnaires were breathing in Philadelphia, what a difference it might have made to all those lives. The speed of *using* the right device, as well as *having* the right device, are matters of life and death. As I wrote, the tiredness, the cold, and the quirks of the borrowed typewriter all faded into the background as unimportant. "If only they can see . . . . If only *we* can see."

When and where did I write? In the hall of a hotel with people walking by—when the room had no proper light; after business hours in a manager's office—when I had no other typewriter; in the TV room of someone's home after others had gone to bed; in the office of another lovely home (served sandwiches and milk on a tray while others were eating lunch); upstairs—when people were arriving for a meal I was supposed to be cooking; or at the kitchen table—when others were sleeping; in a seminary president's home office on his ancient typewriter—when everyone else had gone to the reception; on a train in an empty car; in an airport. Some I wrote on vacations, others on speaking trips—late night, early morning—no pattern as to *when* or *where*.

A Way of Seeing is really more like your stopping in to interrupt me at any time during these past three years—and letting me wipe my dishwater-wet hands on a towel before shaking hands and sitting down on a stool near me—as I talked to let you know what was going on in my head while I scrubbed the pots and pans! It is not really a book, it is a way of seeing life. In our miniscule glimpses of seeing the wonder of the truth of the Word of God, the realization comes that what remains to be seen and understood is endless.

A Way of Seeing

1

Limited or Unlimited?

Oil is limited now. What far-reaching effects this has. Switzerland has banned driving on Sunday, and quiet roads wind down the mountainsides—empty except for walking people or flying birds. City streets are the scene of roller skating and horseback riding. One feels on Sundays as if the clock has turned back to a time before automobiles were known, and people passed each other slowly enough to speak.

But time doesn't turn back, and limitation of one product like oil demonstrates the dependence of a whole culture or civilization on a limitless supply of a variety of things. Come to the end of one thing and many other *things* are affected. But even more than "things," are human beings affected. Suddenly there are no jobs in some industry and like a chain reaction other factories become silent. Depression! Depression within one country, spreading to other countries. "World depression" is an idea in men's imaginations today, a fear in men's hearts, a cold feeling in the pit of men's stomachs. Limited oil, limited energy, limited warmth, limited shelter, limited food, limited transportation, limited supply of every need. What a bleak future men feel they face.

Individuals in the midst of mass limitations are also bowed down, depressed, frustrated, or at least annoyed by their *own* limitations, depending on the vividness of the conscious limitation at the time. People with too much to do are frustrated by the limitation of time. People with too many places they feel they need to go, too many places screaming for them to be there, are frustrated by the limitations of space. People with many talents and ideas, enough to fill twenty-four hours a day, are frustrated by the limitation of energy—by the frailness of the human frame and the constant need of sleep and refreshment. People with a myriad of ideas, but an inability to execute them, are frustrated by a limitation of talent or ability to carry them out. Individuals with a limitation of blood sugar or other purely physical inadequacies are frustrated by a limitation of the smooth functioning of their own bodies. People, suddenly realizing that the sheer passing of weeks, months, and years does make a difference to them personally, are frustrated by the limitations of the qualities they have seemed to have an unlimited supply of during the past. "I can't do what I used to do!" is a surprise limitation which speaks of a limitedness of life as a whole. Limited human beings—and the limitations in various areas—bring about a chain reaction in other human beings, as well as in history. Limited joy, limited peace, limited quiet, limited supply, limited strength, limited interest, all combine to affect not just one, but others whom that one touches.

Why dwell on the gloomy idea of limitedness? First, because it affects every one of us, and second, because there *is* a solution. We have an unlimited God who created a limited universe. There is not an unlimited supply of oil in the ground, and there is not an unlimited supply of energy in a human being. We are dependent upon an unlimited God, who is *able* to supply the desperate needs we each have in a variety of areas.

Paul writes in Philippians 4:19, as God makes real to him the need for us to know: "But my God shall supply all your need according to his riches in glory . . . ." A supply dependent only upon His riches. A supply as varied as our need is varied. A promise from the unlimited Living God to His limited, needy children of every century. What sort of things does He promise to supply? (In this limited space, only a few of His specific promises can be listed.) In this day of empty store shelves, empty oil tanks, and empty gas tanks, consider again the words of Matthew 6:25, 32, 33: "Take no thought for your life, what ye shall eat, or what ye shall drink; nor yet for your body, what ye shall put on . . . . for your heavenly Father knoweth that ye have need of all these things. But seek ye *first* the kingdom of God, and his righteousness; and all these things shall be added unto you." An order is given—first, stop worrying and stop being afraid in the middle of the night. This is a negative order if you like to think of it that way. In the place of worrying, however, a positive action is commanded. So the second thing to *do* is to put *first* the realities of true truth concerning the existence of God and our truly being in His family. This doesn't mean quoting little platitudes to each other, but honestly crying out to God in our need and feeling, as we cry, the wonder of having an unlimited Person to cry to and to come to with our needs. However, in the reality of having someone to come to, the practical outworking of that is meant to be a demonstrable area of putting *Him* first in some way. How? I would say by allowing His interruptions to come first, before our own definite schedule.

We have a deadline to meet in our gathering in the wheat, making the candles, selling the insurance, cooking the meal—whatever is in our today's schedule—and suddenly a phone call, a person at the door, or a letter presents us with an urgent need to give some spiritual help, teach a Bible class, talk on the phone, write a letter, or sit down and talk to someone or give someone a meal. We "spend" our supply of time, energy, ideas, talent, and money for something the Lord has injected into the day, which *could* be either brushed aside as an interruption or recognized as His plan. What do we do? It is in these practical moments when it will cost us time, energy, ideas, money, that we make the decision to put the Kingdom of God FIRST. It is when a factory owner has a choice of making more profit—or being a really loving example to his employees of what a Christian employer can be like in sharing with his workers—that a man has a chance to put the Kingdom of God first. Yes, "seeking first the kingdom of God" does not mean a comfortable giving of a couple of hours a week in church, and writing a check to a "cause," but rather an openness, a sensitiveness to be led by the Lord in ways that interrupt the putting of our own way or interests first— materially, physically, psychologically. There is this *condition* placed upon "all these things" being added to us or provided for us. The third part of the condition is seeking His righteousness.

How can we know anything about His righteousness? We are so very limited in being righteous. We are limited by being "fallen men"—or "fallen people," if you will. His righteousness is perfect, as well as unlimited.

We find that out in Philippians 3:8, 9, as well as in many other places. Think of this the next quiet moment you have—perhaps as you are waiting for a traffic light to change: ". . . I count all things but loss [I count everything as unimportant] . . . that I may . . . be found in him, not having mine own righteousness, which is of the law, but that which is through the faith of Christ, the righteousness which is of God by faith." Tie into your thinking the beautiful picture of the future, in which we are told that one day we are going to stand "faultless before the throne, dressed in His righteousness." We shall be clothed in that which is described in another place as sparkling white linen, the righteousness of Christ. He has given us this to look forward to because He died to make it possible. He took our filthy clothing in exchange for His white linen, at the moment He died to give us the possibility of accepting His death as a free gift to get rid of our sin.

The righteousness which we are meant to be seeking is something He has already supplied for us, an unlimited supply. He has told us that His strength is made perfect in weakness, and that His grace is sufficient for us. This was given to Paul after he had asked that a "thorn in the flesh" be removed. The answer God gives His children is always a real answer. Sometimes that answer is the supplying of the actual thing asked for, specifically and definitely. At other times the answer is the supplying of grace to bear the thorn—quietness in the middle of a continuing storm, victory in the middle of a continuing battle, comfort in the midst of a continuing sorrow. It is, however, when we *ask* the One who has the supply in an unlimited way that the answer is given which provides what we need at the moment. We need not continue our depression, frustration, or annoyance, as we are caught by a limited supply—spiritually, physically, materially. Middle of the night, or while waiting for the traffic light: Don't worry anxiously, but in *everything* by prayer and supplication with thanksgiving, do let your request (for any limitation) be made known unto God. And *then* the peace of God which passes the understanding of yourself—others watching, demons waiting for you to be destroyed, angels watching to see if you'll have a victory—will keep your fearful heart and your mind that fills so easily with nagging worries. And it will all be through Christ Jesus— the Christ who is the Second Person of the *unlimited Trinity*.

2

What Is a Father?

Unhappily, the word *father* has a garbled sense to many people of this century. It needs redefinition—not just in words, but in understanding and in day-by-day life. People may shiver a bit or stiffen up inside when you say that God is a Father to us. Often the word *father* has a negative emotion connected with it that has grown out of thinking of *father* as the definition of a person with whom there is no communication, who cannot understand one's thoughts, feelings, or actions, and who must be avoided or from whom one must run away. Without realizing it, people transfer to God the imperfections and even the sins of earthly fathers they have known. Even Christians often portray the very opposite qualifications to what a father is supposed to be, and give their children a warped response to the word. A fact which is lost sight of is that time is relentless, and the person who has reacted against the *word* for father, and the *concept* of father may suddenly be a father himself. Where is his pattern? How can either he or his children know when the pattern is being followed or deviated from?

It is all backwards when a torn pattern—a spoiled pattern—is followed and handed down year after year, and people forget what the original pattern was like. It is all backwards when men turn from God because they can't stand the word *father* and thus attribute wrong things to God. The "Everlasting Father" is also the "Prince of Peace." When He came, Jesus said, "He that hath seen me hath seen the Father." But the Father, as Jesus demonstrated Him to men, is the same One who promised in Jeremiah 31:9: "They shall come with weeping, and with supplications will I lead them: I will cause them to walk by the rivers of waters in a straight way, wherein they shall not stumble: for I am a father to Israel . . . ."

A father is meant to be one to whom his children come when they are in trouble or deep sorrow, to whom his children run when they are being pursued by an enemy, and to whom they come for shelter from any variety of storm. A father is supposed to be a person who can be trusted to understand and care, who will listen to any kind of communication when others turn away. Listen to David as he speaks in Psalm 61: "Hear my cry, O God; attend unto my prayer. From the end of the earth will I cry unto thee, when my heart is overwhelmed: lead me to the rock that is higher than I. For thou hast been a shelter for me, and a strong tower from the enemy. I will abide in thy tabernacle for ever: I will trust [take refuge] in the covert of thy wings. Selah" (vv. 1–4).

A father should be the first one the child would think of communicating with when overwhelmed by physical woes, psychological problems, confusing philosophies, conflicting ideas as to what to do next. A father is meant to be a shelter. A shelter shuts out wind, rain, ice, cold, heat, sand, pursuing mosquitoes, or armies of men. A father is meant to be a strong tower of protection. The very word father should conjure up a feeling of safety and security. The shelter of God the Father shuts out dangers but also shuts one *in* to the realities of fulfillment. The fulfillment pictured by a family around a fireside—communicating and sharing ideas as well as experiences in an atmosphere of warmth and caring—is meant to picture in a minimal way the perfection of God's fatherliness in being ready to listen and advise, give counsel and guidance. "In His presence is fullness of joy." We are told that an eagle flies under the baby eaglets in order to catch them if they fall while learning to fly. In this way, God pictures the ready refuge we may expect from Him. He not only is ready to gather us under His wings to shelter us from dangers, but He cares enough to stay close, as the eagle flies directly under, in order to be ready when the moment comes. This is a far cry from the father who waits to pounce upon his child's every mistake and to make the child fear to be anywhere near the father when he falls. God's perfect fatherliness is one of loving care, realizing that falls will come. When is a child to learn that this is what a father is? What pattern is the child to have when he becomes a father—and a new generation is suddenly using the same word *father*—with what connotation?

Too often "discipline" is all the word *father* means to some people. The right discipline is to be so *fair* that Jesus causes fathers to stop and think before acting, as when He says through Paul: "Fathers provoke not your children to wrath" (Ephesians 6:4). Fairness in the relationship of father and child is designed to produce a tremendous admiration and appreciation, rather than wrath and separation.

God the Father shows us clearly that a father is meant to be the one person who can always be counted on to *care*. "I will never leave thee nor forsake thee"—"He that cometh unto me I will in no wise cast out"—"I will guide thee to the end." The caring—materially, physically, spiritually, emotionally—that the Heavenly Father gives is in keeping with His being the Everlasting Father. Earthly fathers are finite and limited, but the caring is to be for as long as the father lives. Compassion, love, concern, and true caring are not to be terminated at a certain age. A father-son, parent-child relationship has a pattern to follow which indicates that it is not to be diminishing in reality as years go on, but increasing in depth and closeness—increasing in understanding and true communication.

God as our Heavenly Father has promised not only to supply all our needs according to His riches in glory, but has told us that He wants us to ask specifically for special things, to make our requests known to Him. Part of the pattern given as to what a father is to be is that of providing with love and imagination the needs of the child, for his or her joy, as well as his or her best good. The pattern of the perfect father includes an open ear to requests and a delight to respond to specific desires made known to him. Of course the answer is sometimes "No!" or "Wait!" but there must be many times of demonstrating love, concern, understanding, and compassion by answering with a provision of what was asked for.

The word *father* should bring a tremor of real excitement in the assurance that this one is making hidden preparations for the future. Jesus has said He is going to prepare a place for His own. In Hebrews 11:16 we are told that God is not ashamed to be called our God, because He has prepared for us a city. Our Heavenly Father is in the midst of preparing fantastic surprises for His children while they are suffering difficulties now. An earthly father, in requiring difficult things of his children at certain moments, should at the same time be planning and preparing the wonderful summer vacation together, the special trip alone with one child in special need, the camping trip to the mountains or seaside. The word *father* should bring thoughts of one who is full of marvelous plans for the joy of his children—little joys day by day: the lunch together, the walk in the woods together, the game together, the book enjoyed together, as well as plans for longer periods of special fulfillment ahead.

The pattern we are given of what a father should be includes availability. God is infinite as well as personal, and so we have the completely available Father at all times. Fatherliness in a human being must include availability to the best of the man's limited possibility. Our Heavenly Father is strong. The word *father* should give one a sense of strength. Strength can be depended upon in the need for protection, but God says He will share the strength of which He speaks: "My strength is made perfect in weakness." An earthly father cannot share strength in this unique way, but he is meant to remember to try to share his strength for the child's good in the child's weakness, not to use his strength to bully the weaker one.

All this can *not* be perfect in an imperfect man. But this, and more, is the pattern to be followed, and there is to be a recognizable likeness to this pattern in a Christian father if a child is to grow up with any idea of what the sentence *God is our Father* means. If you have never *had* such a father, determine by God's strength to *be* one. Throw away the spoiled pattern and look to the Perfect Pattern.

And if you are inclined towards Women's Lib, consider for a while what a shattering thing you are doing to the next generation by trying to erase all possibility of men being true fathers. God is a God of diversity as well as of unity. Human beings are equally important and significant, but not alike. One of the basic differences is that of masculine and feminine creatures. Blur them and the blur blots out both fathers and mothers so thoroughly that the question "What is a father?" becomes a genuine one born out of ignorance—ignorance of knowledge and experience.

3

Who Do We Think We Are?

People's minds are so quick to jump into a position of judgment of others, feeling that they are secure on some sort of platform from which they look down. Somehow the very spelling out of another person's faults or failings seems to separate the one speaking—or thinking— from being included in the searchlight of inspection. It is easier to hide from one's own memories of faults, failings, sins, and shortcomings when one is in the middle of accusing someone else. It is a form of "passing the buck" when a person's thoughts can be entangled with dark accusations and doubts of another's actions or motives, and thus freed from questioning one's own actions or motives.

In Romans, Paul speaks of this sort of thing with tremendous force: "Therefore thou art inexcusable, O man, whosoever thou art that judgest: for wherein thou judgest another, thou condemnest thyself; for thou that judgest doest the same things" (Romans 2:1). Like a whiplash this strikes each one who will listen. When we wallow in judgment of others, we are condemning ourselves. The things we so piously pick out to judge, gathering the skirts of our minds and emotions around us like a protective blanket, are the very things which God says will come around and hit us. "And thinkest thou this, O man, that judgest them which do such things, and doest the same, that thou shalt escape the judgment of God?" (v. 3).

These are sobering words. To think of judging other human beings and thus being in the position of condemning oneself, point by point, is a fearful thought. We too easily push this away from our minds and conversations and carelessly indulge in outlining lists that could be presented to us in a different context—when suddenly we are the ones to be judged, rather than the judge!

With whatever measure of reality this forces us to stop and consider our relationships with other human beings, and our slipping into the place of the Pharisee, there is another kind of judgment and criticism which is far, far worse.

Over and over again one hears people say, "I can't believe in a God who would have only one way to approach Him. What about the heathen nations? What about other religions and philosophies? God cannot be a loving God or a compassionate God, if He allows people to be lost." Yes, unbelievers use as an excuse not to come to God the fact that they believe they have within their *own* minds and hearts a more compassionate and loving attitude, feeling, and action toward the people of history, than God does. They set themselves up to criticize God, the Creator of the Universe and the Infinite Personal Trinity, feeling as they judge God that they would have not only a better plan, but also a greater love, compassion, and justice. It is a titanic thing to think of the lack of awe and fear on the part of a finite, miniscule creature—with a span of background which could not be more than one century of his own lifetime—presuming to judge the Eternal God so lightly and easily, rather than seeking to discover something of the marvel of the love of God, the wonder of His compassion—which is compassion not for friends but for enemies. Natural man is at enmity against God. That is, man is really an enemy of God before he becomes a child of God through what Jesus the Lamb did for him in taking his punishment. The love of God is such that the Second Person of the Trinity died for enemies! This is a love which man cannot fathom.

However, it is not just those who are non-Christians, atheists, or people caught in false religions who set themselves up to judge the compassion and love of God. Christians often slip into thinking and feeling that they have more love, more compassion—more willingness to suffer for other people's sake, more sensitivity to the world's sorrows, more hate of the ugliness of the spoiled universe, more agony over the results of sin and the abnormal world, more willingness to do something costly to themselves, more ideas as to a solution which would help more people—than God. Perhaps Christians don't put this into a clear outline in their own minds and feelings. But in conversation, that which is in the wells of their hearts comes out in the buckets of their verbalized questions and doubts. The dark doubt in many Christians' minds is a form of judging God. The murky fear in many Christians' times of aloneness is a form of criticizing God. To judge and to criticize is to set oneself up as at least equal, if not above, the one being criticized. How dare we!

We should pray with David in Psalms 86:15: "But thou, O Lord, art a God full of compassion, and gracious, longsuffering, and plenteous in mercy and truth," and mean it, asking for a greater trust of His compassion as being infinitely greater than ours.

We should be careful in our thinking, as well as in our conversation, to remember that we are responsible for the attitude of the next generation—to remember that our carelessness is affecting this next generation, and we have responsibility.

> One generation shall praise thy works to another, and shall declare thy mighty acts . . . . They shall abundantly *utter* the memory of thy great goodness, and shall *sing* of thy righteousness. The Lord is gracious, and *full of compassion;* slow to anger, and of *great mercy* . . . . The Lord is righteous in *all* his ways, and holy in *all* his works. The Lord is nigh unto all them that call upon him, to all that call upon him in truth.
>
> Psalms 145:4, 7, 8, 17, 18

How can we set ourselves up to criticize, judge, look down upon the Infinite Holy God who is perfect in His love and justice? Just who do we think we are? Such thoughts should send us to our knees, if not literally then inwardly, to worship the God who has made us in His image, with compassion as a part of *our* makeup—but with a fraction of love and compassion giving us only an inkling of His perfect, eternal, and limitless love and compassion.

And if we are troubled with agony over the lostness of the world, if we are sleepless at night because of the suffering, what should the solution be? First, a realization that God has given us access to Him through communication. We are not allowed to criticize, but to come asking, pleading, interceding for others. We are given the possibility of affecting the history of others through our prayer and our willingness to be involved. Rather than simply weeping, we should weep *and* pray, asking that God would use us in some very real way in this moment of history.

Second, we should recognize that our "feelings" should give us compassion towards God. If we suffer because of other people's suffering, we can understand in a small way how Jesus cried, "O Jerusalem, Jerusalem . . . how oft would I have gathered you under my wings as a mother hen her chickens, but ye would not!" (*See* Matthew 23:37.) We can understand in a tiny way Jesus' anger and hatred of the sin which destroyed life as He wept at the tomb of Lazarus.

Then we should come to Lamentations 3:21–23 and pray with the writer of these weepings as we say to God, "This I recall to my mind, therefore I have hope. It is of the Lord's mercies that we are not consumed, because *his compassions fail not.* They are new every morning: *great* is thy faithfulness."

Our Judge is compassionate beyond our imagination. *Trust* His compassion and love—first for ourselves and then for those for whom we long. When we slip into the area of judging God, literally stop and ask: "Who do we think we are?" Ask this not of another person but of ourselves.

4

The Most Dangerous Pollution of All

Many of the world's beaches look romantically beautiful at sunset or in the light of the moon. The gorgeous streak of apricot light comes through the turquoise and green of water to one's feet, as sun dips into the sea. The silver path crosses darkening water and lights up the white froth of waves as the moon's beauty lends enchantment to the rough twists of cedar—or, if you are elsewhere in the world, to the fronds of palms moving in the breeze. Nothing seems to have been changed for centuries. *Still* the breathtakingly pure beauty of Creation!

Ah—but in the relentless glare of the noonday sun, the pollution of plastic mingled with oil shows up in ugly drifts at the edge of the waves. The lovely feel of sand is so mixed with sticky blobs of greasy tar that not only are fingers soiled with brown-black smears, as bits of leaf or stone are picked up and scraped against the offending gummy wads of icky stuff on one's feet, but later the air is filled with some sort of benzine—as no water can budge the heavy stains, and a perfumed bath is *not* the answer.

Pollution! Pollution: spoiling, marring, and staining beauty of sight and smell—and even the beauty of hands and feet and bodies which in past days could run, walk, lie, and be buried up to the neck in this same sand. Pollution: spoiling a certain kind of pleasure and freedom. Pollution: changing and limiting the former fulfillment of a day at the beach.

Ugliness is not the most serious result of pollution, however, nor is discomfort, nor is disappointment. The deception (covered up by moonlight and sunset and separation of distance), which is discovered in the noonday sun, is bad enough when it results in spoiling a long-awaited vacation, but is less serious than pollution, which is more skillfully deceptive and more disastrous in results.

Polluted air can be a gradual thing, and—as one day follows another with slight difference and unnoticeable change—whole cities full of people can be breathing a certain amount of poison so destructive that some become ill, and others even die as a direct result of the variety of lung problems which arise. Unless someone could strain the air through fine white cloth, leaving a visible stain, no one might be able to realize how thoroughly the air was polluted. It would be hard to compare the polluted air with fresh air, if people had never breathed fresh air.

Polluted food and drinking water can be deceptive to the point that poison can be taken into the body without recognizing its presence. A prolonged time of taking poison into the body could be unnoticed if there were no people pointing out the dangers or testing the contents of the food and water. If people have no pure food and water to use as a comparison, they are not apt to question that there might be a connection between their illnesses of one kind and another and the food and drink they are taking into their systems. Death can be a result of the illnesses which result from polluted food and water. But there is a shrug of the shoulders among many kinds of people in many parts of the world, because the only possible answer seems to be a shrug of the shoulders. What else *is* there to eat and drink? What else *is* there to breathe?

But there is a pollution more to be feared than polluted beauty, polluted swimming water, and ruined sand castles—more to be feared than polluted air, dangerous drinking water, poisoned food. The extreme results of shorter life spans—death of fish, animals, and people—are *not* the most disastrous results of pollution.

There is another pollution, the most dangerous of all, the pollution of true truth, the pollution of the absolute Word of God, the pollution of the Bible. Insidiously, there is a dangerous pollution going on, sometimes with delicate deception. The music and the light through the stained glass seem the same. Phrases seem the same. Only a little is removed: a word there, a meaning somewhere else. This portion is deleted from history and changed into myth or parable. That portion is turned away from as unimportant, open to question. The early part of Genesis is treated with a shrug, and the reality of God's speaking in the Epistles is dismissed with a phrase attributing what is being taught only to the man who is writing. *Infallibility* is a word that becomes suddenly an embarrassment, and Satan whispers, "Hath God said?"— over and over again in different tones of voice and with fresh sneers, as he speaks *not through a serpent* but through pastors, professors, teachers who lend themselves to Satan's twisting of the Word of God. Satan twisted God's Word to Adam and Eve: "Hath God said? God hath not said—ye shall surely *not* die" (*see* Genesis 3:1–4). And as Satan polluted the verbalized spoken teaching of God to the first man and woman, so he has continued to pollute the written Word, the Bible, from one moment of history to another.

One disastrous way in which pollution of the Bible takes place is when people no longer teach as *true* the areas of the Bible that deal with history and science, but leave people with a floating religiosity.

In this moment of extreme concern on the part of some people for pollution of other created things meant for our daily enjoyment but in danger of now harming us, we need to be made aware that the purity of the teaching of the Bible is the most important purity of all. Poisoned translations, poisoned teaching, poisoned writing, poisoned preaching, poisoned commentaries, and poisoned Sunday-school lessons take the pure Word of God and pollute it so that people are "breathing, eating, and drinking" polluted spiritual air, food, and water. The resulting death is eternal, not merely a shortening of this life. This is the most dangerous pollution of all. Matthew 10:28 gives us Jesus' strong warning, "And fear not them which kill the body, but are not able to kill the soul: but rather fear him which is able to destroy both soul and body in hell."

God is so fair, because He carefully warns us that there is danger in tampering with the specificness and completeness of His Word. In the final chapter of the Bible there is warning against adding anything to God's Book, and against taking away anything from the words of this prophecy. In Second Peter, we are told that the Scripture is "a more sure word of prophecy" than even the audible voice these men heard with their ears. We are warned to ". . . take heed, as unto a light that shineth in a dark place, until the day dawn, and the day star arise in your hearts: Knowing this first, that no prophecy of the scripture is of any private interpretation. For the prophecy came not in old time by the will of man: but holy men of God spake as they were moved by the Holy Ghost" (2 Peter 1:19–21). We are being warned that the Bible is the light that shows us, in the midst of the darkness of men's words, what true truth is, and that it is the Word of God which judges, which gives light—rather than men who add polluted additions, or deplete portions of meaning by critically subtracting, even as the subtraction of algae from the sea destroys the ecological balance of oxygen in the air! We are told that God has spoken, and we are meant to have His Word in a pure form.

John 20:31 states to us very forcibly: "But these are written, that ye might believe that Jesus is the Christ, the Son of God; and that believing ye might have life through his name." The result of knowing not only the Gospel of John, but the complete Bible, is having sufficient knowledge and understanding to believe that true truth is true, and acting upon that belief to have *life* through Jesus Christ. This One is the Bread of Life, and the Water of Life. He is to be our atmosphere as we live in His presence. How? We are told that by abiding in Him, and having His word abide in us, we are prepared to be in His presence, ready for communication. Jesus prays in John 17:17: "Sanctify them through thy truth: thy word is truth," as He intercedes for us. But there are clear warnings that false prophets, unfaithful shepherds, and pastors who "scatter my flock" are to be avoided and not allowed to pollute the direct Word of God to us.

Can't we see that it has never been different? The Word of God is pure, it is true, it doesn't change—but there has been no time in history when someone has not been deceived by Satan and then stepped into the place of trying to pollute God's Word for others so that they would be destroyed unawares.

Don't step into the gucky black waste oil that spoils the beauty of your walk with the Lord. Beware of the *polluted* Bible in any form. Heed God's warning—that you and your children might live eternally.

5

⊂∾ ∾⊃

"Meditation" or Meditation?

We hear a lot about meditation these days. People learn eagerly to sit in just the right position—toes curled up over their thighs, hands at rest in the lotus position, palms up, shoulders relaxed, breathing deeply, pulling in their abdomens, exhaling in exactly the proper rhythm. Perhaps it will come soon. "Meditation." Some learn to slow down their heartbeat and triumphantly announce that it came to such a slow rate it was negligible. Others help along the arrival of meditation by taking some sort of powdered chemical substance into the stomach. Yet others smoke with what they feel is correct puffing of various plant substances, and with clouded eyes and minds wait for the great meditation to commence. Mystical, cloudy, floating, unreal—separated from earthly sequence of logical thought, separated from understanding and answers to questions, separated from verbalized explanations— modern meditation drifts in ebb and flow with no defining framework. Blurred, misty, with no sharp lines is this meditation. A student in an American seminary writes a friend firmly, "Don't mention the word *prayer* to me anymore. We don't pray. We meditate. Often we find it is necessary to smoke pot to meditate properly." A pastor in Sweden selects certain nights of the month to teach the accompanying bodily positions for Transcendental Meditation. A church opens its doors in an eastern American city for serious lectures on this subject. Meditation—a mélange of mystical, mythical, baseless peace—a state separated from the interruptions of reality—a state in which one can float into an "experience" of some vague sort.

What is the word *meditation* supposed to mean to us, as those who have come into communication with the Living God through the One Way He has opened up into His presence? What does the Bible teach us—born-again children in the family of the Living God—about meditation? *Is* there a difference? Are we in danger of being drawn into something false without understanding the difference?

We need to look at a few verses to see. Psalms 119:97: "O how love I thy law! it is my meditation all the day." Here is no special position in which to put the body, for this meditation is taking place all the day, during the time in which normal daily life is being lived. Here is no empty mind, no slowed-down pulse—but a mind filled with the content of God's law. What is being referred to as "thy law"? Not the Ten Commandments in stark outline, but the full verbalized richness of the Scripture's explanation of the commands of God. Oh, how I love the Scriptures, the true Word of God, as I read it and think about it and come to fresh understanding day by day. Never do I come to the end of the possibility of meditating upon *that*. Sentence by sentence, phrase by phrase, idea after idea, and understanding after understanding drop into the fertile, tilled ground of my mind, and, as I dwell in conscious thought, the seeds of God's law and God's teaching burst and send forth shoots of green understanding that I can put into words of my own. All the day long, as I walk in fields or city streets, as I sit at the typewriter or make a bed with fresh sheets, as I converse with professors or tiny eager human beings wanting to learn—three-year-olds with endless questions—as I work in a lab or scrub a floor all day long in office or factory, I can meditate upon the law, the Word of God which my eyes have read or my ears have heard or my fingers have felt in Braille. This meditation has a base, a changeless base which is as meaningful as it was centuries ago—and as true.

Then on to verse 99: "I have more understanding than all my teachers: for thy testimonies are my meditation." *How* can I have more understanding as a child, as a primary-school or high-school person or a university student? By meditating upon the testimonies of God! The Bible is the place where we can have enough content to give us understanding which is complete in being true. What we meditate upon—as we read day by day and think about what we read—gives us understanding beyond whatever of man's knowledge we are being taught which may cut across this understanding. We understand with our minds full of things to understand. We do not understand with empty, vague, drifting feelings changing with the weather. A foggy day brings depressed feelings—but the facts being thought about and dwelt upon in one's mind are not affected by weather changes. The admonition to meditate during a lifetime upon the content of God's Word is not an airy, fairy thing, nor a thing which is reserved for older and more brilliant times of life. Listen to Paul's admonition to Timothy in 2 Timothy 3:14–16 "But continue thou in the things which thou hast learned and hast been *assured* of, knowing of whom thou hast learned them . . . . From a child thou hast known the holy scriptures . . . . All scripture is given by inspiration of God, and is profitable . . . for instruction in righteousness." Yes, meditation—with the content of the Bible in one's mind in order to understand further—is possible from childhood to old age, and can give understanding of what really is true in the universe and in oneself, beyond any human teacher.

Yes, all the day and throughout the days of my life, I am to meditate at certain times of need—even in the wee hours when others are sleeping. "Mine eyes prevent the night watches, that I might meditate in thy word." Here in Psalms 119:148 we are given the picture of one being unable to sleep and using that time to meditate *in* the Word of God. In comfortable bed with the bedside light on, in the hospital ward with pain or fears making sleep impossible, in long times of waiting for news when sleep will not come, in prison where cold floor and hideous odors drive sleep away, we can and must meditate in the Word of God, the Bible—His true truth which gives us what we need to know for comfort and direction. God is communicating to us as we think for periods of time upon what He has given in written form. It is in this way that our help comes from Him time after time.

In Psalms 63:6, 7 David makes this more vivid to our understanding: "When I remember thee upon my bed, and meditate on thee in the night watches. Because thou hast been my help, therefore in the shadow of thy wings will I rejoice." Here, if we follow David in our times of worry about violent death, rise and fall of governments, taxes larger than our incomes, we meditate rather than worry. Meditate upon God. But God is not just a word, a misty idea of our own—we have His Word telling us who He is. We read of His Creation and power, we read of all He has done in centuries gone by, and we can meditate upon Him and the help He has been through the ages, and the help He has been to us individually, too. And the reality of being in the protective shadow of His wings becomes so clear that before the time is over a real rejoicing follows. How seek comfort in the "white hours of night worries"? By meditating in the Word of the One who we suddenly remember is really *there.*

Then in Joshua 1:8, God speaks to Joshua and to all of us as we read the next day's frightening news in the paper. God has said, "Be strong and of good courage" just before this. Joshua is faced with leadership in a very difficult moment. He is weak in his human limitations and finiteness. What is the *practical* admonition and advice given before the direct guidance is unfolded? "This *book* of the law shall not depart out of thy mouth; but thou shalt *meditate* therein day and night, that thou mayest observe to *do* according to all that is written therein: for then thou shalt make thy way prosperous, and then thou shalt have good success." Joshua and you and I are told as clearly as human verbalization can make clear to a mind—that is not spoiled by breakdown of some kind—that we are to read and know the content of the Bible and then constantly *meditate* upon it, so that, as we speak, the true truth will come out in words others will hear and understand. How can Joshua or any one of us *do* God's will if we don't know the base of His law, His teaching, His character, His history? We have been given sufficient preparation in order to be ready to understand His will and then to do it. But what we *do* is to be action based on that which has been written in human language, understandable to brains which can think and follow sentence after sentence during times of meditation. *Doing* God's will, action based on God's teaching, will follow after a person meditates— hour by hour, day by day, year by year—upon that which God has carefully given and protected so that it might be available to anyone.

Is there a difference? Is there danger in trying out the wrong kind of meditation? Yes, there is danger. Satan's traps are sharp steel which tear the flesh of those who pull away! *Both* kinds of meditation cannot take place in one portion of time. One kind drives out the other! Which meditation will we have? How precious is our time? How serious is it to waste minutes, hours, days, when God has so clearly commanded us to do that which is a solution to our deepest needs? How much other time exists apart from "day and night"? Meditate day and night that you can *know, do, rejoice,* and have success spiritually and in God's plan for you. What a promise! What a direction! Which meditation will you choose?

6

Safe Storage or Sure Loss?

News magazines and newspapers scream at us with headlines predicting worldwide depression. An anxious scrutiny of the stock reports shows a general decline in value. The tiny box telling the exchange value of the money of our country shows a drop which makes money for travel worth a fraction of what it once was. Prices soar, and rice, margarine, and dried beans have little tags on them which seem like a week-by-week joke as new packages are brought home and put on the shelf beside those purchased weeks before for half the amount of money. Rumors float around by word of mouth as to what might be a safe thing to do with cash, as to what land might be a good investment, as to how to protect what one has.

Have you ever had moths get into the drawer of your best sweaters and lay a series of eggs on cashmere, only to find that your discovery came too late, and the lovely soft warmth knitted in your favorite pattern is now merely a rag of ugly lacy holes? Have you had what looked like strong wood in a house wall be discovered to be only soft, wet pulp because of years of leaks from rusty pipes—or have you come upon the telltale line of sawdust left at the edge of a wall when termites spew out the waste as they eat their way through to hollow out beams?

What *is* safe? How can we feel secure? Mugging is common in many American cities. So many people have been hit on the head and had their bags stolen. So many have found themselves in an elevator with a person bent on attack. Twisted ideas of idealism cause modern Robin Hoods to turn into violent criminals with little real accomplishment of any relief to the "oppressed," but with a great display of oppression of innocent bystanders. "Riches" stored up in banks, stocks, or even in bags on one's person are very literally a source of concern and worry for people in many parts of the world today.

As we look into the Bible, our source for practical knowledge of what to do day by day and how to live according to God's specific advice, we are hit by the truth of how well God knows us, as well as the definiteness of His commands. We can't one day say, "Why didn't You *tell* us?" He has told us so clearly, but we are so often blind and deaf, or we let words flow over us like rain—feeling the fresh, cooling drops, putting our tongue out to catch a drop or two, then shaking ourselves and getting a towel to rub dry, and we are free of any effects. Words—words—words—like drops of water or music, pleasant but temporary in effect. The Word of God is *not* meant to be like that. If it is not cutting us deep, sharper than a two-edged sword, then we have not really listened or seen.

Look, listen to Proverbs 23:4, 5: "Labour not to be rich: cease from thine own wisdom. Wilt thou set thine eyes upon that which is *not?* For riches certainly make themselves wings; they fly away as an eagle toward heaven." What a description of today. How up-to-date the warning. The stocks which suddenly are "not," because they have dropped to half the value. The bank accounts which suddenly are "not," because taxes have diminished them or money exchange has dropped. The rise of prices which causes the money in one's handbags to suddenly be "not," because it cannot pay for half of what one expected to buy. Oh, yes, people are daily clutching with their eyes and with their hands that which is "not," which is suddenly going to turn into ashes in the midst of the clutch. "Riches make themselves wings"—what a description of the ratio of income and taxes, disappearing income and suddenly-breaking depression. The more riches one has, the greater the flight. Picture stocks, bonds, bank accounts, and incomes suddenly rising as a flock of birds going south—taking wing. God has warned His people for centuries. God has meant His people to be aware of the trap of spending *time* like a crazy spendthrift, a drunken sailor. The people who pride themselves on being prudent and wise about money are so often spending the precious commodity of *time* figuring out how to clip the wings of their riches, to keep them from flying away—and they are going to fail; so God warns! Riches certainly will make themselves wings! Time must be spent wisely because we have only a certain measure of it and no more. Riches may seem to increase—but what good does it do? What then *are* we supposed to do in order to "cease from thine own wisdom" in this area?

Come to the man in Luke to whom God said, as he was drawing up blueprints of safe storehouses for his riches: "Thou fool, this night thy soul shall be required of thee: then whose shall those things be, which thou hast provided? So is he that layeth up treasure for himself, *and is not rich toward God*" (Luke 12:20, 21). Jesus does not leave His disciples or us pondering what on earth He means when He says this. He goes on to be very explicit about what it means to be rich toward God. Turn to Luke and read on. Read Luke 12:15–34 and think about it as if you had never seen it before. Think about it in relationship to the stock-market report, and the tax bill. What *are* we to worry about? Anything? What are our minds to be full of to replace worry? He gives us things to fill our minds, not a vacuum!

We are to take no time to worry about tomorrow's prices, what we are going to eat or to put on our bodies. We have been given the birds to think about. Look out the window, go into the woods, watch the birds. They fly, they eat, they have glossy wings which God has provided for them. We are to measure ourselves and think for a while as to how we can't be taller by trying to plan it. That should hit us with the realization that our powers aren't very great in any area. We are to think about the flowers. Walk in an Alpine field if you can; look at daisies, violets, gentians, wild roses. Look at pictures if you can't get near the flowers. Think awhile about the fact that God designed these diverse textures and colors as "clothing." "Oh," says Jesus, "how small is your faith if you can't trust with specific reality [even with excitement] this same Person to clothe you." Verse 29 shows us that He wants us to think not about a coming depression and how it might affect our daily need of food and drink. We are not to be "doubtful" or worried as the world would worry. If we lose everything, we are not to react in an anxious way. Why? Because here is a practical place for us to demonstrate to Satan, the demons, the angels, the "nations" (all the people who are not in the family of the Lord) that we really do believe the truth of true truth in a *practical* way. We are to remember that the difference will show up in remembering that our Heavenly Father knows we have need of these material things and that he will "add" them to us, if we put first things first. And what is first? "But rather seek ye first the kingdom of God." (*See* vv. 30, 31.)

How? Again we are given *one* area of practical direction. How can I know God's will? In one area it is surely clear enough—in the area of material things. I am, in a very specific way, to share what I have. I am to "lose my life in order to save it"—but I am also to give away my money in order to save it. The early church did this to such an extent that there were no people in want among them. They bought shoes and food for each other, they stopped worrying about hoarding against times ahead, and really tried to be practical about what Jesus had said, as recorded for us in Luke.

"Provide yourselves with bags which wax not old" (see v. 33). What marvelous bags are these? When we give as unto the Lord, feeding the hungry, clothing the naked, sharing with people we see daily, as well as giving so that the Word of God might go forth—suddenly we have saved all that much in special bags that are forever new and cannot be snatched! But more is said. It is not just in a supernaturally safe bag. But this actual dollar, franc, cash, yen, florin, this actual money, so Jesus says, when given away is now stored in heaven. We can actually put treasures in heaven which will very practically be discovered to *be* there someday! No one needs to be "poor" this way, but Jesus says that some will be. The widow, Jesus pointed out, who put her "all" in the box, had given far more than the gold of the Pharisees, because of the *proportion*. The treasures in heaven are proportionate. The sharing which Jesus is talking about is proportionate, but the results will be proportionate, too. Results in heaven? Yes. The Bible says so. Results now, too, however—for "Where your treasure is, there will your heart be also" (v. 34).

Wait a minute. Be quiet in some hidden place in the woods or alone in a room. *Is* your heart, my heart, really in heaven? Are our thoughts filled with excitement as to how our treasures are growing *there*? Do we look forward to what is being prepared for us by Jesus who said He had gone to prepare a place—but do we also spend time thinking about the treasure stored there? Or, because the largest amount of our "treasure" is here—in banks, stocks and bonds, land, and so on—do we grow white and tremble with each daily newspaper, because it is all so *unsafe*? Can we really shrug our shoulders and say to the Lord, "Thank You for the warning. I expected the riches to take wings. I love You, Lord, for being so open with me about this. Thank You for telling me where to store a good proportion of my goods. I'm full of thoughts about heaven. It's really true that my investments are all there."

And then next will come, "Blessed are those servants, whom the lord when he cometh shall find watching . . ." (Luke 12:37).

7

Who Is Ashamed—God or Me?

It was an icy day in January many years ago in Grove City, Pennsylvania, when our first little girl was skipping along beside me as I did our grocery shopping. Arms clutched around a huge brown bag, unwieldy on my feet because of being heavy with our soon-to-be-born second daughter, my feet suddenly slipped on a sheet of ice, my arms flew out, my legs went up in the air, and I landed squarely on the side of my forehead. I painfully sat up, gathered my scattered belongings, put my hand up gingerly to the side of my right eye, and felt a rapidly rising lump which was soon to close that eye and turn blue-black. A passerby helped to steady me, but I assured him I was all right and that I would go "not to the hospital, thank you," but to the fish counter of the A & P, where I was sure they could give me a lump of ice, and I could sit down until the dizzy feeling stopped.

Four-year-old Priscilla was flooded with embarrassment and shame at being connected with a mother who had a blue lump on her forehead and a blackening eye. Her feeling was one of wanting no connection discovered between herself and this person who could be an object of ridicule. She ran to the other side of the store to put a safe distance between herself and the fish counter, so that no one would think she belonged to me.

How quickly Peter disassociated himself from Jesus when he saw the Lord being led off by soldiers to be tortured and examined. Not only fear but shame swept over him as he disclaimed any connection with this man whom he loved and had believed to be the Messiah. The apparently unkinglike weakness of being spit upon and slapped blotted out temporarily his loyal love and trust, and Peter was ashamed of his former connection with the One who was being led off to judgment. This is the same Peter who such a short time before had answered Jesus by saying, "Thou art the Christ." It was also the same Peter who had "rebuked" Jesus after He had told His disciples that ". . . the Son of man must suffer many things, and be rejected of the elders, and of the chief priests, and scribes, and be killed, and after three days rise again" (Mark 8:31).

It was following Peter's rebuke that Jesus made strong the fact that following Him included the need for denying self, taking up a cross, and being willing to lose one's life: ". . . whosoever shall lose his life for my sake and the gospel's, the same shall save it."

So often one thinks of martyrdom of a physical sort in connection with this statement and the question which follows it: "Or what shall a man give in exchange for his soul?" (Mark 8:37). But it is very important in this moment of history, when disciples of Jesus are tempted to deny Him rather than denying self, to see what comes next in the context of what Jesus is saying to His people—then and now.

"Whosoever therefore shall be ashamed of me and of my words in this adulterous and sinful generation; of him also shall the Son of man be ashamed, when he cometh in the glory of his Father with the holy angels" (v. 38). There is a coming time when Jesus will no longer be rejected and spit upon and no longer be the One for whom there needs to be self-denial on the part of His disciples. There is a coming time when there will be blazing glory surrounding the Second Person of the

Trinity as He comes in His magnificent beauty accompanied by angels. The desire *then* will be to be claimed by Him as one of His people. There is a serious warning connected with the future promise.

What is involved in fulfilling the admonition to "deny self," and to be *not* ashamed? There is involved the promise that there will be moments of danger during which other people, described as "this adulterous and sinful generation," will be full of ridicule and criticism of the sort that would threaten the ego and make it easy to deny the words of Jesus—the Word of God—rather than denying self. Human beings love the acclaim of other human beings. Jesus is pointing out that the very fact of following Him will bring about situations in which it will be easy to feel ashamed and to choose to be more comfortable with the sneering, jeering people by giving in to the desire for acceptance by people, rather than remembering that acceptance by Him is the eternally important thing.

"But I'm not ashamed of Jesus," we might say, without thinking of the strength of this statement: "Whosoever therefore shall be ashamed of me and of my words . . . ." John describes Jesus: "In the beginning was the Word, and the Word was with God, and the Word was God. The same was in the beginning with God. All things were *made by him*; and without him was not any thing made that was made" (John 1:1–3). And God had Moses write in Genesis: "In the beginning God created the heaven and the earth . . . . So God created man in his own image, in the image of God created he him; male and female created he them."

It is easy to be strong and brave about the past. It is especially easy to fight battles after they are over. The danger is in slinking away in the present moment of discomfort or attack. "No, no, no, I don't really believe all that literally. I believe in a spiritual application. You see it is all religious. No, no. Of course, I do not take the biblical view about science and history. But I do believe in all this spiritually." Who doesn't "believe" some kind of "spiritual" thing today? Mysticism of some sort is easily accepted by twentieth-century people. The Bible can be placed with many other things as acceptable, as long as it is equated with other religious pronouncements in keeping its "place."

Jesus is not talking about an airy, fairy, spiritual moment when He speaks of the coming time of His return. He means *something*, not *nothing*, by His warning that there is danger of our missing the opportunity to be not ashamed of His *words*. The moment will be past one day, and there will be no more opportunity to be not ashamed. We can't go back and do it over again. It is a serious thing to be told that we have a period of time during which we can be *not ashamed* of Jesus and of His words.

Paul says so strongly in Romans 1:15, 16: "I am ready to preach the gospel to you that are at Rome also. For I am not ashamed of the gospel of Christ: for it is the power of God unto salvation to every one that believeth; to the Jew first, and also to the Greek." What *is* the "gospel" of which Paul declares he is not ashamed? What is the "gospel" that is making him a target for persecution and ridicule?

In 1 Corinthians 15:45, the connection is clear, even as it is in John. The need is always to go back to the beginning and understand the continuity. "The first man Adam was made a living soul . . ." is important in understanding that Jesus is "the last Adam." The One who is coming back again in glory is the One who was there in the beginning and who *made* all things, who made man in His image.

In Romans 1:22, 25, Paul goes on to speak of how people "professing themselves to be wise" became fools and "changed the *truth of God* into a *lie,* and worshipped and served the creature more than the Creator . . . ." Is there a sweeping desire to be praised by men, to be thought of as scholars and intellectuals, able to discover clever substitutes for the explanations given in God's Word—relegating all that to a "cultural idea" which can be reduced into being *ashamed?* Being ashamed is a subtle feeling. A child can easily be embarrassed into a kind of "denial" which is temporary and not serious. A child of God can also become embarrassed, and Satan works on this sudden embarrassment to pressure God's people into outward actions based on the feeling. These actions then speak to God and the angels, giving a declaration of our being *ashamed.*

Who matters most? Who are we trying to impress? "And ye shall know that I am in the midst of Israel, and that I am the Lord your God, and none else: and my people shall never be ashamed" (Joel 2:27). May we take our opportunity now to stand before the accusations that hit us from strange sources, and be most concerned by the reality of the briefness of the moment of crunch! The time of the Lord's return is too late to fulfill the resolve to never be ashamed. Before many or before few, the sneers of "this adulterous and sinful generation" are *now,* and the time to be not ashamed of His Word is now. When we can do no more about it, will He be ashamed of us—at His coming? Which moment matters most? Now? Or then?

8

~~~ ~~~

Unequal Equipment

The estimated power of destruction bound up in a hydrogen bomb causes us to gasp, if we really let the thought penetrate our minds enough to think of "bomb matching bomb" over some imaginary battlefield. What nation is really properly equipped? Football helmets and suits come with more complicated padding these days, and the two teams need to be equipped fairly equally to start with. Technology provides deep-sea divers with more and more complicated equipment to delve into the depths, even as spacemen soar off into the atmosphere surrounded from the skin out by tested equipment. Men drive off in the morning in fully equipped cars, and women stay home in fully equipped houses—or vice versa—and children play in fully equipped playrooms with buttons to push for a variety of results.

Matching equipment is a concept that is carried into every area of life these days, as people press on to be equipped to the same degree, or more than other people. It takes longer and longer to be prepared for whatever each person thinks he is preparing for—because the preparation is more complicated, and the future keeps being pushed farther off. One can imagine people soon all waddling on through life so weighted down with equipment and bound up in it to the extent of completely forgetting what they were getting ready for—and never arriving at the starting place! The complicatedness of technical, educational and psychological equipment—and keeping up with everybody else's equipment—throws many people into such a state that they fear to *do* anything without "one more year" of getting ready, or earning enough to buy the "latest" before starting.

It is not only interesting but very important to consider how God has equipped the people He has given especially difficult tasks at crisis moments of history. When men equip men, the emphasis has always been on attempting to equalize the equipment to match the opponent in battle or confrontation. God's way has been the exact opposite.

When we are told in 1 Corinthians 1:27 that God has chosen the weak things of the world to confound the things which are mighty, and the foolish things to confound the wise, we are reminded of many examples of God's doing exactly that. We see lovely, slim, young David, a sensitive harpist and a poet, a conscientious shepherd lad refusing to put on the heavy armor and helmet. With only his shepherd's rod, walking out simply in his ordinary clothing, picking up five stones for a little slingshot, he stands facing the scornful, jeering Goliath, a giant warrior equipped with the heaviest of armor. What a confrontation! How unequal! After listening to the giant's taunts and threats, hear David's confident statement: "Thou comest to me with a sword, and with a spear, and with a shield: but I come to thee in the name of the Lord of hosts, the God of the armies of Israel, whom thou hast defied" (1 Samuel 17:45).

Think of Gideon's equipment against thousands of Midianites. Not only did God remove his troops, leaving only 300, but his technical equipment was made up of pitchers, lamps, and trumpets. Another unequal confrontation! Combine with this your memory of Moses going before Pharaoh with a stick of wood, and Joseph going before the Pharaoh of his time with no past study of dreamology or magic tricks. Think of Jonah's spiritual weakness as he ran away from God, yet had to redouble his tracks and preach the only message which the large city was going to have an opportunity to hear if they were to be given the true truth. For that matter, think of the twelve apostles and the first disciples, given the task of telling the whole world the Gospel, as Jesus ascended to heaven. No flashing equipment had been given them to lend them special standing in the eyes of men.

When are we in danger of telling God, "Oh, I can't—I'm not equipped. It would be unequal for me to stand against professionally trained people."—"Oh, I'd make a fool of myself. I can't be president [peasant, general, private, composer, soloist, or one of the least violinists]."—"I can't do that; it's too much for me"? What kind of things hit you and hit me and cause us to feel that the equipment is outdated and insufficient and that we have to back out? Perhaps it is when Satan attacks us as he did Job, and we feel too weak to love and trust God in the midst of cancer, flood, famine, depression, loss of bank accounts, spoiled crops, burned-down houses. We feel we are not "noble" or "spiritually strong" or "emotionally ready" for difficulties which Satan has thrown at us, and we don't want to win any spiritual battles nor do we want to be used to prove anything to angels or demons. Or perhaps it is something God is thrusting upon us which places us in what seems to be competition from a human viewpoint, with "giants" in a variety of fields, equipped with a long list of Ph.D.'s. Perhaps we are alone, surrounded by scientists and historians with marvelous "equipment," who laugh at us in scorn as we defend the Word of God. Perhaps we feel we have not been equipped to fight for family life—or a Christian factory setup if we are left a business to head up. Whatever the "confrontation," one thing is sure: Not once, but many, many times in our lives we'll be finding ourselves saying, "I haven't the equipment to stand before the well-equipped giant [or the army so very much larger]," in *some* sense of that statement. Time after time, Satan attacks to bring about that very defeat, and time after time, God calls upon the "weak things to confound the mighty."

Why? Come to David's explanation of his plight, so fearful to behold as he looks so vulnerable. "This day will the Lord deliver thee into mine hand . . . that all the earth may know that there is a God in Israel. And all this assembly shall *know* that the Lord saveth not with sword and spear: for the battle is the Lord's and he will give you into our hands" (1 Samuel 17:46, 47). Come to stand beside Gideon and listen to God speaking to him: "The people that are with thee are too many for me to give the Midianites into their hands, lest Israel vaunt themselves against me, saying, Mine own hand hath saved me" (Judges 7:2). Listen to Elijah's prayer as he puts water on the wood and the sacrifice and prays for the fire to fall, "Hear me, O Lord, hear me, that this people may know that thou art the Lord God, and that thou hast turned their heart back again" (1 Kings 18:37). Come now to First Corinthians again: ". . . God hath chosen the weak things of the world to confound the things which are mighty . . . . That no flesh should glory in his presence . . . . That, according as it is written, He that glorieth, let him glory in the Lord" (1:27, 29, 31).

Yes, there is a purpose in the inequality of the equipment. The unequal equipment has been a demonstration of God's existence and power and glory, time after time in the past—and is now in the present in a diversity of places and people, and will be in the future until Jesus comes back. If we pray, "Oh, God, use me that men may know that You are there," and God answers us, then we will be involved in various kinds of confrontation, through which watching men who are "seeking" will know that the power is God's and not ours, and which will glorify God and not ourselves.

What is it that our God who promises that His "strength is made perfect in weakness" says to us when we begin to tremble in one kind of a circumstance or another as we look down at our feeble equipment?

"For I the Lord thy God will hold thy right hand, saying unto thee, Fear not; I will help thee" (Isaiah 41:13). One day we shall be equipped to perfection in our new bodies. Right *now* is the only time we have to be weak, and—to show forth His glory—don't let's muff our opportunity by spending our whole lives trying to prepare an equal equipment!

9

Fearing or Afraid?

There is a tremendous difference between "the fear of the Lord" and being afraid of God, and it seems to be mixed up into a mélange of misunderstanding in many people's private moments of wondering what God is like. Small children are given misconceptions so often, and adults' insensitive remarks or attitudes which send forth waves of doubts or worries surround the words "the fear of the Lord" with an ominous mystery. The ordinary use of the word *fear* causes it to be synonymous with "terror," and the emotion which accompanies terror is apt to flood one's being, even if it is pushed away into a back area of the mind.

How can one exchange the desire to shrink away from thinking about "the fear of the Lord" for a desire to experience the richness of what God means His children to have, as we dwell upon this important area of understanding our relationship with the Lord? For me, Psalm 147 is a place where a special excitement accompanies the glimpse we have as a curtain is drawn for a moment and gives a very real perspective.

"Praise ye the Lord," the psalmist begins—and tells us it is good, pleasant, and appropriate for us to praise the Lord. He then gives us a pattern of praise which lists specific things which the Lord does for His people, which should cause us to suddenly be filled with a rush of praise and thanksgiving like water rushing through a break in a dam. The "dam" which holds back our excitement about the Lord needs to be broken through time after time, as we are often so complacent. "He healeth the broken in heart, and bindeth up their wounds," is the first reminder of why we should praise the Lord. This One *cares* about brokenhearted, wounded people in His family. This dear Father not only looks for the proper "gauze and ointment" to bind up the wounds—psychological wounds, spiritual wounds, emotional wounds, as well as physical wounds—but He also is *able* to do something about heartbreak.

Next we are taken to His fantastic knowledge, as we are told that He not only knows how many stars there are, but has a name for each one of them! Those who study the stars are in awe of the endless number and of the time it takes to learn the names of the few which men can distinguish and name—but He knows them *all*. What admiration should come forth in our attitude towards this God. The next verse speaks with trumpet notes: "*Great* is our Lord, and of *great* power: his *understanding* is infinite." This infinitely great One understands *us*. Yes, He understands everything, and that includes us. We are understood. Our little fears, doubts, excitements, hopes, imaginations, ambitions, pains, joys, battles, struggles, disappointments, sins, faults, weaknesses, strengths—all are understood. What a comfort to communicate with One who understands us, and to be alone with that One. A desire for praise should be a natural result of thinking even a short time about such a reality. With all the misunderstandings of my friends and family—there is One who understands. I am not alone. How very crass of us to not want to praise this One—to not discover that praise is pleasant!

We go on to discover that the Lord lifts up the meek. Lifts them up where? Well, we speak of our being "lifted" out of depression, don't we? We speak of being "lifted" out of dullness and humdrum, don't we? We speak of being "lifted up" spiritually, don't we? It is His promise to lift up the meek. He lifts up others, too, in different needs—those who are His children looking to Him for help. Is it any wonder that the psalmist now urges us in the next verse—yes, even *commands* us—to *sing?* "Sing unto the Lord with thanksgiving; sing praise upon the harp unto our God." We should burst into song with thanksgiving and praise. Maybe you have the voice of a Jenny Lind, maybe you croak like a crow, but bursting into a song of praise is what each of us should do at times, simply and spontaneously as we think upon some of the wonders of what God promises to do for us and also consider *who* He is. Maybe you have a harp or a banjo or a piano or a recorder—if you have an instrument, it can give forth praise to accompany the song. God says so. The important thing is the reality of spontaneous expression of praise and thanksgiving, not just in church, not just formally, not simply with other people when it is expected, but alone with the Lord—speaking to Him with some amount of understanding of how much there is to admire Him for.

This psalm adds more description to open our understanding of God. He is the One who covers the skies with clouds, who sends the marvel of crop-watering rain, who makes the grass grow upon the mountains. Ah, what grass! He filled the Swiss Alpine slopes with purple-blue gentians, creamy-white edelweiss, myriad varieties of wild flowers mixed with the grass and the moss. He always gives abundantly *more*. This same One gives food to the beasts and cares about nourishing the ravens. He is a gentle Person, caring to fulfill the needs of hungry people and even the birds and beasts.

We have been prepared in these verses to meditate upon the positive things which God does for us, and given specific things to praise Him for. We should be flooded with warm feelings of trust, confidence, and expectancy—ready to pray on a background of praise for the immediate difficulty, whatever it is.

In the midst of this preparation which draws us toward the gentleness of God and fills us with a certainty of open arms and loving care, we then come to something in verses 10 and 11 which may bring us up short, if we are not careful.

> He delighteth not in the strength of the horse: he taketh not pleasure in the legs of a man. The Lord taketh pleasure in them that fear him, in those that hope in his mercy.

What are we being told? The very first thing to fix in our minds is that, with the background of things God is reminding us He does for us, we are brought to thoughts of God's own pleasure. We are being told that there are things we can do to give God pleasure. This is a two-way relationship, and as God desires to bring us pleasure and, of course, is preparing fabulous things for us in eternity, He now tells us there are things we can do for His pleasure right now.

The negative is given first. He does not take pleasure in human strength, even though He made man to have marvelous legs such as can leap over the high jump and win races in the Olympics. Part of God's Creation is the beauty of the human body's possibilities in a variety of achievements. But here we are told that it is not our perfection of achievement which brings pleasure to God. Oh, dear person who feels inferior to others in talents of any sort, and oh, dear one in a wheelchair or with other handicaps—God is saying that to bring pleasure to Him you don't need to have your legs healed. That which brings the Lord pleasure is not what any person is to do. That which brings the Lord pleasure is not what necessitates special basic strength in any area of body or mind, or education or equipment which puts one above another. That which brings the Lord pleasure is within reach of the maimed, the halt, and the blind—within reach of anyone, of any age, anywhere. What is it we need to do?

"The Lord taketh pleasure in them that fear him, in those that hope in his mercy." We need to understand and attempt to do something which the Lord says will give Him pleasure. This must *not* be passed over. What is this fear? In the context of Psalm 147 we know it is NOT being *afraid;* it is rather a mixture of awe, adoration, appreciation, and some degree of understanding of the titanic reality of God's being infinite. It is bowing as a creature before the Creator, recognizing that perfect wisdom, perfect love, perfect justice, perfect compassion, and perfect creativity need an emotion in response—which the Bible calls fear. The word *fear* must cover so much that, as we realize some portion of it all, we *feel* like praising and singing but at the same time feel like falling flat on our faces in worship.

Coupled with this great combination contained in the word *fear,* we are in the same moment to have hope in His mercy. We are to realize afresh, as we fear God, that this Lord is the Lord of compassion and of great mercy. This, then, is the One to whom we can pour out our requests for the needs of ourselves and other people. We must recognize that all who come to "fear the Lord" in this deep and full sense are those who know that He "is," and who have come to Him through the Lamb who died to make it possible. There is no need for anyone who *fears* God in the real sense to ever be afraid of Him. There is a need to pray for all who do *not* fear God, because one day they *will* be afraid when they see Him and cry out for rocks to hide them.

Fearing or afraid? Be sure we are among those who fear Him and ask Him to use us among those who will one day be *afraid*—unless they are taught the fear of the Lord.

10

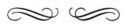

Commanded Love

Love without reason is sometimes pictured as a meeting of personalities in some mystical blending of baseless emotion. The intellect is put on the other side of a high gray stone wall—where a chilly dull atmosphere is contrasted to the riot of colored flowers and warm sun-drenched grasses on the "emotion" side of the dividing wall. One is given an impression of needing to make a choice between "mind" and "heart," as if to choose one is to deny the other. "Come away from the harsh use of logic, you over there on the cold side of thinking—as you search for answers," shout some who think the wall is rigid and never to be crossed. "Love, feel, experience. Don't ask, don't question, don't use your mind. Just let yourself go; don't seek for a logical base for love." Love is thought of as so delicate a wisp of cloud that it will be blown away by any wind of verbalized reason.

Is love there? Is it not there? Shhh—don't ask. The very *asking* may drive it away. Jump into some experience with your eyes shut. Close the eyes of your mind and feel—feel—feel. Don't define. Don't verbalize any reason why. Don't give any form. Throw away any hindering words of proof as to what might bring forth this love. The stark use of intellect will nullify the reality of love.

Is this true to what exists? What about human love which is so limited and imperfect and yet which can grow and deepen through the years? How does it grow? It grows through verbalization and deepening understanding, which comes from coming to *know* the other person. In a human relationship the other person is never perfect, so there are weaknesses and faults which could hurt or destroy the love if dwelt upon. If one discovers a new reason to admire, enjoy, and be stimulated by the other person, one would do well to verbalize this discovery: "Oh, I do love the way your mind works."—"I do admire the compassion you have for the minority people."—"You have such sensitivity to my need of music right now."—"Thank you for getting those concert tickets for tonight."—"How special of you to think of making those tapes for Johnny in the hospital. I love you for that."

Concrete reasons for loving another human being not only need to be expressed to that person, but will also help the person who is doing the verbalizing. Dwelling in one's mind on logical reasons for love does not diminish the feelings of love, but increases them. Making new discoveries of qualities in the other person's character, through recent things he or she has done, gives increased reality in the area of *knowing* the person. Verbalizing these discoveries fixes in the memory some of the reasons that should logically increase love. Love will grow as reasons for love are discovered, thought about, dwelt upon in the mind, expressed verbally, and remembered. As time goes on, the memory will become rich with increasing vividness and warmth in storing up facts and reasons behind the increase of love.

The question is asked: "How can I experience love for God? I want a flood of warm love for Him, but He seems so far away, and I feel nothing." Is the answer to be one of urging each other to wait for a mystical, spiritual experience during which we will be plunged into a riot of color and sunlight on the "emotion side of the wall"? Are we to put away intellect and logic?

Listen to the First Commandment as Jesus speaks in Matthew 22:37. Jesus is being asked what the "great commandment" is. What is the basic and First Commandment as Jesus clearly explains it? Listen carefully: "Jesus said unto him, Thou shalt love the Lord thy God with all thy heart, and with all thy soul and with all thy *mind*."

The whole man is to be involved in loving God. This is a command to not only love God, but to love Him with heart and soul and mind. The whole person is to be blended together in this love, not divided into compartments. The mind is to have an important part in this. How can we experience a growing love for God? By discovering logical, reasonable, understandable reasons for loving Him. We can constantly verbalize our discoveries and express our love to impress upon our memories the reasons we have for loving God. "Oh, God, I do love You for Your compassion to Nineveh in sending Jonah to make truth known, to warn the people in time."—"Oh, God, how I love You for letting meople come to know Jesus personally day by day, so that they could also know You, the Father."—"Thank You, Father, for keeping a record of the many prayers You answered in detail centuries ago, and just a hundred years ago as Hudson Taylor went to China."—"Thank You for Your gentleness in supplying our need for food—and for adding the roses yesterday."

Love for God increases as the reasons for love are verbalized, spoken aloud, written on paper, considered in the mind, dwelt upon in the wakeful hours in the night. Love for God sometimes burns low, as a dying fire of pale pink-and-gray coals. It needs to be blown upon with a breath of air—with the breeze of one's thoughts carefully worded. When reasons for loving Him are expressed, they fan the dying embers into a glow. Reading His Word, looking for fresh understanding of what He is like—as Isaiah is reread, as Psalm 90 is meditated upon—brings with the breeze some fresh fuel to catch and flare up. "Love the Lord thy God with all thy mind." It is a command which increases love when we attempt to follow it.

How foolish we are in human relationships when we continually dwell upon each other's weaknesses and mistakes. How easily love is squashed and the fire dimmed with a dash of cold water, when the sensitive deed, the proffered rose, the cup of tea, or the concert tickets are ignored, and instead a stream of criticism blasts the air with "Why did you forget to mail the letter?—"Why did you drop that dish?"—"Why have you brought mud in on your feet?"—"Why didn't you tell me first?" The lack of appreciation certainly hurts the person being screamed at. But the one doing the screaming is losing the possibility of experiencing the growing love that would have taken place had the mind been filled with the obvious and very logical reason for expressing love—and either waiting for a quiet moment to discuss whatever really needed discussing or putting aside the criticism altogether. Searching for reasons to express love, thinking about them, and formulating appreciation into words takes time. "Time" can be so completely absorbed by dwelling on each other's mistakes that there is *never* time to increase love. The *mind* needs to be involved in blending the whole person into a reality of growth in the areas of feeling. Emotion needs a base if it is to be a solid, continuing experience. We can help ourselves to have a continuity in our life relationships when we come to recognize that there is no *wall* between intellect, mind, logical understanding—and the warmth of growing love.

There is a danger in people's dwelling on things they find in God's Word or in their knowledge of the conditions in the abnormal universe which distress them. God is perfect. God's love and compassion, His wisdom and holiness, His creativity and diversity, and His gentleness and kindness are perfect. When we come up against anything which causes us to feel critical and which makes us begin to "feel" the criticism like a scream of annoyance that bursts out against another human being, we can know we have not understood the thing that bothers us. *If* we allow the things which bother us to absorb all our time—if we read and reread the lines which we do not understand (and which bring feelings of fear, criticism, coldness, uncertainty) and verbalize them, think about them in connection with present sufferings we don't understand, the effect will be one of throwing cold water on the embers of our love for God. Our minds will be occupied with the thoughts which distort the reality of the character of God. Our minds will be spending time—that will never be recaptured—in disobeying a specific command.

We are commanded to love. We are commanded second to love our neighbors, but first to love God. That command gives within it the key as to how to increase the reality of that love. That command shows how to pull down the wall that has been falsely built between intellect and faith, reason and trust, understanding and feeling, mind and love. Within the command itself is given the way of fulfilling the command. God is so fair in His dealings with us. How we can love Him for His fairness, as we discover more and more about it. "Thou shalt love the Lord thy God with all thy heart, and with all thy soul, and with all thy mind." Search for an increasing number of things with which to fill your mind with memories which will give continuity to love—before you are in His presence—and the difficult things become clear.

11

Who Is the Snob?

Snob class. Snob value. Snob schools. Snob hotels. Snob clothing. Snob cars. Snob judgments. Snob perspectives. Snob attitudes. Snob treatment. Snob advertising. Snob training. Snob professions. Snob recreation. Snob clubs. Snob churches. Snob families. *Snobs.*

The dictionary may imply that the word refers to people who go to universities or private schools—but that this usage is now archaic. It may go on to say that it is a word referring to people with exaggerated respect for social position or wealth. It may continue its explanation with speaking of people who feel ashamed to have any connection with others who are thought to be socially inferior to them. The dictionary may then end by saying that when you add *-ish* and make it *snobbish*, you have an adjective which describes someone who judges people by exteriors. Reading this, it is easy to close the dictionary and feel that the description fits a certain type of person, but "certainly not me!" One's memory may bring a parade of types to march across the path in front of the mind's eye—strutting in finery with noses held high—the kind of people who have hurt us with varieties of snubbing, with squashing remarks in accents which have cut us like a lash. "How glad I am not to be a snob." The dictionary is shut. The memory fades out. A warm glow of satisfaction fills one. "I am so glad I am not like that!" is the happy conclusion.

But—are we safe from being judged snobbish by God? How often do you and do I look down from a pinnacle of self-satisfaction upon the lowly, miserable people "below" our mountain. "Oh, but I feel warm and especially loving toward all minority groups," says one with fervor. And a friend nearby pipes in, "I'm careful to be like Jesus was; I go to be with outcasts and sit right down on the sidewalk with beggars or junkies. I just couldn't be snobbish." A military friend might chime in, "Me, too. I'm a captain, but I don't mind inviting privates for dinner." And another, "No class barriers for me. I work with my hands. Nuts to my university degree; I'm going to be a shoemaker."

There is a very real breaking of barriers going on, but the danger is that subtle new "mountains" are being piled up, with the despised people "below" being made up of very new categories. New divisions are being made, and the judgments taking place are as excruciatingly sharp as ever before. The same old feelings of superiority are being felt, although the outward appearance of people looking down may have changed. In fact, the changes are so swift and frequent that one might picture the mountain and valley as a seesaw of gigantic proportions. Have we been unwittingly swooped up into the place of being the snob?

Think soberly for a moment. Many brought up going to public schools really "look down" in their emotional reactions to those brought up in private schools or those who speak with a different accent. People who have never been in government circles feel a kind of superiority to those who have won the elections. There is a "ganging-up" in the emotions of people in city flats against people who have farms or any large property, but an equally superior feeling on the part of the new back-to-nature people toward businessmen or factory owners. There is a "looking down" on parents by children, and a superior feeling on the part of the "liberated" woman toward men. There is a feeling of great intellectual superiority on the part of the critics toward those who have painted the artwork, written the music, given the lectures. There is a judgment of the judges on the part of the masses, as well as a superior feeling of prisoners toward the guards. The upswing takes us, if we are in a rowboat, to a place of scorning the ones on a yacht and holds us high as we ferret out the weaknesses of the employer under whom we work. A daughter can flaunt her superior attitude over her father to the place of purposely "breaking" him, as recently a high official in the army was forced to resign because of his daughter's purposeful revenge by getting into trouble with drugs. Whether in seeking vengeance or in the hidden unseen place of emotional reactions, the seesaw is *real*, and there is not one of us who is not in danger of being a *snob*. High-low, poor-rich, young-old, man-woman, black-white.

Jesus spake this parable unto certain people who so trusted in *themselves*, that they were self-righteous and despised others:

> Two men went up into the temple to pray; the one a Pharisee, and the other a publican. The Pharisee stood and prayed thus with himself, God, I thank thee, that I am not as other men are, extortioners, unjust, adulterers, or even as this publican. I fast twice in the week, I give tithes of all that I possess. And the publican, standing afar off, would not lift up so much as his eyes unto heaven, but smote upon his breast, saying, God be merciful to me a sinner. I tell you, this man went down to his house justified rather than the other: for every one that exalteth himself shall be abased; and he that humbleth himself shall be exalted.   Luke 18:10–14

> And why beholdest thou the mote that is in thy brother's eye, but perceivest not the beam that is in thine own eye? . . . Thou hypocrite cast out first the beam out of thine own eye, and then shalt thou see clearly to pull out the mote that is in thy brother's eye.   Luke 6:41, 42

What danger we are warned of! As we go into the presence of the Creator of the universe who is all-wise, perfect in His understanding of us, perfect in His justice and love—needing no dictionary definition to make clear what is taking place inside our minds and hearts, thoughts or emotions, needing not to have us explain to *Him* whether we think more highly of ourselves than we ought to think—do we not feel frightened if we never examine ourselves to see whether we are coming across as *snobs?*

How often are we in the place of the Pharisee? "I am so glad, dear God, that I haven't cheated like that man did; that I haven't lied as this one has; that I haven't been leading a majority group but have always been in a minority one; that I have eaten poor food and slept in a poor bed. Oh, God—how glad I am that I am so humble." "God, I am thankful for my education and understanding, so glad not to be like ———." "Oh, God—how thankful I am that I have not been segregated." "Oh, God—I am . . . ."

What is it? What is the "beam"? The beam can be the sin of neglect, the sin of omission as well as a wicked thing we have done or thought. The beam can be pride in humbleness, as well as pride in riches or power. The beam can be feeling superior to people "above us" socially, as easily as feeling superior to those who have *less* in goods or education. The beam can be found in Jesus' words that day, trusting in *ourselves* that *we* are righteous and despising *others*. The puffing-up of self is very subtle. People have leaned upon it in many ways in history. People once thought that buttons were a source of pride, and as time went by the ones who did not wear buttons were in danger of having more pride in *not* wearing buttons than anyone ever felt in having buttons. There are all kinds of "buttons" that people put aside. And in the causes we espouse, we are in great danger of taking pride in putting aside the former source of pride. People are proud of long—or short— hair. People are proud in a wrong way of being white or black. People are proud of being old or young. People are proud of being negative against everything or being positive toward everything. People are proud of being humble, or proud of being in power. People are proud of knowing other people—and people are proud of *not* knowing other people. There are all sorts of "buttons." And the "buttons"—whether we wear them or do not wear them—are the source of turning us into *snobs* as we come to the Lord.

There are conditions placed upon us in our approach to the Living God. He means us to take these conditions seriously. We are not to brush them aside. When we come to the Living God in prayer, our first requirement is to come with our sin cleansed away because we come through Jesus, who died that we might have access to God. As he died,

Jesus made it possible to take away the wall of separation which sin built between man and God. We *can* come and communicate with God the Father in Jesus' name. But, as we carefully read His communication to us, we are warned that there are certain things we need to ask forgiveness for, to be careful to recognize in ourselves, and to openly speak to God about. These things are the "beams" in our eyes which are so very, very huge to God, but which we are so apt to rationalize or not even see. We see a tiny speck in someone's eye which we try to remove, so God tells us, while we ignore the enormous log in our own eye. "Take time to look for the log, and be honest with yourself. Don't be easy on yourself. Don't be embarrassed to tell yourself how inconsistent you are being." This is what we are being told. Then when you and I have discovered something which needs to be different to be in line with the drastic teaching of God's Word, we need to speak audibly about it to God, and ask with the publican, "God be merciful to me, a sinner."

One clear sin that separates us from the reality of being free to pray is the sin of snobbishness. How easily we delegate that sin in our categories of men to a "proud elite" to which we do not belong. But the seesaw has undoubtedly taken you—and taken me—to a swing upwards with a whoosh of air in our faces which we thought was just a pleasant breeze. We are "looking down" on someone or some group, unless we ask God's help in showing us how unbalanced we are at the moment—*and ask His forgiveness and His strength in this particularly universal kind of weakness.*

12

❦ ❦

What's Going to Happen to John?

"She has a bigger sandbox and swing set; I want bigger ones, too."

"Oh, his bike is nicer than mine; it has fancier brakes and a headlight. I need a new one!"

"Their car is bigger than ours. We need a new one. Why should we all be so squashed?"

"They have two houses—one at the beach and one in the city. We ought to have two by now, too."

"That company has the men work only five days a week. Why am I working five and a half?"

"Let's strike for more pay and longer vacations!"

"That mission board gives its missionaries refrigerators, cars, and better schools for the children. Why can't ours?"

"Those professors have a whole year off to study. I want to study, too."

"I'm older than that person. Why shouldn't I get more time off? I want as much rest as he has."

"What is she getting in that envelope? I want something just as much; it's my birthday, too."

Comparisons start with toddlers and continue throughout life. Children compare—what they have, what they can do, what work they are being made to contribute, what privileges they will be given—with brothers and sisters, neighbors, and people they have read about. Teenagers do the same thing, but no more than those in their twenties, thirties, fifties, seventies! Organizations compare themselves with organizations, labor unions with labor unions, churches with churches, mission boards with mission boards. Often we human beings are so busy craning our necks to try to see what is happening to someone else and what we might be missing by comparison that we never compare ourselves with ourselves. Does that sound like nonsense? How can we stand alone and have any kind of helpful productive idea of what is "enough" or "right" or "just" or "acceptable"? What ingredients are needed for contentment?

Come to John 21, to the time when Jesus in His resurrected body had just been eating fish and bread with His disciples on the seashore. You remember that the men had been fishing all night and had caught nothing. Jesus called out from the shore to ask what they had caught, and when the answer came in a disappointed negative, He told them to put the nets on the other side of the ship. Now when they did this, there were so many fish they were not able to draw the net into the ship, so they dragged it along to shore. Peter couldn't wait for that and impatiently jumped into the sea and came in first to see Jesus. It was an exciting thing for Peter to see the risen Lord once again and to rush in to touch Him and be served bread and fish by Him. Don't you think it would have been natural for Peter to be thinking in terms of how easy it had been to fish after Jesus told them where to put the net, of how splendid it was to come in wet and tired from the night to be served fresh bread and sizzling-hot fish straight from the coals? He could have been feeling relaxed and expectant of easy times ahead. The One, who had died in such a tragic way as to crush his hopes, was now risen and in a splendid body. He could do even greater miracles, and here He was with them. Difficulties and agonies were behind. What a glorious future lay ahead! I feel sure that Peter's emotions were in a state of blissful certainty as he interpreted to himself what the Resurrection would mean in peace and joy immediately ahead. What happy bites of fish and bread were probably chewed with vigor and appreciation in those moments. The others would have pressed around, flinging themselves down for a lovely, refreshing time with Jesus who had died, for whom they had wept and mourned, and who was now alive and caring for them. And the sound of chewing and swallowing was probably interspersed with cheery words and contented murmurs, such as one hears at a meal of welcome when someone returns from a time of long separation. They had been through such terrible fears and doubts. Now they were eating together and all was well.

Immediately following the meal, Jesus spoke to Peter, singling him out for a serious time of questioning. "Simon Peter, Simon, son of Jonas, lovest thou me more than these?" And again, "Simon, son of Jonas, lovest thou me?" Each time, Peter answered, "Lord, you *know* I love you" (*see* vv. 15, 16). The third time Jesus asked the question, Peter was really hurt, we are told, and insisted that Jesus who knew all things *must know* that he loved Him. As each answer was given, Jesus told Peter to feed His sheep, His lambs—to feed not with bread and fish, but with the spiritual food Peter could give from God's Word—the people who would believe on Jesus and become His lambs and sheep.

Peter, well fed, dry, warm, and full of love for Jesus, accepted this commission to feed the lambs—with pleasure, I feel sure. It seems so natural that a feeling of satisfaction would flood him as he imagined sitting and teaching gatherings of hungry people with the spiritual food they longed for. He would be glad to do this. Suddenly, in the midst of his satisfied contemplation, Jesus' next words would come crashing in like a bomb, shattering the peaceful emotions with fragments of fear and shrinking back.

> Verily, verily, I say unto thee, When thou wast young, thou girdedst thyself, and walkedst wither thou wouldest: but when thou shalt be old, thou shalt stretch forth thy hands, and another shall gird thee, and carry thee whither thou wouldest

not. This spake he, signifying by what death he should glorify
God. And when he had spoken this, he saith unto him, Follow
me.

John 21:18, 19

What is Jesus saying? He is letting Peter have a glimpse of his
future—a future which includes death by crucifixion, martyrdom! And
in the midst of Peter's fearful dismay, the words continue. *Follow Me.*
Very direct. Simply, *Follow Me.*

Peter's first reaction was to crane his neck and look around. There
were all those other disciples there, wiping the crumbs from their lips,
looking satisfied. It would be quite natural to imagine Peter thinking, "I
wonder what is going to happen to each of *them.* What is in *their* future?
Why should I—?" Whatever was going on in his head, what he did was
to look suddenly at John. John had leaned on Jesus' breast at the Last
Supper, Peter remembered, and John was especially loved by Jesus.
Peter burst forth to Jesus, "Lord, what shall *this* man do?" Or, "What's
going to happen to *John?*" Can't we each feel the question inside our
emotions? "What about this person living so long on that quiet
farm?"—"What about that one in Hawaii?"—"What about the one who
has no dangers at all in his country?"—"What about that man and
woman who haven't known serious illness?"—"*What's going to happen to John?*" The idea is comparison, of course. The feeling is: "It's all
got to be equal—equal—equal."

What was Jesus' reply? "Jesus saith unto him, If I will that he tarry till
I come, what is that to thee? follow thou me" (v. 22).

Jesus did not hurry to make an explanation of how *equal* all the
stresses and strains were to be. He did not say that, because He is
perfect love and perfect justice, each of His children was to have equal
experiences, with no diversities among them. He used the most extreme contrasts He could have used—between the two earthly futures,
the two earthly experiences, the two life plans and purposes—to show
that *each child of the Living God has a specific plan to be unfolded by
God, important to Him and to the whole future of God's total plan.*
Jesus was saying, "If John is to live until I come back a second time, that
is none of your affair. You are to follow My plan for your life. You, Peter,
are to love Me enough to trust Me and follow Me wherever that following leads, even to martyrdom for God's glory."

There was misreporting in those days as there is now. The next verse
says that people reported that Jesus had said that John would never die,
but would live until Jesus comes back. But it is carefully pointed out

that this is *not* what He said. Jesus was only saying, *"If*—if John is to live until I come back, and you are to be martyred, it is not a reason for you to make comparisons. The only comparison to be made is between what I *tell* you to do and what you *really* do. Follow Me."

We are brought up short. Each of us is in danger of craning our necks to see whether God is giving someone else more—an easier life, bigger things, more exciting events. And in the process we are apt to take our eyes completely off the directions the Lord has given us. We can miss our own signposts, our own guidance, by being too anxious to compare. Our eyes can be so completely on the points of comparison that we miss what the Lord would show us as to our own next step.

John could have done the same thing. Perhaps he didn't want to live so long. He was to write the Book of Revelation on the Isle of Patmos in his very old age. He lived in a concentration-camp type of surroundings, and it would have not been easy. Perhaps John wished inside at times that he could have been up there in heaven under the throne of martyrs, which he saw as he was taken to see what was ahead.

John heard them crying out, Peter among them, "How long, O Lord, dost thou not judge and avenge our blood on them that dwell on the earth?" (*See* Revelation 6:10.) John saw them in the special white robes reserved for martyrs and heard the reply giving such *importance* to martyrs, as he was told that they needed to wait for Jesus' Second Coming, until the last martyr would die as they had died.

John might very much have wished to have a place among them, but his task was to be shown this, to write, and to continue to be exhausted for years longer in his own waiting to be with the Lord. What appeared to be a harder thing for Peter actually meant a shorter time of affliction. Today there are martyrs joining those waiting martyrs. Many are arriving there from Africa and many from other parts of the world. Who of us is to be martyred? Who of us is to suffer other things? God alone knows, but He does have the same word for each of His children: "Follow Me. Never mind about John; you follow My plan for you. If you love Me, follow Me."

13

~~❦~~ ❦

Computers or God?

"Now look, darling, I think Penelope ought to get married soon. She needs to be fulfilled, and more involved in *life*. I mean she just needs *something*, anyone can tell. So—I got her to fill out that card to take to the computer place where you stick in all the things that are *important* like whether you like peanut butter and if you can't sleep with the windows open and what kind of attitude you have toward animals and what you are allergic to. She's already got an answer back—from just the right person; the computer *said* so. The wedding ought to be soon . . . .

"*Darling*—the wedding is *tomorrow* and everything is ready: the gorgeous dress, a fantastic cake, flowers in the bathtub keeping fresh to trim the church. But the most disastrous thing has happened. You can't believe it. Well, wait, I'll go back a bit. These two are so perfect for each other. You know the computer doesn't make any mistake, and then they decided they both wanted to be missionaries, and the mission-board computer took their cards and that showed they were just right for India. So here they are, all ready to go after their honeymoon to the school where they are to train first. Oh, but the disastrous part comes next. The school for their training has a psychiatric test each one has to take to get in, and the most horrendous results were found out about Conrad (that's the one Penelope is marrying). He's turned out to be a "sesame seed!" Well, a sesame seed is a *type*, you know. It is the type that has a need to be admired by Indian women. It seems India would be the wrong place altogether. In fact they'd be divorced within two years. A sesame-seed type is always like that. It's just a known fact.

"So, what on earth are we going to do? I mean, when the computers and the psychiatrists clash, there just isn't anywhere to go next! *Something* must be wrong. I thought it would all be so easy with the progress that has been made in recent years. No trial and error like our grandparents' day. But . . . ."

Exaggerated? Something out of *Brave New World?* Not very exaggerated, and not far off, at all. It is the direction evangelical groups are in danger of being sucked into, as particles are sucked into the vacuum cleaner from your rug, day by day. It is difficult to stand against the pull of twentieth-century solutions.

It is so easy to take the first steps away from the *reality* of God's existence. It is so easy to take the first steps away from any practical difference which God's existence makes in our choices, and in our day-by-day lives. It is so easy to go "down into Egypt" for help, and to forget that our help is really supposed to come from the Lord who made heaven and earth.

Do you remember what Isaiah was given by God to say to the people of Israel at that time? There was a danger about which the people were given fair warning. This danger was not limited to one period of history. There was danger of their accepting help as a substitute for God's help. The form of proffered help which *could* be a substitute for God's help differs from time to time, but the fact that a substitution is being made for God continues over and over again through the centuries. When other help is accepted and counted upon so that the need for crying out to God is erased or shoved aside in area after area in life, one needs to be afraid. Afraid of what? Afraid of having ignored God's warning and of having turned to another form of "Egypt." Listen:

> Woe to the rebellious children, saith the Lord, that take counsel, but not of me; and that cover with a covering, but not of my spirit, that they may add sin to sin: That walk to go down into Egypt, and have not *asked* at my mouth; to strengthen themselves in the strength of Pharaoh, and to trust in the shadow of Egypt! Therefore shall the strength of Pharaoh be your shame, and the trust in the shadow of Egypt your confusion.
>
> Isaiah 30:1–3

This is a warning in the shape of a promise. The promise is that if we as children of the Lord don't come to Him for counsel, and don't ask Him for help, the strength of the help apart from Him will one day be our shame, and the trust in the help apart from Him will be our confusion. This is the picture of our pushing aside the truth of the fact that access to the Living God, the Creator of all the earth, the One who has all wisdom and understanding, the One who knows the future and can give counsel in the light of what is coming, is *really* open to us. We are told He will help us; we are told to ask Him for help; we are assured that, as the Lamb died as our substitute, He also died to open the way directly to the Father with our requests. To spurn this offer of help, paid for with a costly sacrifice, and to seek "counsel, but not of me" is to bring about an opposite result. This contrast is made clear in another place in Isaiah:

> For the Lord God will help me; therefore shall I *not* be confounded [or confused]: therefore have I set my face like a flint, and I *know* that I shall not be ashamed . . . . Who is among you that feareth the Lord, that obeyeth the voice of his servant, that walketh in darkness, and hath no light? Let him *trust* in the name of the Lord, and stay upon his God.
>
> Isaiah 50:7, 10

Yes, we may come frequently to foggy, dark places where we can't see one step ahead, but this is the repeated place of showing God practical reality in our trust of Him, and in our taking literally the possibility of asking, then waiting for Him to answer. These two verses combined are a contrast to verse 11, which is another warning of the same sort. Here is the picture given very vividly, along with another promise of a strongly negative result: "Behold, all ye that kindle a fire, that compass yourselves about with sparks: walk in the light of your fire, and in the sparks that ye have kindled. This shall ye have of mine hand; ye shall lie down in sorrow."

A strong promise! If we refuse to wait in the dark place with our hand in God's in trust, asking Him to show us the next step, really depending upon Him in prayer to answer us in this moment of history, and instead make all our own plans to unscramble our difficulties with all the modern helps we can find, God will not stop us. We can go on and light our own sparks and walk in the light of them. However, we can expect Him to be speaking the truth when He says that the result will be to "lie down in sorrow."

Ask of Me—is given us over and over again. We are to be shown marvelous things as a result of asking. When can we be shown, if we never ask in times when there is drastic need of having God's solutions? As individuals, as twos and threes in a variety of relationships—family, friends, groups, churches, organizations—we need to demonstrate that we really believe God is there, and that He is accessible, and that His promises are true. We need to demonstrate that we believe His negative promises, as well as His positive ones, by the way we react to the need of help. We need to stop and consider whether we are in danger of demonstrating that we really think "Egypt's help" is more dependable.

To whom will we go? To whom *else* can we go? How can we today demonstrate to the angels and demons, as well as to anyone who might be affected by our manner of reacting to a difficulty, that we really *believe in the existence of the God of the Bible?* Prayer is to be made "without ceasing." How much more thoroughly can prayer cease than when we turn our backs on any practical reality of God's answering prayer?

"And call upon me in the day of trouble . . ." (Psalms 50:15). God speaks to each of us in our diversity of problems—trouble in making a decision, trouble in finding the right house, trouble in knowing what we are fitted to do. "And call upon me in the day of trouble: I will deliver thee, *and thou shalt glorify me.*" Here is a result that does not speak of shame or confusion; here is a result to be excited about, as given in the Word of God. If we lack wisdom, we are to ask of God. To whom shall we go? Computers or God?

14

Starvation and Dry Bones

Picture after picture, paragraph after paragraph, the description of starving people of the world becomes an indelible image in our brains and an unforgettable shudder in our emotions. Starvation! Skeleton figures with gaunt, haunting eyes staring out of sockets too well defined. Bones covered with the merest coating of skin, walking, still moving. Bodies stretched out in death, quickly turning into valleys of dry bones. Famine bringing on starvation. Starvation disposing of flesh. Skeletons dropping into piles. Piles of dry bones scattered in the dust of a desert. Dust returns to dust.

> And the Lord God formed man of the dust of the ground, and breathed into his nostrils the breath of life; and man became a living soul.
>
> Genesis 2:7

And he said unto me, Son of man, can these bones live? And I answered, O Lord God, thou knowest. Again he said unto me, Prophesy upon these bones, and say unto them, O ye dry bones, hear the word of the Lord. Thus saith the Lord God unto these bones; Behold, I will cause breath to enter into you, and ye shall live: And I will lay sinews upon you, and will bring up flesh upon you, and cover you with skin, and put breath in you, and ye shall live; *and ye shall know that I am the Lord.*
Ezekiel 37:3–6

God who made man and woman in the first place—not just as physical bodies which could breathe and walk and live—made them living souls with the possibility of having spiritual life. This marvelous Infinite Creator has watched through centuries the reverse take place as sin has brought the abnormal situation of famine, starvation, death, and return to bones and finally dust—body after physical body, and soul after spiritual soul. "For I have no pleasure in the death of him that dieth, saith the Lord God: wherefore turn yourselves, and live ye" (Ezekiel 18:32). The centuries of people dying have brought God no pleasure, have brought sorrow to the Creator, as demonstrated in the weeping of Jesus over Jerusalem's turning away. The reverse of making man out of dust and breathing life into him has been death—death of physical body and of living soul. Slashed artworks bring pain to the artist. How much more the return of living souls to valleys of dry bones would bring pain to the Creator of life itself!

For I have no pleasure in the death of him that dieth, saith the Lord God: wherefore turn yourselves, and live ye. What is He talking about? Physical life? Spiritual life? *Both.* He who created human beings created them with both kinds of life, and as sin separates people from God, the resulting death is a double one, spiritual and physical. Many people alive, well, with flesh firm and skin a healthy color, are rattling dry and dusty bones spiritually. Many people spiritually alive and well are losing their flesh and soon will physically be skeletons of drying bones. The death of the Son of God, the Second Person of the Trinity, the long-promised Messiah Jesus, brought about the specific and absolute result of life in exchange for death. Those who believe Him and accept what He died to make possible will once more experience the breathing of God into their nostrils the breath of life. Each one who believes becomes a living soul, alive to God, and a fresh reborn creature who will live forever. Each one of these living souls will one day experience the changing of a set of dusty bones, dead body, or dying body into a resurrected body that will live forever! The breathing of the breath of the Lord God into all the bodies as they are resurrected is a fantastic reality we have to look forward to. He who breathed into Adam will then once again breathe into each body which has become "dust," and into the ones who will be alive at Christ's return, but who await the changed body. Dusty bones to live forever, covered with sinews and flesh:

> So I prophesied as I was commanded: and as I prophesied, there was a noise, and behold a shaking, and the bones came together, bone to his bone. And when I beheld, lo, the sinews and the flesh came up upon them, and the skin covered them above: but there was no breath in them. Then said he unto me, Prophesy unto the wind, prophesy, son of man, and say to the wind, Thus saith the Lord God; Come from the four winds, O breath, and breathe upon these slain, that they may live . . . . and the breath came into them, and they lived, and stood up upon their feet, an exceeding great army.
>
> Ezekiel 37:7–10

We are told in Ezekiel that God made clear that this was a vision and explained what the vision meant. The dry bones were Israel. Israel was saying, "Our bones are dried, and our hope is lost." God was speaking through Ezekiel to say very sharply and clearly, "One day I am going to bring you up out of your graves and bring you into the land of Israel and you will *know* that I am the Lord God, and that I am the One who has brought you up out of your graves, so that you can live in your own land. I will put My Spirit in you, and you will live and you will *know* that I, the Lord, have spoken it, have also performed it."

God is making known to Israel that He, who made people in the first place and breathed life into Adam, can take a dead people, physically dead or spiritually dead, and bring them back to life—a victory over the terrible separation Satan brought about. God is also saying that He is going to complete the promises He made to Israel, and that one day there will be a fulfillment of all He promised concerning the land: ". . . and [I] will cleanse them: so shall they be my people, and I will be their God. And David my servant shall be king over them; and they all shall have one shepherd . . ." (Ezekiel 37:23, 24).

> And as he [Jesus] sat upon the mount of Olives, the disciples came unto him privately, saying, Tell us, when shall these things be? and what shall be the sign of thy coming, and of the

end of the world? And Jesus answered and said unto them, Take heed that no man deceive you. For many shall come in my name, saying, I am Christ; and shall deceive many . . . . For nation shall rise against nation, and kingdom against kingdom: and there shall be famines, and pestilences, and earthquakes, in divers places. All these are the beginning of sorrows.

Matthew 24:3–8

Yes, the famines were definitely foretold. God is fair with us. We have been warned of wars and pestilences, of earthquakes and famines. We have been given a deeper more serious warning, however, and this is that "the love of many shall wax cold" (*see* Matthew 24:12). The warning goes on: "Therefore be ye also ready: for in such an hour as ye think not the Son of man cometh" (v. 44).

The famines may cause us to shudder. The famines may cause us to feel the responsibility to do all we can about helping the starving peoples. The famines may bring us to a sudden realization that perhaps we *are* living in the time close to the return of the Lord. But the sight of dry bones scattered in the deserts of the world ought to be a sober reminder of something very personal to each of us who are children of the Living God.

What about my own spiritual life? How starved am I in the Lord's sight? Am I myself in a valley of dry bones, spiritually. Am I without flesh and sinews and breath, a sight which would bring horror to anyone who could see? Because I belong to the Lord and can never be separated from Him, have I taken for granted that I will be well fed without eating? That my love will stay warm without verbalizing it or demonstrating it in any way?

Starvation can take place because there is not any food—or because the food is not being eaten. If people's sympathies are out of balance, they can refuse to eat because others have no food and grow so weak that they can never prepare or grow or find food for the starving ones. A measure of good health must be kept in order for the well to care for the sick, the strong to care for the weak, the living to care for the dying, the fed ones to bring food to the starving. We are given the Bible, the Word of God, to "eat" in its unpolluted form. We are to drink the uncontaminated milk of the Word, with no drops of poison in it to weaken us. We are to eat the strong meat of the Word, unadulterated with new preservatives, which some people think is needed to keep it "modern." God has supernaturally given milk that does not go sour, meat that keeps forever fresh. We are to feed on the Bread of Life as we stay close to the

Lord, and truly communicate in prayer and receive all He has to nourish us with. An unfed person has not the strength to love and communicate as he or she should.

Think for a moment how utterly serious it is that we *may* be the very Christians who are needed to "blow the trumpet" of warning in the midst of the most devastating period of history of the centuries. How can we "blow" if our breath is all gone? God has provided food for us to feed on, day by day. The Holy Spirit will prepare it for us to digest, as He opens our eyes of understanding as we read. But we need to eat. Let each picture you see of famine, starvation, scattered bones, bring you to a full stop of contemplating how to care for the physically starving, but also a pause to reach out for the Bible and drink a long draft of the milk of the Word, praying, "Breathe on me, breath of God, that I may be warm and alive and ready to be used, and not in danger of being in a spiritual valley of bones right now."

> . . . O ye dry bones, hear the word of the Lord . . . .
> Behold, I will cause breath to enter into you, and ye shall
> live . . . . And shall put my spirit in you, and ye shall live,
> and I shall place you in your own land: then shall ye know that
> I the Lord have spoken it, and performed it, saith the Lord.
> Ezekiel 37:4, 5, 14

15

Castor Oil and Nutrition

A dear friend of mine, born in Indonesia of Dutch parents, was caught with her mother in years of concentration-camp living during the growing-up period of childhood. She missed out on a whole period of life, not only in the area of education and childhood toys and games, but in basic nutrition. The most horrifying part of the food in this particular Japanese concentration camp was the misnomer which attached the name "food" to what was served in bowls to the prisoners. Hunger causes people to eat almost anything that is provided. The feel of something in the mouth, the need of something sliding down the throat, and the desire to have something in the stomach cause people to swallow without analyzing what is being swallowed. And if nothing else is in sight, what good would analysis do, anyway? What was offered daily in this place was a mixture. True, there was a certain amount of grain, meal, or rice, so that if anyone asked, the minimal amount of basic food was being given to prevent starvation. Statistics as to content, if only part of the story were told, would undoubtedly satisfy some sort of regulation.

What was the rest of the story? *Castor oil.* Yes, castor oil was mixed with all the bowls of mush, so that digestion would be prevented. The food would be expelled before very much nourishment could be absorbed into the system. Starvation was being assured, in the midst of giving that which could be camouflaged as sufficient food. It was a way of reducing the number of mouths to feed. The castor oil worked more rapidly in some cases than others. People's systems differed enough so that some lived longer than others. One by one, however, people died because the castor oil had removed the possibility of the food accomplishing what it could have accomplished in each body, had it been given in its original state—pure and unmixed with a purgative.

How was it that this little girl, her mother, and some others lived to tell the tale? Because of the variety of work to be done, some people worked in the gardens or in the kitchens—weeding lettuce or peeling vegetables for the nonprisoners' meals. The little girl's mother (and others) were able to put bits of food into their mouths and to hide a few leaves of lettuce or scraps of things to share later in the day. Thus, some who were able to have some untainted food to eat and digest kept up enough strength to live. At the end of the time they were malnourished and depleted in every way, skin and bones without energy, but they were still alive and slowly able to gain a measure of health, as proper food was provided. My friend is an adult now. The lost years, however, can never be given back to her in this life. Not only is there a memory that cannot be erased, but her physical and psychological system has certain inevitable scars from the ordeal.

"Did you have a good day of prayer?" I asked a young theological student who had shared in our special day of fasting and prayer. "No, I can't say that I did. Really, you know I find it difficult to define the difference between prayer and meditation. I can't find the reality of trust for prayer," he said hesitantly, and then went on: "Reading Tillich and some of those men can't easily be forgotten, and somehow the doubts keep coming back, and you just wonder about things."

Prayer—mixed with the wrong connotation of meditation. A Personal God with whom one made in His image can communicate—mixed with a God afar off, unattainable, the "god" behind God. A created universe made by the Creator—mixed with a chance universe that evolved by random through eons of time. A literal Adam and Eve who really made a choice and literally fell—mixed with a myth that takes its place with other tales. A literal "second Adam" who really lived forever and came to be man, to make it possible for people to be conformed to His image—mixed with a nebulous, unreal Jesus whose coming is a romantic, emotional story without substance. A *mush* with the castor oil of liberalism and unbelief—mixed with phrases from God's Word that are true. A mush of biblical quotations—mixed with the castor oil of denial and dished out in the same bowl. A murky, oily mélange of God's truth and Satan's lies spooned into open mouths by the same Satan who wanted to purge all the truth from Eve's system in the first place. Mush—cancelling out spiritual nourishment.

As this student's struggles were unfolded in a small measure to me, I suddenly saw the concentration camp's bowls of starvation food and realized that *this* was the picture of this dear fellow's diet for a long enough time to give problems which will not disappear immediately. When someone has had the mixed diet for a long time, how quickly can the system begin to digest the pure grain of God's Word without intestinal troubles?

Who is being fed such spiritual mush, in which the good food cannot be separated from the castor oil which is driving the good grain right out of the system? Many theological students are in situations where things are blurred—and the wrong concepts bring subsequent results. In such situations, the spiritual body grows thin and people are unaware that their food is having an opposite effect from nourishment. But it is not just the theological students who find they are robbed of strength and trust, because these are the ones who become the writers, the speakers, the pastors, and the teachers—and the mixture is then spooned out in the "bowls" of books and sermons and fed to a variety of people of all ages and sizes, who open their hungry mouths expecting food. These people swallow what they are fed, and faith is purged out of an emaciated body.

God speaks in Jeremiah: "For the pastors are become brutish, and have not sought the Lord . . . and all their flocks shall be scattered" (Jeremiah 10:21). He continues firmly:

Woe be unto the pastors that destroy and scatter the sheep of my pasture! saith the Lord. Therefore thus saith the Lord God of Israel against the pastors that feed my people; Ye have scattered my flock, and driven them away, and have not visited them: behold, I will visit upon you the evil of your doings, saith the Lord.

Jeremiah 23:1, 2

He goes on to say that these scattered people are to be gathered up out of all countries and brought again to the fold: "And I will set up shepherds over them which shall feed them: and they shall fear no more, nor be dismayed, neither shall they be lacking, saith the Lord" (v. 4).

"Oh, yes," you may say. "This is speaking of Israel in a future time. They are the people being spoken of." Right, but the Lord also has sheep who are meant to be fed day by day, week by week, as shepherds "pastor them," in Christian churches now. Shepherds are meant to be feeding their flocks with food which nourishes spiritually, with the unadulterated truth of the Word of God. Doubts are not meant to be mixed in. In fact, the good food of the pastors' preaching is meant to cast out the fears. Those who are well fed in this way are to be *not* dismayed. There is not to be a castor-oil mixture which takes away all the food and leaves nothing but gnawing fear and sick hunger. Those who are fed what God intends for pastors, shepherds, to feed them are to be *not* "lacking."

What has happened? How does it all start? Jeremiah is given something to explain to Israel and to us: "For my people have committed two evils; they have forsaken *me* the fountain of living waters, and hewed them out cisterns, broken cisterns that can hold no water" (Jeremiah 2:13). It is a double message. God has been forsaken. The *Personal Infinite Creator God* has been denied, turned away from, said not even to exist. Then the teaching stemming forth is like a vessel that is broken and cannot hold the water. The water of the Spirit cannot be poured out of a broken "pitcher." Empty of water, the cracked pitcher pours emptiness into cracked cups! Another picture of the same thing—food mixed with that which will not let it nourish.

God calls out to professors and students, pastors and people, to every one of us who is in grave danger in the twentieth-century spiritual threat of being thrown into this "concentration camp." God calls out: "Go and proclaim these words toward the north, and say, Return, thou backsliding Israel, saith the Lord . . . . And I will give you pastors according to mine heart, which shall *feed* you with knowledge and understanding" (Jeremiah 3:12, 15).

God makes it clear that the true food which will give us spiritual health and strength and cause us to grow and have spiritual energy and power is described by the words *knowledge* and *understanding*. How fantastic! God has made it undeniably clear that the teaching and preaching of pastors is to bring knowledge. There is to be "content"— the full content of the whole Word of God. This is to give comforting and satisfying knowledge which will push away fear and dismay. There is to be "understanding" of that knowledge. Questions are to be answered as well as possible. Things are to be put in several ways by patient teachers, desiring to make it possible for Sunday-school children, college students, seminarians, or congregations to really *understand*. And this understanding is not to leave huge gnawing pains in the intestines because of the lack of "grain" remaining. This is the kind of understanding which will be fulfilling and lasting.

How sobering it is to realize that Jesus speaks to all His disciples down through the centuries when He says to Peter: "Lovest thou Me?—Feed My lambs. Lovest thou Me?—Feed My sheep."

It is a serious responsibility to feed the flock—the very little lambs as well as the older sheep—with nourishing, lasting food, the whole-grain, full-bodied wheat of the food which God prepared in His Word. The need to be aware of not eating food that has been mixed with "castor oil" is also serious. Sheep or shepherd, the strength to accomplish and the possibility of fulfilling our responsibility—or of being properly aware—are not impossible if we listen to God's Word in this context:

> Fear thou not; for I am with thee: be not dismayed; for I am thy God: I will strengthen thee; yea, I will help thee; yea, I will uphold thee with the right hand of my righteousness.
>
> Isaiah 41:10

Whatever we need to ask forgiveness for, to begin again and do, or whatever we need to go on doing where the going seems hard and knees are wobbly, as we pick the bits of lettuce and take the crumbs of food in the face of possible attack, let us keep on! *His* promise to help applies. Be fed. Feed others. Turn away from the devastating effects Satan wants you to have from the castor oil! The source of food has *not* been removed from the world. It is available. Analyze and turn from the "mush," but remember that the effects have left a weakness that is more devastating in some than in others. "Lord, I believe; help Thou my unbelief," can be the beginning prayer, time after time. His strength is made perfect in weakness. Verbalize this weakness to Him. If you ask *Him* for bread, He will not give you a stone—or meal mixed with castor oil to remove the effects of the meal.

16

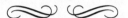

Sponge Cake or Noodles?

"I've really blown it now! I'm sorry—but what good is being sorry when it is impossible to pick up the pieces? It is impossible to go back and live that time over again. I wish I could, but time can't be wiped out. The things I've done can't be undone; the things I've said can't be unsaid; the effect I've had on history has already taken place. I feel like a gluey mess that ought to be tossed in the garbage pail. Life is just impossible."

Have you ever said anything like that? Have you ever felt an overwhelming wave of finality as regrets washed over you, threatening to drag you out into a sea of hopelessness? Such final feelings of worthlessness can turn into egotistical introspection for the Christian, failing to remember that the One who made the universe out of nothing is not limited and does not look at any human being—broken as that one may be—and see a "blank" or a hopeless mess ready for the trash pile. God—the Creator of all things out of nothing—is a God of diversity and without limit in His creative ideas. He can take any one of His children in the midst of history and at that point create an amazing work of art with what looks like "the end." The end can become a surprise beginning, when placed in the hands of an expert.

Listen carefully to this true story. Some years ago, a lovely girl, Jane, was helping to prepare food for the weekend meals at Chalet les Mélèzes. As we looked over the menus together, I wrote out my favorite sponge-cake recipe for her to make, while I rushed around to do other things. After a time a puzzled-looking Jane came to show me a very strange mixture, yellow, sticky, gluey. "Is this what it's supposed to look like? Shall I put it into the pan now?"

"Oh, no," I said in a rather horrified tone. "Please don't. It's not right at all. You have left something out, I'm sure."—"No, I followed your instructions perfectly. I know I did."—"Here, let's look at the book, you *must* have forgotten something."

So we read and checked each item—once, twice, three times. "But I'm sure it's all in order. I mixed it just as it said. The white of egg was beaten light, but it just disappeared into the mixture and it all got heavy and sticky. Oh, dear; what's wrong?" she wailed. Once more we slowly read the book's directions—and suddenly she remembered. "I know now. I didn't put any sugar in it. Shall I throw the mess out? Shall I start with new stuff?"

"No, wait; we can't afford that," I said hastily, putting out my hand to take the bowl, protect the "mess," and stir it thoughtfully. "Let me think—egg, salt, baking powder, flour, water. What can I do with that?" Silence and patience for a moment. "Wait while I think." Suddenly I exclaimed with excitement, "I *know*, I *know*. Noodles! I can turn it into noodles." While Jane watched in wonder, I added flour, first a little, then a little more, mixing, kneading first in the bowl, then turning it out on a floured board. When the mixture would take no more flour, I got out the rolling pin and rolled it out vigorously. Thinner and thinner the pale-yellow stiff mixture spread out on the board until it was almost paper thin. "Now," I exclaimed in satisfaction, "we'll put some heavy weights—those cans will do—on each of the four corners, and let it dry awhile." After the right period of time I took scissors and, folding the dry paperlike mixture, cut it in fine thin strips—which rapidly piled up in lovely heaps to be tossed with our fingers so they could separate and dry. There—not a sponge cake, but noodles—perfectly beautiful, fresh, wonderful homemade noodles. No, not for dessert, not to put under the strawberries, but to make a marvelous chicken noodle soup. With broth made from boiling leftover chicken bones for hours and hours—with some chicken bouillon added, some finely chopped onion and celery added with the homemade noodles and a dash of soy sauce—steaming bowls of soup were placed before thirty famished people. "What fantastic chicken noodle soup!"—"I never tasted such good noodles. May I have the recipe?"

I smiled at Jane across the table. "Not sponge cake, but marvelous noodles which are just as important," I remarked. "Don't ever forget this, Jane."

Don't ever forget what? Don't ever forget that if you can't be a "sponge cake" because of having spoiled something which you can't go back and do over, the Lord can make you into marvelous "noodles." Just say it to yourself, anytime you feel you have "blown it"—"I can't be a sponge cake now, but I can be noodles."

The Bible gives us a similar illustration to emphasize the wonder of what God can do for us as we put ourselves into His hands, letting Him take over and do with us what He is able to do. In Jeremiah 18, we have the vivid picture of a potter taking a pot or a vase or a pitcher he had made and, seeing that it had been marred by something, molding it over again into something else, ". . . as seemed good to the potter to make it."

> Then the word of the Lord came to me saying, O house of Israel, cannot I do with you as this potter? saith the Lord. Behold, as the clay is in the potter's hand, so are ye in mine hand, O house of Israel.
>
> Jeremiah 18:5, 6

The Lord is able to do what He will with His children, if they turn to Him and become clay in His hands, but He does not force any one of us. "Ye have not, because ye ask not," is something to be thought of in this connection. As one who has been born into God's family through coming to Him in His accepted way—through Christ—it is also necessary to turn to the Father when a "mess" has been made. To ask forgiveness? Yes, but also to ask, "Please take me and make me into what You would have me be, *now*, at this point of history, on the basis of what I can*not* be, make me into what you *now* want me to be."

Listen to comforting words: "Remember ye not the former things, neither consider the things of old. Behold, I will do a new thing; now it shall spring forth; shall ye not know it? I will even make a way in the wilderness, and rivers in the desert" (Isaiah 43:18, 19).

What wilderness have you been wandering in recently? What dry and dusty desert has been your walking place? What kind of a gluey mess in your life has replaced the fluffy sponge-cake mixture? Are you about ready to give up and say, "What's the use . . ."? There must be a literal, specific, definite coming (as Jane came to me) and a turning over of the "bowl of your life," asking for fresh direction, acknowledging you have missed the way, turned aside, plowed on stubbornly in the desert. "Please—I'm sorry. Do a new thing. Make a way; let rivers gush in the dry spot of right now. Make me into the noodles of your choice!"

And what if the gluey mess is not just one life, but a relationship—one and one—or a group that is ready to fly apart—or a church where things are dry, dusty, or sticky and gluey? The two people or the group or the church ought to come together to the One who can take the whole "bowl," the whole situation, and add the needed ingredients—whatever that might be—to blend together the ones who are bowing, asking, and seeking His help realistically after making a mess. He is completely capable of making a whole churchful of "noodles," to be marvelously appreciated by the surrounding community who need to be fed!

> And they that shall be of thee shall build the old waste places: thou shalt raise up the foundations of many genera-tions; and thou shalt be called, The repairer of the breach, The restorer of paths to dwell in . . . . Then shalt thou delight thyself in the Lord . . . .
>
> Isaiah 58:12, 14

We are to be delighted with what the Lord has done with us, but first we need to let Him do it. What if Jane had secretly thrown the mess away without asking? Be careful to own up to your need of help. Sponge cake? Or noodles? Or the garbage can?

17

Careful Conversation

Love is a much misused word and misunderstood even by Christians whose "mark" is supposed to be love shown in a variety of ways. At present, many valentine cards are flying about the country, speaking of one or another sort of affection, and the day of many grandmothers and grandfathers—as well as mothers and fathers, children and young people—is a bit cheered up by a reminder that someone was thinking of them and cared enough to express it in a way that took a bit of time, thought, originality, and communication which could be felt and observed. However much we may scream "commercial" about sending some sort of a squeeze of the hand across the miles, *something* is better than *nothing* in reminding us to be thoughtful and to care what sort of an effect our still being alive today has on a number of people who love us—and on some who are lonely and may have nobody else to indicate that their feelings matter to *somebody*. Yes, even an "artificial" (as some would call it) day or period of time to bring forth communication can be a helpful reminder to stop in the too-busy hour-by-hour, day-by-day life and say to someone, "I love you. You are significant to me. You matter. It is important that you are alive," or something in that direction.

Conversation is supposed to have an effect on the people who are hearing what we are saying, even as writing is supposed to have an effect on the people to whom we are writing. What kind of an effect? In 1 Corinthians 13, the strongly worded admonition to us is that we are to speak with love. The strong picture here is that even though a person can speak with the tongues of men and angels—if it is without love, it is like the clank of brass or the tinkling of a cymbal. Speaking is to be in love, with love, and to be prompted by love. Chapter 14 goes on to say that we are to follow after love, so that we can speak in a way that will build up people in their understanding and give them comfort. True comfort can only come from knowing the true truth and the true hope and the true promises of the Living God who tells us that one way to comfort one another is to converse about the coming of Jesus again someday. Our compassion and love are to prompt us to *comforting* conversation, but also conversation which leads to learning something that will help us take a step forward (if we think of the Christian life as a walk) or to start the shoot of a new leaf (if we think of the Christian life as a plant).

We are often tempted to let our conversation go on for hours when we are tired or feel relaxed, and we just let subjects go on and on with no consideration for anyone else and no thought of what someone else might need. Such conversation can be full of "weed killer," spraying the plants all around us with a poison that stunts growth, instead of fresh water and a little proper fertilizer to encourage growth. What devastation often takes place in an evening's careless conversation—with doubts and bitternesses, gossip and criticism slashing the tender growth of understanding, ideas, creativity, or fresh love for the Lord and desire for His will in others. People can walk home, go to bed, and lie awake full of doubts as to whether it is worth bucking the criticism about the book, article, painting, landscape-gardening project, open house on Wednesday evenings, meal planned for an old-folks' home, willingness to give a day a week to visiting a blind person to read aloud, sketches to illustrate a Bible story, or fresh way of telling true truth to prisoners. There are doubts even as to whether it is worth trying to find the Lord's will at all or to pray about anything in life—whether it is worth the effort needed for any alive, fresh, new, loving, compassionate desire to glorify God and help people to find Him, or to show kindness. While tossing and turning in bed, the careless remarks, the unkind blasts, and the raised eyebrows of "That's impossible!" spoken louder than words can bring such discouragement that the result is the death of some precious seed which the Lord had planted in His plan for someone's next step.

Second Timothy 2:17 says sharply to us all, "And their word will eat as doth a canker . . . ." The sleepless night of tossing over what has been carelessly said or argued can be pictured as a block of quiet time eaten up by an ugly canker sore—spreading and spreading until the time has been destroyed.

A Christian's careless conversation can be used in the devil's plan to hinder or delay the plan which God is unfolding step by step to His children, even in areas covering the basic following of the most important things of truth. In Galatians, Paul says, "Ye did run well; who did hinder you that ye should not obey the truth?" (5:7). Someone's conversation is hindering the following of the One "that calleth you" (v. 8). It happened in Paul's time, and it happens now, hour by hour. We need to spend time in conscious prayer that we may not "hinder" someone else from following what the Lord is calling that one to do, whether it be for a day or a year. It is a serious thing to hinder carelessly another one of the Lord's children from quickly obeying. It is a serious thing to do the very opposite of what God admonishes us to do. When we are told in Galatians 5:15 that there is danger "if ye bite and devour one another," it is in the area of conversation. We are being warned with a flashing light that there is danger when we *depart* from talking with love, kindness, long-suffering, concern, compassion, and a desire to help rather than to hinder the Lord's leading.

However, there is a danger not just in long times of talking together with careless disregard for what we might be doing to each other. Questions can be completely without compassion, totally unloving, and without any fraction of love for the lost. Yes, honest questions deserve honest answers. But there are two things to think about before asking a question in a group of people who have come together as a class, discussion group, gathering of friends, Bible-study group, or casual gathering on a beach: (1) Is this an honest question of mine or a tricky question designed to upset the person answering, as the Pharisee's questions were labeled by Jesus? (2) Is it an honest question, but are there people present who do not know whether or not the God of the Bible is really existent—who may not have another opportunity to hear their own deep questions dealt with, and who will be turned aside by theological hairsplitting?

Consider for a moment that perhaps you have entered a grouping of people where there are a Hindu, a devil worshiper, a Buddhist, an atheist, a confused church member, a materialistic businessman with a minimal interest in spiritual values. They and a variety of others have come because of someone's concern in bringing them or praying for them—and then the question period is opened. With what breathless interest someone may be listening! In front of anyone who does not know whether or not God exists—or anyone who is close to being born again, but who is bothered by a haunting doubt—suddenly a Christian asks a question which sounds like an aggressive attack in hairsplitting vocabulary about some point in which theological schools differ, such as predestination, mode of baptism, or what person's apologetics are correct. The whole evening can be negative in its effect.

But worse than that, the *time* is lost, never to be retrieved. We are responsible for the use of time, and it seems to be doubly so for the use of other people's time. So often it is the Christian who uses up the time during which non-Christians might have drastically needed and received help. Extravagance in money is being talked about because "depression" is near. But what about costly, extravagant use of time— because *time* will never be more abundant until this life is over?

Paul says to Timothy in 2 Timothy 2:14, ". . . charging them before the Lord that they strive not about *words* to no profit, but to the subverting of the hearers." I feel Paul is talking about *conversation* and questions which use up the time of a whole period during which the "hearers" need some positive help. It isn't that Paul is saying that discussion and asking questions is ruled out when he goes on to speak of "vain babblings" in verse 16 and "foolish and unlearned questions" in verse 23, but he *is* warning each of us who is a child of the Living God to show forth our love and compassion for each other and for the lost ones of the world when we sit conversing and asking questions. He goes on to urge and command (as he speaks with the authority of God because this is the Bible): "And the servant of the Lord must not strive;

but be gentle unto all men, apt to teach, patient, In meekness instructing those . . . that they may recover themselves out of the snare of the devil, who are taken captive by him at his will" (vv. 24–26). There is to be a positive result from conversation, and question-and-answer times, as well as in teaching-preaching times.

Love expressed is not simply a valentine, not simply the words *I love you* said at the end of a phone conversation, an evening, or in public acclaim—but it is to be expressed in the content of our conversation, in the careful choosing of when to ask a question and when to keep quiet, in considering other people before one's self as we use precious time never to be relived. "The greatest of these is love."—"Follow after love." These can be shown by each of us today and every day.

18

The Security of Insecurity

Anyone who has seen an avalanche thunder down a mountainside—sweeping strong rocks and trees, chalets and barns along with it as though they were pebbles and matchsticks in a stream—or anyone who has looked at the devastation caused by a cyclone such as the one which destroyed Darwin, Australia, knows what insecurity *feels* like. The sight of normally solid, dependable old landmarks suddenly shifting, sliding, and crumbling brings a reaction usually accompanied by an action! The action would in most cases be one of escaping (on foot or by airlift) to more solid ground, the most dependable, safe area available.

These days, our news media report to us the crumbling of far more than mountainsides, houses, and towns. The crumbling economy and shifting value of money fill with dismay any who have looked with satisfaction at bonds and stocks or bankbooks as something to be counted on for a period ahead, to fulfill the plans for an account book full of notations.

Security is so often defined as a comforting amount of material goods in a house or bank, or plots of garden or lands. Security is daydreamed about with blueprints for the use of time and talents for years ahead, as well as with the certainty that the safest place has been discovered in which to be hidden from famine, flood, fire, pestilence, or war. Security conjures up a picture of warmth, comfort, settledness, with no "risk" blowing in a chill air to bring a shiver.

Who wouldn't prefer to be "secure" rather than "insecure," whether one is speaking of material things, health, emotions, talents, self-assurance, or human relationships? Yet—there is a danger signal flashed to us which needs to be given very definite attention. You probably read in the accounts of the Australian cyclone that warnings had been given which had not been heeded because they seemed so impossible. We are warned that if we are secure in this world's things, we are in danger of being insecure in that which matters most. We can be lulled to sleep by a false sense of security. If we are rich enough, have health that is satisfactory, are young and strong enough, have a great deal of energy and talents, have food enough, and land and houses enough to feel a protection from the specter of "want" in its usual forms, then we can be harmed by the sweet drowsiness of warm security. If we have in our hands (held figuratively behind our backs) a human secu-rity, we are not apt to experience the sensation of *insecurity* which is so important to feel.

"How ridiculous!" you may exclaim. "Who would find *in*security a good thing?" Paul says, "Therefore I take pleasure in infirmities, in reproaches, in necessities, in persecutions, in distresses for Christ's sake: for when I am weak, then am I strong" (2 Corinthians 12:10).

These things are a list of very insecure realities. They are not theoret-ical things. Paul has already listed shipwrecks, prison, beatings, and hunger as happenings which would make anyone feel insecure about provision of the natural means of bodily comforts! Why is he taking pleasure in further difficulties? What double-talk is: "When I am weak, then am I strong"? It seems to me that Paul is saying in other words, "When I am insecure in this world's things, then I have a reality of my security in the Lord." Paul makes clear that it is when he is crying out to God in prayer—in the midst of the insecurity that the thorn in the flesh gave him—that God's strength is promised to be given to him in his weakness.

Come to the writer of Psalm 91, as he speaks of the secure place which is the only completely dependable place to be: "He that dwell-eth in the secret place of the most High shall *abide* under the shadow of the Almighty. I will say of the Lord, He is my refuge and my fortress: my God; in him will I trust" (v. 1, 2). But wait a minute—a fortress speaks of protection, and there must be an awareness of the reality of a situation in which protection is needed. One runs to find refuge only in a moment of need.

> Surely he shall deliver thee from the snare of the fowler, and from the noisome pestilence. He shall cover thee with his feathers, and under his wings shalt thou trust: his truth shall be thy shield and buckler.
>
>   Psalms 91:3, 4

Could we run to hide under His wings if the noise of difficulty did not hit our ears with some kind of fearsome insecurity? As we read our news magazines or hear the news on radios, as we groan over the loss of money or lands and over the unsettled state of affairs in city or nation, are we not alerted to the fact that we may have been expecting a security for our lifetime in earthly things? We need to acknowledge quietly before the Lord the fact that insecurity in earthly things can open the way to our literal running to *Him* and find filling us the actual emotion of security under His "feathers" in His care.

> Thou shalt not be afraid for the terror by night; nor for the arrow that flieth by day; Nor for the pestilence that walketh in darkness; nor for the destruction that wasteth at noonday.
>
>   Psalms 91:5, 6

It is not meant to be theoretical that in troubled times God's children will one by one find the reality of His care—it is to be a part of history. The truth of what God has spoken will take place literally in life after life.

> He shall call upon me, and I will answer him: I will be with him in trouble; I will deliver him, and honour him.
>
>   Psalms 91:15

When will we "call," when will we "run"—seeking His security? Only when we are insecure in some portion of this world's "necessities" of daily life and safety. How secure a spot was Daniel's in front of those lions? How secure do you think the three young men felt with their hands bound and their feet unable to walk with ropes around them, as they were on their way to the door of the fiery furnace? How secure do you imagine Elijah felt as he sat by a wilderness brook during a time of famine? What security did these men have—from the world's viewpoint? What security did Hudson Taylor have, as he set forth by sailboat for China for the unknown future of his young life?

It is when worldly or earthly security is shaken to its core that we are ready to cry out without a comfortable bit of "something to fall back on" clutched in our hands. The *reality* of trusting God comes when our entire security is really *felt* (by our emotions as well as our minds) to be in Him.

These days are troubled ones. *Newsweek*'s and *Time*'s looking back over the year's events may have made you feel ill. Predictions by a variety of brilliant men may strike fear into your heart. But together let us be thankful for the fact that we are being made aware of the insecurity, so that we can have the very specific result of security. Thank God for the security of insecurity!

"When I said, My foot slippeth; thy mercy, O Lord, held me up" (Psalms 94:18). Our action must be to run to God—to more solid ground, the most dependable, safe place available in the universe. All other ground is sinking sand.

19

~~~

What Is My Mess of Pottage?

Do you remember the story (in Genesis 25:29–34) of the day when Esau came back from his tiring day of hunting—exhausted, ravishingly hungry, with only one burning desire which filled his whole being, driving every other desire away, as well as every logical kind of thought or reason. Esau desired food! His blood sugar was low, his stomach was causing him gnawing pain, his imagination was filled with thoughts of what a bowl of hot food would *taste* like and *feel* like going down, and how comfortable a full tummy would be once the meal was over. His passion was rising, all in the direction of physical satisfaction in the area of all that would accompany sitting or lying down and guzzling food. "My kingdom for a bowl of my favorite food!" was literally his violent and exaggerated summing up of the worth of an immediate satisfaction. "I want what I want at any price!" was his set of mind.

Jacob was cooking, and as Esau heaved into sight the "red lentile" minestrone filled the air with drifts of tantalizing odors. This was Esau's favorite meal. "Feed me some of the red pottage. I'm about to faint with starvation, please dish me up some of that minestrone!" was the kind of request Esau made. Jacob set forth to make a bargain on the strength of what he felt would be the extent of his brother's violent, greedy desire. Jacob was sure the price could be high. "And Jacob said, sell me this day thy birthright" (v. 31).

Now, the birthright was a most important inheritance and would be something that would change the whole future of Esau's life, as well as his children's and children's children's lives. His decision would affect many people, and his thoughts should have been of others as well as himself. But Esau's price was not counted; he didn't care in the least how costly a bowl of soup this would be. He wanted what he wanted—with a violent disregard for the future and with no pause to think what would be a proper evaluation of the worth of what he was asking for. There was no consideration of priorities or the need to take a more balanced position. Determination filled him, and his reply was blurted out with a frightening finality: "I am about to die: and what good shall this birthright be for me?" (see v. 32).

Jacob made him "sign on the dotted line," so that he couldn't go back on this rash statement. "And Jacob said, Swear to me this day; and he [Esau] sware unto him: and he sold his birthright unto Jacob" (v. 33).

Oh, frightening sight—had we been there to see it! A costly bowl of soup being sloshed into Esau's mouth, dripping from his beard. What slurps of satisfaction would have come forth, to disgust us with the ghastly imbalance of the price just paid for a temporary satisfaction. "What an exchange," we exclaim to ourselves. "What a horrible thing! How awful to watch a man eating a bowl of lentil soup which he has just paid for with a birthright which would have affected generations of people, as well as the rest of his own life. It is as bad as watching someone burn up his own creative artworks to warm his hands for a second. I don't want to look any longer."

"Then Jacob gave Esau bread and pottage of lentiles; and he did eat and drink, and rose up, and went his way: thus Esau despised his birthright" (v. 34). Despised his birthright! This is the description of an attitude of heart. Rather than feeling that no hunger, no difficulty, or no sacrifice could be too great to protect the birthright for himself and his family, he "despised" or kicked aside his birthright. The truth of the future meant nothing to him. Only the existential moment counted. No price was too high to pay for the abandonment of feeling responsibility and acting on the assumption that one might as well eat and drink for "tomorrow we die." The enormity of the imbalance did not cut through the violent passion of his desire enough to make him stop short in exchanging a birthright that affected years and centuries ahead for immediate satisfaction which would last only a few minutes or hours at the most.

Oh, stupid Esau! But what about me? What about you? What about us? "What is my mess of pottage?" How often do we ask this question of ourselves? It is important to verbalize the question. We are in constant danger of having the temptation to exchange something very precious—a priceless reality—for indulging our sudden violent desires. The violent desire may be involved with greed for eating and drinking, passion for money or material things, letting loose our anger in action and abandoning reason, giving in to depression without check, cursing God in despair or disappointment without even thinking of the trap which Satan set for Job and is setting for us, yielding to a sweeping sexual desire without waiting for the right framework. The "mess of pottage" that is dangerous to you and to me is any temptation to give in to violent speech or action or choice of direction, based on the fulfillment of the "feelings" of the immediate moment which will demonstrate vividly to anyone watching—angels or human people or demons—that we despise the promises of the Living God for our future. Time after time we have the opportunity for demonstrating the reality of our belief in the *truth* of truth, of our trust in God's promises. Time after time we can demonstrate by our responses and our choices that we really believe that no suffering for the present can be compared with the glories that are ahead of us in the plan of God. We have a miniscule amount of time to demonstrate this in times when it is hard to do so. We have such a short time to "run with patience," because when the race is over, the patience is not needed and cannot be a proof of our love and confidence in God.

Come to the twelfth chapter of Hebrews where we are being warned that people are watching us with eagerness. "A cloud of witnesses" is watching to see if we are going to lay aside sin which easily besets us, and "run with patience the race that is set before us" (v. 1). The possibility of doing this is outlined in the second verse as the way is given: We are to look unto or keep our eyes on Jesus, who endured the cross and who despised something—but that "something" was the *shame* of all the agony he had to go through, so that *we* could be handed the birthright! The extreme imbalance (if one could put it that way) is the excruciating cost of the Messiah's price paid to give us the birth-right. What double responsibility is ours to treat not like dirt that which He paid to give us. We are told to consider *Him,* think about what He endured, when we get faint and weary in our minds. Yes, *minds.* When we are swept by violent desire, we still have the possibility of making a choice in our minds to resist—or to accept and slurp the pottage greed-ily as did Esau. The choice is there. We can look to Jesus for help, but we are responsible for making a choice.

The warning is clear as we go on in the chapter. We are to follow peace and holiness diligently so that we will not allow bitterness to spring up. This is really a bitterness of imbalance—a violent bitterness we are being warned against, which can be compared to Esau's stupid, costly exchange. There are things we can do, choices we can make, that will remove from us the fulfillment of the things God has for us in this race. As we kick aside the cost of running with patience and dart off into the bushes to get out of the race for a while, the result will be something lost!

We who believe strongly that God will keep His promise of everlast-ing life, based on the completeness of the price Jesus paid on the cross to wash away our sins, know that nothing shall "separate us from the love of God," and that the words of Romans 8:38, 39 stand unchanged. However, we are told in that same chapter of Romans that if we hon-estly *hope* for that which we do not now see, we *wait with patience* for it (vv. 24, 25). We are not in danger of losing our salvation, but we are in danger of losing something that can never be had again, the actual fulfilling and living in this earthly period with some measure of pa-tience. We are constantly demonstrating something. There is not a "neutral" time. We are either demonstrating that we honestly believe what God has said—or we are demonstrating that we despise it.

> Looking diligently lest any man fail of the grace of God; lest
> any root of bitterness springing up trouble you, and thereby
> many be defiled; Lest there be any fornicator, or profane per-
> son, as Esau, who for one morsel of meat sold his birthright.
>   Hebrews 12:15, 16

Oh, how often we must bring ourselves up short. Verbalize the words as we ask, "What is my mess of pottage?" Then conjure up a vivid picture in our minds of a cloud of witnesses watching us slurp the soup of the moment, kicking aside, in the very act, the precious things God has for us.

20

Faith—God's Definition

"I wish I had faith to pray for a house with the space we need, in the right location."

"I wish I had faith to pray for an apartment at a rent we could pay."

"I wish I had the faith to pray literally for food, as it is becoming a real problem these days."

"I wish I had the faith to pray that our garden crop would grow."

"I wish I had faith to believe God could intervene in history in answer to prayer."

"I wish I had faith to take God's promises about prayer literally in just *some* area of my life."

"I wish God's existence and presence were real to me. I guess I just don't have the right kind of faith, because when I pray it seems like a recitation of words."

"I wish I had faith to pray for the needs of my children with expectancy."

"I wish I had faith to pray for our church, or other people I know, with the certainty that there would be *some* results."

"I wish I had faith to pray for the Lord's return with the excitement of real hope."

Is there some magic formula to be discovered for manufacturing "faith"? Is there a key to unlock a supply cupboard containing the faith some people seem to have discovered? Is there a mysterious level to be reached, which only the properly initiated can reach, where faith is then freely given?

By whose definition has the word *faith* come to have a mystical twist, so that it conjures up a hushed atmosphere with sights, sounds, and feelings enveloping the fortunate ones and driving out ordinary thought forms and logical understanding? Who has spread the idea that faith is separated from reason and mind—to be "experienced" even as people experience a light show with rock music, or a drifting "spiritual" floating by means of some sort of chemical or plant substance which is swallowed or smoked? What definition opens the way to faith for an elite who have had some sort of an experience (with a capital *E*) which others must either duplicate or be left in the cold outside a shut door? Is there a beginning place for exercising faith, as one would the muscles of the leg, when one *is* a Christian? Upon whom can we depend in sorting out possible reasons for lack of faith to carry out the literal admonition to "ask" rather than to "ask not"?

God speaks to us clearly concerning the base for faith, and the primary exercise for our faith. "So then faith cometh by hearing, and hearing by the word of God" (Romans 10:17). *Hearing* has to do with physical ears, first of all—but with the mind simultaneously. Hearing is accompanied by some sort of action in our minds, if words in a language we understand are being used. Ears and mind are simultaneously involved. In case we might think of music flowing through us without touching a thought process, God carefully speaks here of verbalized sound. It is the *Word of God* which is truth being unfolded by the use of a succession of meaningful words in human language.

The Word of God is the Bible. What makes it different is that it is what God has revealed to man, and is therefore true truth. What makes it different is *not* a floating, mystical, spiritual kind of "feeling," which bypasses language as it is normally used. Language can be used to say things that are *not true*, to deceive, to stir up responses that are wrong, to twist people's thinking. But when God's Word is spoken of, the basic difference is one of pointing out that there is a trustworthy, perfectly just and holy Person verbalizing something that can be depended upon. Here is something to "hear" with the eyes, enabling us to speak the words inside our own heads and think about them, or to hear as someone reads it to us. We are to be really shaken with the realization that we are not reading something another human being has said, so that we have a right to our opinion. We are sitting in awe, shaken with a recognition that we are to be listening with a different kind of awareness, ready to believe what is being said is accurate Otherwise we are judging, even as critics judge the writing of other people.

We are to listen to God's definition of "faith" with careful expectation of discovering what we have overlooked before, of really learning something that is true. However, it is to be learned with the same equipment with which God has created us to learn arithmetic, spelling, or how to bake a cake, plant a garden, or build a house that will stand the storms. Understanding does not come immediately and completely in the learning process in most areas of life. Understanding usually takes some amount of time, but the first requirement of understanding, as parents often stress to their children, is hearing—listening and paying attention to the content of what is being said.

God tells us in Hebrews 11:3: "Through faith we understand that the worlds were framed by the word of God, so that things which are seen were not made of things which do appear." What a staggering statement of fact, as well as a definition of what we are to start with in our exercise of faith. We are forcibly thrust back to the beginning of the Bible: "In the beginning God created the heavens and the earth," and we are told to *believe* that the Living God has spoken the truth when He has said He created the heavens and the earth. We are told to have faith demonstrated or exercised before God Himself and any others who know about it, by believing that God has spoken the truth when He said that He created all things. We are to read with eagerness the Genesis account, thrilling at the opportunity to have faith, to begin at the starting place God has given, and to state in the most emphatic way we can (in such individual diversity as playing an accompaniment on the piano, flute, violin, or with poetry or painting, prose spoken or written): "I have faith to believe You, Creator God, that You have made what I see, taste, smell, and hear. I believe what You have verbalized in Your Word. I believe in Your Creation of the universe. Thank You."

In 2 Peter 3:2–4, we are warned of scoffers who will make fun of and be scornful about the literalness or truth of the promises of the Second Coming of Jesus—saying that nothing has ever changed in history and that things will simply continue as they always have. In verse 5, a sharp finger is pointed at us in warning for this moment of twentieth-century temptation to Christians: "For this they willingly are ignorant of, that by the word of God the heavens were of old, and the earth standing out of the water and in the water." Here is the negative of the faith set forth in Hebrews 11. Here is a willful putting aside of the "beginning point," and a demonstration that then the "ending point" is also gone. Can we have faith for the present moment of literally trusting the promises connected with prayer? Can we have assurance and expectancy and literal hope of the Second Coming?—and willfully forget or turn away from, push aside and ignore the command to dwell on Creation? As the psalmist speaks of praising God and singing unto Him, his song is based on believing, having faith that: "By the word of the Lord were the heavens made . . . . For he spake, and it was done; he commanded and it stood fast" (Psalms 33:6, 9).

It is the God of Creation in whom we are to have faith. It is His spoken

Word we are to believe when He tells us He created the universe. It is our faith that the Creation actually took place which is to be our exercise of faith as a foundation to having the faith so that we can "ask." As we come with our requests "with thanksgiving" and thank God for what He has done in the past, we are to include thanksgiving for the act of Creation. "Let them praise the name of the Lord: for he commanded, and they were created" (Psalms 148:5).

"Through faith we *understand* that the worlds were framed by the word of God . . . ." Let us cast ourselves on our faces in the midst of twentieth-century discussion, and cry out for a reality of that faith to be such as will be pleasing to God. He has clearly given us the starting place. It is His definition of faith.

21

❧ ❧

Faltering Trust

When the coals are red on the hearth, or the logs are blazing in a wide fireplace, the chair is deep and comfortable, and a hot cup of one's favorite evening drink—chocolate, coffee, or herb tea—is being sipped slowly, even a wild wind howling around the house or making a moaning noise through the eaves can be an exciting sound, emphasizing the comfort and security of the snug little spot. A warm bed is the next place one expects to go to, deep and peaceful sleep is ahead—the shriek of the wind or the rattle of the shutters can be a lullaby giving new appreciation of the smoothness of the covers to be pulled around the shoulders. The slash of rain against the windows simply makes one appreciate the dry comfort of the blankets. If the wind seems to be blowing in two directions at once, it doesn't matter; the *feeling* of being protected is only more vivid.

Strong wind frequently changing direction and high waves tossing spray with a greater drive than rain are different matters when one is in a boat that pitches and rocks with sickening creaks of the wood, as if it were about to split in two. If it is a small open boat and the waves are washing in, fear and not pleasure is a natural response to such a storm. The little ship in which the disciples were tossed in the middle of the sea was being driven to and fro by a "contrary wind." Can't you imagine the chill of wet skin and clothing as the wind whirled around the men, destroying any possibility of directing the ship, and threatening to overturn it? Then suddenly the men caught sight of a form coming towards them. Could something be going wrong with their eyes? No, it was a man, but it couldn't be; it must be a ghost! Perhaps their teeth chattered with something more than cold, as sudden terror was added to their natural fear, and their screams arose above the sound of the wind and sea. There was no other boat in sight; there was no place from which help could come.

"But straightway Jesus spake unto them, saying, Be of good cheer; it is I; be not afraid" (*see* Matthew 14:27). I love the "straightway" because it portrays the gentleness and tenderness of Jesus and of God the Father. Jesus said He came to make known the Father. Jesus cared about quieting the fears immediately. Did He change the force of the waves and stop the wild wind right away? No, we know He didn't at this time. What then was the meaning of *be of good cheer, be not afraid* in that context? It carries us back to Psalms 46:1-3: "God is our refuge and strength, a very present help in trouble. Therefore will not we fear, though the earth be removed, and though the mountains be carried into the midst of the sea; though the waters thereof roar and be troubled, though the mountains shake with the swelling thereof." The reality of the presence of God with us, His tender love for us, and His trustworthiness as our Guide is to dispel our natural fear, even in the midst of storm and earthquake—while the waters are still roaring and the wind is still buffeting our faces and whipping our clothing around us. God is our Refuge during the time no visible change has come in the circumstances. Our complete trust is to be in Him alone, not merely in what we suddenly see Him doing for us. We are given moments of opportunity to demonstrate a steady trust.

As we continue reading in Matthew 14, we see that Peter was the one who answered Jesus with an impulsive and sudden feeling of faith in the power of the One who had made heaven and earth: "Lord, *if* it be thou, bid me come unto thee on the water." *If this is really the Lord,* thought Peter, *He can do anything. He can make me walk on the water too.* It was with faith that Peter stepped out of the ship into the midst of those wild waves in response to Jesus' command, "Come." Jesus was responding to Peter's requests which were based on faith. Peter had asked, requested, and made known his desire to Jesus, and Jesus had answered, "Come." In the midst of answered prayer, when we ask for guidance—"Shall I do this, Lord? If You want me to do this thing, let me know, and I will do it. Please lead me, Lord; I promise I will follow, if only I know. Guide me. Anywhere, Lord."—does the answer, "Come," insure us of a smooth walk ahead?

When Peter stepped into the waves, we are told that he walked on the water! Oh, fantastic moment—Peter is walking on that deep, wild, crashing sea! We are told so. "And when Peter was come down out of the ship [Do we think the ship held still? No, no; it pitched and tossed as much as ever!] he walked on the water." Yes, for a distance it was real walking on top of shifting water, huge waves piling under his feet with the motion you have felt if you have ever been swimming out in the sea. He believed Jesus could make it possible for him to do this impossible thing. The faith in the One who can do all things was present in Peter.

But when he saw the wind boisterous, he was afraid . . . . It was the immediate circumstance that caught his attention, and he "shifted his weight," so to speak. He realized that nothing had changed that he could *see*, as far as wind and waves went, and he shifted into thinking about the impossibility of it all. "It's impossible. I can't do it. I can't, I can't—I am going to drown. Help!" No, Peter, you can't do it. Did you think that *you* had been doing it for this distance you have already walked?

What is it that hits me, that hits us all when a scream arises within us and fear takes over and we cry out in a silent cry that no one hears but God, "I can't. It is impossible. What am I doing? What have I gotten into!"? If we have asked the Lord for His will, and He really has shown us, then what we have started to do is a double thing of looking at the waves, the unchanging circumstances, and then taking a measure of credit for what we already have been doing, rather than dwelling on the wonder of the fact that He has been doing it for us or through us. There has to be a sustaining trust, a continuing trust, a moment-by-moment trust in the Lord in whom we have put our faith when we have asked Him to call us, to tell us to *come*. If the Lord has said, "Come—do this, do that," we have to remember that, of course, it will be impossible to us, but we must continue to believe that *He* is able. The trust must be an active, unfaltering reality—or we will also begin to sink, because there is no promise that the circumstances will always change.

. . . Blessed are all they that put their trust in him.

Psalms 2:12

But let all those that put their trust in thee rejoice: let them ever shout for joy, because thou defendest them . . . .

Psalms 5:11

O Lord my God, in thee do I put my trust: save me from all them that persecute me, and deliver me: Lest he tear my soul like a lion, rending it in pieces . . . .

Psalms 7:1, 2

O taste and see that the Lord is good: blessed is the man that trusteth in him.

Psalms 34:8

Peter began to sink when he concentrated on the fierceness of the unchanging storm of difficulties and realized he couldn't continue by himself. Every one of us begins to "sink" when we do the same kind of thing—when we look at the enormity of the "impossibility" of what we are in the midst of, and we realize we cannot do it. We are not strong enough or clever enough or rich enough or brave enough or wise enough. *We can't go on.*

But then Peter ". . . cried, saying, Lord, save me." We are carried back to Psalms 34:6: "This poor man cried, and the Lord heard him, and saved him out of all his troubles." Yes, Jesus heard: "And immediately Jesus stretched forth his hand and caught him . . . ." The help came, but there was a rebuke! Peter need not have cried for help that time, if he had not faltered in his trust of the One in whom he had put his faith in stepping out. We can take comfort that the help came tenderly and immediately—but we must also listen to the rebuke and pray for a *longer* time of walking on the waves with a sustained trust in the power of the One who has told us to *come.* ". . . O thou of little faith, wherefore didst thou doubt?" (Matthew 14:31).

We are in danger of sinking. Ah, but that is not the worst danger; we are in danger of spoiling the marvelous demonstration that *God is able to do it.* What a beautiful sight it would have been to have seen Peter walk longer, in answer to Jesus' "Come." Only his faltering trust in the One in whom he had stepped out in faith stopped him. Our waves may be high right now in this moment of history. Let us pray for each other and each for ourselves that our trust falter not, that our faith be not so "little" as to last only a few steps. *O thou of little faith, wherefore didst thou doubt?*

22

⚜

Expectation—Vague or Vivid?

Jaapjan Berg is bending his blond head and earnest face over a piece
of grained wood as he is very carefully carving letters as well as his
eight-year-old skill can do them—really very even for his age. Come
closer and you will see that the letters are the beginning of a street name
in Holland. What can it be? An address, if it is completed, the address of
the new apartment where Jaapjan and his mother, Marry, and little
brother, Steven, have just recently moved, leaving their beloved larger
house because Daddy now cannot drive Steven to his school, and they
needed to be many kilometers closer. Hans was a most sensitive and
careful Christian father. Steven is a very handicapped, cerebral-palsied
child and in his special school he must learn to point out the pictures he
is matching, with his chin, because he cannot use his hands or legs and
is deaf.

Here has been a family drawn closer together because of great
difficulties, and their amazing closeness to the Lord. The resurrection
of the dead, the coming changed bodies of all living believers, handicapped in so many big and little ways, has taken up much time in family
conversation—around a beautifully set table with flowers always in the
center, or during outdoor walks where leaves, ferns, butterflies, a special tree, or a bird on a bush have been looked at carefully and enjoyed.
In the midst of enjoying the tiny things for which to say, "Thank You,"
and really appreciate daily, this family has looked forward with the
most vivid expectation to the return of Jesus: "For *then* Steven will run
and jump, make and feel things with his hands, be able to hug us, and
jump over things like that log. Steven will do wonderful things when
Jesus comes and all believers are changed in the twinkling of an eye,
and when we are finally in the new heaven and the new earth!"

Now Jaapjan is carving his new address and wants to place it on his
father's grave site, so that "if Jesus comes back, and Daddy rises first
[Scripture says that the dead in Christ shall rise first], he can find us

easily." Marry explains, "But Jaapjan, Jesus will bring us all together quickly. Jesus knows where we are." Little Jaapjan persists, "But Mommy, please? May I? I would feel better if I knew that Daddy could find our new address there right away." Marry is a sensitive, understanding mother. She has not denied this eight-year-old's request just because someone else might think the carved address marker on the cemetery grave was out of place.

On a gray morning only a few months ago, the rain was driving across the Dutch landscape and Hans Berg was on his way to work, having left his little family in a cottage where they were to have had a week's vacation in the woods. Suddenly a young truck driver made a wrong movement, skidded into the front of Hans's car, and Hans was plunged from the land of the living into death. He was absent from the body and present with the Lord, only his broken body left behind. Death is not beautiful. It separates soul from body, husband from wife, father from children; and Jesus let it be known that death is not beautiful when He stood at Lazarus's grave and wept.

Jesus wept not just with sympathy, not just with sorrow for Lazarus's sisters and friends, but also with anger at the enemy—death. Satan brought death with his taunting temptation to Eve and Adam to choose to believe him rather than God's warning. Jesus wept with a strong emotion, not with polite tears as if to enter an "atmosphere of mourning." His tears were real, and the strength of emotion behind them was real. The amazing thing to me is that Jesus wept *after* He had already said to Martha, "I am the resurrection and the life: he that believeth in me, though he were dead, yet shall he live: And whosoever liveth and believeth in me shall never die. Believest thou this?" (John 11:25, 26). He believed completely what He had said, yet He wept.

Jesus was speaking of the *reality* of the resurrection of bodies which will be changed bodies—just as He himself would later demonstrate with His own resurrected body—as well as speaking of the fact that He had the power to raise Lazarus. Now the resurrection of Lazarus was a miracle, but his body was in the same condition as it had been before. Jesus was speaking of something that no one really understood that day, as He pointed to the future, or they would have been more excited and waiting with *vivid expectation* for *the* Resurrection after His death. Instead of vivid expectation, the disciples had something even lower than *vague expectation*. They had downright depression and lack of any expectation at all. It was all over, as far as they were concerned.

The resurrection of Lazarus was a demonstration, an object lesson of the fact that Jesus could rise from the dead. The "firstfruits" of which Paul speaks to the Corinthians show clearly that the Resurrection of Jesus has no precedent. Jesus after His Resurrection was not like Lazarus at all; His body was the same body, but one that could not ever die or be hurt again.

Listen carefully. In the Book of 1 Corinthians, the true believers were no longer mixed up, but others even then were still just as confused as many had been on the day of Lazarus's death. People can be so very blind to what is being shown them and so deaf to what is being told them. Paul that day said, "Now if Christ be preached that he rose from the dead, *how* say some among you that there is *no* resurrection of the dead?" (1 Corinthians 15:12). He goes on to say that your faith is really a vain faith, your hope is a vain hope, *if* it is only a vague kind of hope in this life: "If in this life only we have hope in Christ, we are of all men most miserable" (v. 19).

Two things are important in Jesus' speaking of Himself being "the resurrection and the life," and then afterwards weeping real tears, with real anger and sorrow. First, it is *not* wrong to weep, and it is not wrong to be angry at death and at Satan who causes death. It is not wrong to long for the change—that will come after Jesus comes back—to come quickly to this abnormal world. Your weeping *in all that* is possible while Jesus is weeping with you. It is when you or I turn away with bitterness and anger *at* God, instead of joining in His weeping, that it becomes a separation and sinfulness, rather than a running into the Lord's arms.

Second, it is also important to believe with vivid expectation *before* we see the resurrection. Jesus was asking Martha to have a double belief: the possibility of His power to do an immediate thing that would be temporary and His power to do that which would be *forever*. Asking us to believe also, Jesus speaks the same words to us. Do we really believe in the lasting resurrection of our bodies? Do we believe with vivid expectation—the kind of expectation that causes us to have practical thoughts about laying up treasures in heaven, about putting the Kingdom of God first, about meditating upon His Word day and night, so that as we read and think, we might find out what it is He means for us to be doing? How vivid is my expectation? Really! How vivid is yours?

Don't you think that the Jesus who said to suffer the little children to come unto Him sees Jaapjan these days as one who is carving his address as a personal demonstration—before angels and demons as well as unto his loving Shepherd—that he believes with *vivid expecta-*

tion that Jesus is coming back? The any-moment expectation of Jesus' return is also the any-moment expectation of the resurrection. What demonstrates *our* vivid expectation? "Be ye therefore ready also: for the Son of man cometh at an hour when ye think not" (Luke 12:40).

23

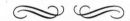

Whose Harvest Is It?

Have you ever had a garden? Do you know anything of the feeling of watching little shoots come up, grow, produce buds and flowers and then pods, peas, beans, limas, ears of corn filling out, or tomatoes ripening? Have you watched for the right moment to harvest *any* kind of crop, when it was *your own crop?* Do you know the sort of nervousness felt by one to whom one's garden is precious, that the wrong sort of person will tramp through the neat rows, crushing plants with rough boots, tearing off peas not quite filling the pods, knocking off delicate blossoms which so soon will mature into tender, ready-to-harvest butter beans? Do you understand the *trust* that goes into saying to another person, "Here, take this basket, and *you* can pick the tomatoes. Be sure they are ripe and ready; and pick two heads of Bibb lettuce. But don't be harsh with it or you'll crush the leaves. Then pick a cucumber, the one nearest the path. But don't knock the three others near it which all need a little longer to ripen"? To hand over the harvesting of vegetables is something I understand out of my own experience, but a farmer with much more experience would know what it would be like to trust someone to go out and harvest his grain, being sensitive to what he had been told to do and following instructions—remembering to come back and ask for directions if he was uncertain. A harvest can be so easily spoiled by people who simply won't listen to instructions or acknowledge their lack of know-how enough to *ask.* One carefree, careless, insensitive person who has no understanding of the preciousness of the harvest to the owner of the field can demolish so much in so short a time, and bent, stepped-on grain presents a sad picture of waste.

We're given two amazing pictures in Matthew 9:36, 37. One is of God as the Lord of the Harvest, yet trusting human beings to be His laborers in this business of harvesting. Another is the picture of Christ, who gave His life for the sheep, being moved with compassion as He looked at the multitudes of human beings, filling the synagogues, fields, and streets of the cities and villages. We are told He was moved with compassion because they were distressed, scattered as sheep without a shepherd. They were distressed and scattered because they were very mixed-up concerning truth and needed to be cared for by shepherds who met their needs daily. Mark 6:34 reveals that Jesus began to teach them many things—these people who were as sheep without a shepherd, and toward whom He was moved with compassion. But He was not going to *stay* on the earth to keep teaching the frightened, "baaaaing" people running to and fro as a flock of sheep left without direction.

John 4:35–38 stresses again the reality of a harvest ready for reaping:

> . . . I say unto you, Lift up your eyes, and look on the fields; for they are white already to harvest. And he that reapeth receiveth wages, and gathereth fruit unto life eternal: that both he that soweth and he that reapeth may rejoice together. And herein is that saying *true,* One soweth, and another reapeth. I sent *you* to reap that whereon ye bestowed no labour: other men laboured, and ye are entered into their labours.

In Matthew 9:36, 37, these two amazing pictures are brought together in two verses. How often have I heard these verses since early childhood in China? How often have *you* heard them? Yet, suddenly at times it is as if lightning streaked across a dark sky, or the sun suddenly came out to split the fog to make a snow-covered scene dazzlingly clear, and we see something new. Fran was reading Matthew 9 to us this morning while we were still in bed, and it was one of those dazzling times of suddenly "seeing" as if I had been blind before. He is the Lord of the Harvest!

"It is *His* harvest!" I exclaimed. "We're being trusted to gather in *His* harvest. What a precious commission we have been given. What trust has been put into our hands." It is as if we had the basket and were on our way down to the most precious of vegetable gardens with the owner's complete trust placed in our carefulness to carry out directions. It is as if we had been given our instructions by the farmer and had been sent into the fields with his expectation of our fulfilling what we have been told to do.

We, you and I, each of us who are the Lord's children—a part of the Bride of Christ, the sheep of His hand, the people of His pasture—are to be harvesters, trusted not to crash in like oafs and spoil things with our ignorance.

How can He trust us? He is compassionate; He has wept over people. They *matter* to Him. Yet He trusts us to gather in the harvest. How *dare* we undertake such a delicately important task—*yet how dare we not?* He has appointed no angels to take over. Human beings are the ones to do it. But how?

He can trust us to do what He gives us to do, because He *knows* His promises are true. *He* knows that He will be faithful to the end, and that we need only to come to Him for the help we need, over and over and over again. He knows that His patience will not give out. He has promised to guide us and lead us to do that which will fit into the whole plan of harvesting the harvest. And as we fit in, we don't even need to count on our own strength and wisdom to do whatever He tells us to do. But how do we find out what our part is? "If any of you lack wisdom, let him ask of God, that giveth to all men liberally, and upbraideth not; and it shall be given him. But let him ask in faith, nothing wavering. For he that wavereth is like a wave of the sea driven with the wind and tossed" (James 1:5, 6). Yes, we have to *ask* what He would have us do, along with the wisdom to do it, but with the kind of faith that is real, that is willing to do what He unfolds, sight unseen. It is faith in *Him* and in *His* plan for *His* harvest that is what this is all about. It is the willingness to let Him be the Lord of the Harvest, and not to tell Him we have a better method we learned in another farmer's land.

Suppose His job for me is sharpening scythes? "But I wanted to go out and drive a tractor!" He knows. We need to acknowledge in some very real way that He *knows*. The same idea can lend an opposite sort of illustration. Suppose His job for me is driving the newest kind of tractor or harvesting machine? Then I am not the one to say, "But I love the old way of doing things, and this is an antique scythe I have had handed down to me for generations. I want to do it in the good old way." This is *His* farm, *His* harvest, and *He* is the One who is giving directions, instructions, equipment, as well as the strength to do what He has for me to do, whatever my part is. I am to trust Him because of *who He is*, and because of the truth of what He says and what He has promised.

But I am the Lord thy God, that divided the sea, whose waves roared: The Lord of hosts is his name. And I have put my words in thy mouth, and I have covered thee in the shadow of mine

hand, that I may plant the heavens, and lay the foundations of
the earth, and say unto Zion, Thou art my people.

Isaiah 51:15, 16

Whether He wants you to be setting type for printing presses, selling
groceries across the counter, driving a laundry truck, painting a house,
making furniture, working in a little underground office of a city building, digging potatoes on a ranch, doing secretarial work, nursing sick
people in a hospital or at home—whatever unlikely looking harvesting
work it seems to be—He really does have a place for each of His
harvesters, and the problem is that He says the "labourers are few."
Somehow or other some of us are not doing what He would have us
do. Somehow or other some of us are not picking the harvest by hand
because we think we need a big machine, or we are not running the
machine because we want to handpick the tomatoes.

It seems to me very right to connect the compassion which moved
Jesus in Matthew 9:36 with the kind of voice He had, deep with this
same compassion, as used in the next two verses: "Then saith he unto
his disciples, The harvest truly is plenteous, but the labourers are *few:*
Pray ye therefore the Lord of the harvest, that he will send forth
labourers into his harvest."

The laborers are few. The harvest is plenteous and it is *His* harvest!
Doesn't anybody care? Do we really care? What about the old song,
"Lord, send me; here am I, send me, across the street or across the sea"?
Do we put limits on what we really mean? Are we too proud? Or too
proud of our humbleness? Why are the laborers few? May the clouds
not gather back over the sun, and a dullness settle down on what we
have seen. "Pray *ye* therefore the Lord of the harvest, that he will send
forth labourers into *his* harvest."

24

"The Just Shall Live by His Faith"

"Just think of Amy Carmichael as a slim, young, brown-eyed, beautiful Scotch-Irish girl, going off to India and pioneering the way she did!" Darkening her face, wearing a sari and sandals, slipping in and out of dangerous marketplaces on her errands of rescue, saving babies that were destined to be sold as temple prostitutes. Imagine her bucking the whole evil custom of Hinduism, with all the weight of men and demons behind it! That tiny little human being all on her own, with only an Indian helper and herself to make a home for the first baby. No money to do it. Praying for the babies to be rescued, for the money to care for them, and for protection from all the forces that would be against her—including some established missions at the time. A rebel against all precedent? No. Though she was a kind of rebel, she was simply one of "the just" living by faith. Her setting forth to *live* by faith began something which brought over a thousand girls and boys out of the "system" into which they would have been plunged to be sold to the temples for evil purposes.

It can be said of her, as Paul spoke of the believers in Rome: "First, I thank my God through Jesus Christ for you all, that your faith is spoken of throughout the whole world" (Romans 1:8).

Note that we are clearly told that ". . . the just shall live by his faith" (Habakkuk 2:4)—not the missionary, the Christian worker, the pastor, the theological student, the enthusiastic new Christian—but "the just" are to live by faith. Not only the poor, the downtrodden, the persecuted, the people wiped out by war or depression, those in the midst of earthquake or plague, but "the just shall live by his faith." Not spiritual Christians, people with special gifts, people with a special calling, but "the just shall live by his faith." The affluent, the rich, and the successful are not barred from living by faith. The young do not have to wait longer, the old are not excluded. There is only one category given—*the just.*

Who, then, are the just? Romans 3:28 reminds us that we are first justified by faith: "Therefore we conclude that a man is justified by faith, without the deeds of the law." The just already have faith which they have demonstrated in actually believing in the Second Person of the Trinity who died that they might be justified, who gave the one way which was possible for sins to be forgiven, in taking the punishment Himself. A *just* person is one who has had real faith in Christ Jesus who came to be born, to live, and to die in history about two thousand years ago, in the geographic spot that today is the scene of such turmoil. A person who has really accepted Christ as his or her Saviour is one of the just.

The verse from Habakkuk is repeated in Romans 1:17: ". . . as it is written, The just shall live by faith." In Romans this follows the verse speaking of not being "ashamed of the gospel of Christ." I feel that not being ashamed of the Gospel includes an active demonstration of *not being ashamed* to do practically, in day-by-day life, what the result of the Gospel is meant to prepare us to do—to *live* by faith. Every single Christian is included in the category of the just. Every Christian is *meant* to live by faith in really practical areas of life. There is a danger of being "ashamed" or "embarrassed" to speak of praying in practical areas of daily living, and to feel that this would be "childish" or "fanatical." Watertight compartments are kept by some people for their "prayer life," for their "Christian activities," and their business or profession—agriculture, medical practice, real estate, government work—as well as their choices of where to live, how to use their money, where to go for a vacation, how to live as a family. There is no mingling of *faith* with practical life, and a shrug of the shoulders says, "All that is for the people called to do it." There is also a danger that churches and Christian groups will ignore the search for practical ways of *living* by faith.

But this is a serious command that each of us needs to consider and reconsider, over and over again. Our lives are shifting and changing. No two periods are alike. The areas in which we were sure we were given an opportunity to "pray" may be removed, and we are in danger of saying, "Yes, I used to live by faith when I was a struggling student, or when we had to pray literally for bread during days of depression, but now—now it is different." It is never meant to be different. There is no softening of the command timewise. It is not: "The just shall live by faith for a little while."

But *how?* True, if you have no job, the house is being taken from you because of the mortgage, there is danger of invasion, stock values have disappeared in the drop of the market, or a flood has ruined your crops, you may be in the place of Habakkuk. He speaks of the loss of everything—no crops, no herds, no grapes—everything gone: "Yet will I rejoice in the Lord, I will joy in the God of my salvation" (3:18). It may be only then that you can "live by faith," simply by continuing to love the Lord, and to pray for the immediate day's little loaf of bread. But *how*—if you have everything you need?

The first consideration in the *How?* of being able to do anything the Lord asks us to do, is what Jesus said to the disciples when they were filled with absolute dismay, after Jesus had spoken to the rich young ruler and stated that it was harder for a rich man to enter heaven than for a camel to go through a needle's eye. Utter dismay was the reaction of the disciples. "Who then can be saved?" was the question. Does it depend on being destitute? Can no one else have saving faith? Jesus' reply was, "The things which are impossible with men, are possible with God" (*see* Matthew 19:23–26). "Yes, it is possible for a rich man to be saved (although it is a difficult thing to contemplate)" Jesus is saying, "because with God all things are possible." A rich man can also come as a child, believing that he has *nothing* with which to pay for his salvation, and that he needs what Christ has paid—to pay for his sins, to be given forgiveness, to be justified. Then the rich "just" can also live by faith; in fact, they are commanded to live by faith.

How? What does it mean. Is it relative? Is there no struggle in prayer for people unless they are faced with *immediate* disaster of some sort? Must there be a danger or a change on the horizon to push us into *feeling* the necessity of carrying out the practical reality of "living by faith"? Is there something needed to make us realize that it is not something just to be sung about in church, to thrill about as the choir sings, to feel with some emotion as the pastor preaches? How do we attempt to have it be *real* in our personal lives, our family lives, and our grouped-together-as-Christians lives?

It seems to me that Hebrews 10:36–38 is incentive enough for every single justified person, each one who qualifies as one of the *just*, each born-again Christian: "For ye have need of patience, that, after ye have done the will of God, ye might receive the promise. For yet a little while, and he that shall come will come, and will not tarry. Now the just shall live by faith: *but if any man draw back, my soul shall have no pleasure in him.*"

Habakkuk 2:3 had already spoken of the time of the end which is to be waited for, but which will "surely come." The connection was already there in Habakkuk, but now in Hebrews it is written in flaming words! *The just are to live by faith, until Jesus returns.* The time may not be long, even though it seems to be. If we "draw back" and stop experiencing the reality of living by faith in some day-by-day practical way, God has said that we *spoil* His pleasure in us. We bring Him, our Father who has done so much for us, the very opposite of pleasure!

It is so easy for us to outline a set of circumstances in which it would be "practical" to live by faith. We can look back with nostalgia to another period of life and say, "Back there—then it was real." Or we can look at other people's lives and think what a realistic opportunity they had to live by faith. "If I had been Amy Carmichael . . . ." But none of us can wiggle out of the category—*we are the just.* None of us can wiggle out of the command in Hebrews *not to draw back.* We need to struggle in prayer to be willing for whatever "living by faith" might mean in today's circumstances. When we trip and fall and smash our ribs, we must recognize *this* as the circumstance in which to say, "May nothing be wasted of what You, God, want to bring out of this," and ask, believing that He can unfold His will, give His victory, fulfill His purpose in the midst of pain.

When the extremes of "success" come, and there seems to be no material need, the day-by-day practice of saying, "I'm willing, O God, to give half away or to do whatever You want with it. Make me real today in whatever this combination of circumstances," is meant to present us with the possibility of living by faith. It is your today and my today that count in practical living by faith. Pray to God for *today's* reality to be demonstrated.

Consciously, with a specific search for reality in obeying this command, there must be the realization that it is only "a little while" before He may come, and that the "drawing back" is a thing we can easily do, but which we will regret when we discover the actual meaning of His words—"My soul shall have no pleasure in him." May we hasten to stop wasting the time we have to bring Him pleasure.

25

⚜

Centuries of Conflict

Big wars, little wars, long wars, short wars, World wars, local wars—wars! Enemies, armies, adversaries, soldiers, destroyers, accusers, persecutors, attackers, combatants, provokers, murmurers, criticizers, troublemakers—*intelligent beings stirring up discord!* Big discord, little discord, long discord, short discord, world discord, local discord—*discord!* Centuries of conflict have come forth from the original conflict—when Lucifer, the highest of the angels, desired to be equal with God and to destroy everything beautiful, to smash everything in his way, in order to try to accomplish his purpose. The war which started in the heavenlies was continued on earth as Lucifer, now Satan, came in the form of a serpent and talked Eve into being dissatisfied with what God had given her, tempted her into smashing the truth of the Word of God, in order to gain something he dangled before her eyes as superior knowledge and education. Satan's war against God was fought through his capturing the minds of Adam and Eve and luring them into believing a lie rather than truth. But it didn't stop there! Satan has continued to twist men's minds to use all their talents, intelligence, and energies of lifetime after lifetime to prove God wrong and to try to prove God's existence to be nonexistence. This basic war has been the birthplace of all the wars and rumor of wars which have continued throughout all the ages, and which God promises us will continue as long as Satan has power. The day will come when that power will be over, but that day has not yet arrived.

The picture of Nero fiddling while Rome burned is a horrible one! An opulent party on a hilltop while a war in the valley is in plain sight—this is a picture often given us in historic novels and actual history books. Constantly, people have been hardened to the tragedy of others' suffering and dying, homes being destroyed, cities being turned into rubble, beauty being ground into trash as museums are torn apart and streets are running with blood. The pages of any news magazine will give the contrast of what is taking place everywhere in the earth's geography, as side-by-side scenes of destruction are pictured near scenes of utter lack of involvement. Seeing eyes are blind to what is taking place, hearing ears are deaf to what is being screamed, feeling hands are empty of touching what is pouring forth. Centuries of blind, deaf, and numb people in their misty silence of separation from reality simper words such as "peace . . . peace . . . peace," when no peace exists. As bombs drop and air sirens shriek, the words will continue to echo emptily—"peace . . . peace . . . peace."

Christians so often feel superior because they are not among those crying, "Peace!" when there is no peace. Christians are apt to think they are being realistic because they *expect* wars and rumors of wars until Christ comes back again. But there is a deafness, blindness, insensitivity of touch and feeling among many Christians who refuse to recognize the war in which *they* are involved, and who are spiritually "playing a violin" while the enemy attacks and scores victories unchallenged, given no resistance. Not only are there wars between nations and civil wars within countries going on in an increasing intensity these days, but Satan is achieving his minor victories in an increasing number of conflicts in Christian circles, schools, seminaries, churches, missions, and groups of all sorts, and inside many of us as individuals. The very cleverest strategy of an enemy is to achieve an attitude of friendliness and to succeed in being accepted within the ranks as a friend. Within the ranks an enemy can accomplish his work unhindered, as he gradually twists and turns ideas and principles into opposite positions and swerves thinking by poisoning minds with tiny bits of poison which bring a mental and spiritual effect as specific as germ warfare in spoiling body and brain cells physically.

God has warned us. We cannot one day say, "Why didn't You tell us? Why didn't You warn us to look out for that fifth columnist? Why didn't You say he would be disguised as an angel of light?" We have been sufficiently warned. The fires of our cities burning down are in plain sight. The whistling bombs can be heard by our ears. The devastating fight of someone wrestling with us can be felt. We are as stupid and negligent as any of the "Neros" who ever lived, if we simply entertain ourselves with Christian diversions and let ourselves and our children be attacked and devoured without entering into the army and setting up the defense we have been instructed to prepare.

What are some of the aspects of the warnings? "Neither murmur ye, as some of them also murmured, and were destroyed of the destroyer" (1 Corinthians 10:10). We are warned not to "murmur" against God by complaining, criticizing, or cutting down any Moses or Aaron within our believers' groups. The destroyer, Satan, is ready once again to destroy murmurers as he did in Old Testament times:

> And all the children of Israel murmured against Moses and against Aaron: and the whole congregation said unto them, Would God that we had died in the land of Egypt! . . . And the Lord said unto Moses, How long will this people provoke me? and how long will it be ere they *believe me,* for all the signs which I have shewed among them?
>
> Numbers 14:2, 11

Here is a strong warning that believers, in their conversation as well as actions, are constantly to remember what God has done and are not to be full of complaint about things they want to be different in the immediate moment. Satan is waiting to pounce on people who use all their wit, intelligence, energy, and talents to "pull down" and turn aside from glorifying God and recognizing the marvel of what He has done and is doing. To neglect the recognition of the work of the Lord in lives and in situations—and to always set up specifications that are people's measuring sticks which wipe out the wonder of what God has done—are dangerous ideas which give the enemy a foothold— dangerous to the people doing the murmuring, as well as to the work of the Lord.

"Wherefore we would have come unto you, even I Paul, once and again; but Satan hindered us" (1 Thessalonians 2:18). Satan accomplished something against Paul because of some neglect in the war on the part of believers in *some* way, and an historic moment was different. Paul was hindered by Satan from coming to this group. Peter both warns and comforts us in calling us to watch out for Satan's wiles: "Be sober, be vigilant; because your adversary the devil, as a roaring lion, walketh about, seeking whom he may devour: Whom *resist* stedfast in the faith, knowing that the *same* afflictions are accomplished in your brethren that are in the world" (1 Peter 5:8, 9). We are warned that Satan is like a roaring lion looking for people to devour, eat up, destroy. We are comforted that it is not impossible to "resist" him, which we can do if we are "stedfast in the faith," and are further comforted that we have company in our war—"the *same* afflictions," the same troubles in this battle with Satan, the devil and our adversary, are being experienced by all those who are in the same family with us, the people of the Lord's pasture. We all, who are the Lord's sheep, have the same horri-

ble wolf rushing at us. No person among "the brethren" is immune from
his attack.

> Finally, my brethren, be strong in the Lord, and in the power
> of his might. Put on the whole armour of God, that ye may be
> able to stand against the wiles of the devil. For we wrestle not
> against flesh and blood, but against principalities, against
> powers, against the rulers of the darkness of this world, against
> spiritual wickedness in high places.
>
> Ephesians 6:10–12

Read on in Ephesians 6 and note that we are not only warned, but also
given instructions as to how to stand and how to fight. We need to be
"girt about with truth"—or there is no use starting! God's Word is truth:
". . . and thy law is the truth" (Psalms 119:142). "And if any man shall
take away from the words of the book of this prophecy, God shall take
away his part out of the book of life, and out of the holy city, and from the
things which are written in this book" (Revelation 22:19). There is no
need even expecting any kind of a victory in the battle, if only a part of
truth is used to "girt us about." We are totally unprotected if we give up
bits and pieces of the Word of God. Satan has so many loopholes
through which to shoot at us that the wounds multiply in fantastic
succession, and weakness is overtaken by further bleeding weakness.

The protecting helmet is salvation, but the sword with which to stave
off Satan's weapon against us is the Word of God. With this sword we
are to attack and to defend. It is the sword of the Spirit, but that sword is
the Word of God. Many people have a sword that is nibbled at—with
nicks in the blade and point bent and broken. It isn't in bright, shiny,
perfect condition because parts have been discarded as unimportant.
No proper loincloth—and a spoiled sword. What ridiculous underesti-
mation of the enemy! What a foolish sight. The shield of faith is the
shield which will quench the fiery darts which the wicked enemy is
able to throw. That faith, which can be as small as a mustard seed, is
nevertheless effective when the further admonition is carried out:
"Praying always with all prayer and supplication in the Spirit, and
watching thereunto with all perseverance and supplication for all
saints" (Ephesians 6:18).

Self-protection and protection of "all the saints" is part of our call to
war! To say that there is no war is to give comfort to the enemy who then
knows he has succeeded in his infiltration. "And they overcame him by
the blood of the Lamb . . ." (Revelation 12:11).

26

Contrasting Responses

Accurate reporters of the flow of news find it hard to write with lightness and optimism about world events these days. Words such as *sorrow, pity,* or *agony* follow each other, accompanied by pictures of wounded and dying men, women, and children; homes turned into rubble; cities and farms devastated while living people stumble in any direction that seems to promise some measure of safety. The great promises of people who were sure the world was getting better and better—with peace just around the next corner, and violence soon to disappear—have become blurred and lost in the roar of cold and hot wars and in the rumble of diverse disasters. Screams of fear, calls for help, and cries of alarm pierce the constant undercurrent of general noise. To whom are the calls being made? Who has ears to hear?

"Wherefore, when I came, was there no man? when I called, was there none to answer? Is my hand shortened at all, that it cannot redeem? or have I no power to deliver? . . ." (Isaiah 50:2). The Lord is speaking. God is asking a question. Why, when He calls, do people not answer His call? God has spoken through the ages, and so many have not responded to His call with anything but silence. "I also will choose their delusions, and will bring their fears upon them; because when I called, none did answer; when I spake, they did not hear: but they did evil before mine eyes, and chose that in which I delighted not" (Isaiah 66:4). It was not only Eve and Adam who did evil before God's eyes; it was not only Cain who chose that in which God did not delight, but streams of people—mobs of people through the centuries who responded by turning in the opposite direction and by acting as if they did not hear—kept silent to His plea. It is not only past centuries of people who did not listen to the Word of God as His prophets verbalized it to them, nor is it only those who heard the Second Person of the Trinity when He walked on earth, who seemed deaf to His call or scorned and spurned His cry. It is now, in this moment of history in the land of the present living people, that His call is bringing no response.

"Hear the word of the Lord, ye that tremble at his word; Your brethren that hated you, that cast you out for my name's sake, said, Let the
Lord be glorified: but he shall appear to your joy, and they shall be
ashamed" (Isaiah 66:5). Is there a trembling on the part of Christians to
really *hear* His Word? Or is there a concentration on the opinions or
power of "brethren" who hate us—and would be ready to cast us out for
the sake of our really believing the supernatural Word of God
sufficiently enough to *act* upon it and to really *hear* His call to us in
day-by-day, moment-by-moment response? Does it matter more to us
that we have the good opinion of men who might cast us out—or are we
literally ready to listen, that we might glorify the Lord while there is yet
time and, to our joy, experience His appearing one day, when we will
not then be ashamed? There is double meaning in the call of God to
men. First, He calls, "Come unto me, all ye that labour and are heavy
laden, and I will give you rest" (Matthew 11:28). He calls with redeem-
ing power and His arm is not shortened today. Second, He calls His
children to live according to His Word, to not do evil but to do His will,
to speak the words He gives us to speak, rather than speaking in human
cleverness or in our own strength. God's people through the centuries
are often *not* answering His call and are turning a deaf ear to His pleas.
Because His children are the ones who so often are not responding to
His call, the lost ones of the world—to whom His call comes for
redemption—are further confused and are without the "relay" of that
call. People who are meant to be sounding trumpets, so that the lost may
hear, are ignoring God's call to them. People who are meant to be living
in accordance with God's Word are not stopping to find out what God's
Word contains. What God speaks so clearly is given no response.
"When I called, ye did not answer; when I spake, ye did not hear" (*see*
Isaiah 65:12).

The silent response of lost men and the silent response of many of
God's own people present a contrast to God's own promises to hear and
to act upon the call of people who honestly cry out to Him. "The Lord is
nigh unto all them that call upon him, to all that call upon him in truth.
He will fulfil the desire of them that fear him: he also will hear their cry
and save them" (Psalms 145:18, 19). There is a condition here, just as
there is in seeking and finding the Lord. It could be stated: "If with all
thine heart, ye truly seek me," which precedes the promise: "Ye shall
surely find me." Here is a strong promise that the Lord will come close
and be with those who call upon Him in *truth*. It cannot be a nebulous
scream into an empty universe, using the name "god" to voice a need of

something somewhere existing in some measure of strength. To call upon God in truth, one must believe that He *is*, that He is there, that He is the Triune God of the Bible who created heaven and earth, that He is *who* He has revealed Himself to be. One must call upon God, not "a god." For the believer who is in need of His God, moment by moment in all kinds of situations, the call must also be in the framework of truth: "But let him ask in faith, nothing wavering. For he that wavereth is like a wave of the sea driven with the wind and tossed" (James 1:6). The mouthing of words, the throaty sounds of the audible verbalization of a "call" to God, must have a reality behind them. The call can not be a dramatic piece of acting, turned on and off with only a surface veneer of involvement. The attitude of "I tried but it didn't work, so now I'll try this other thing!" is in itself a cancellation of any reality. To call upon God in truth is to realize that there is no other place to go. There is no substitute, no other solution. It is a cry which we must echo with honest certainty as in Psalms 73:25: "Whom have I in heaven but thee? and there is none upon earth that I desire beside thee." And as: . . . "Thou art my Lord: I have no good beyond thee" (*see* Psalms 16:2).

A Malayan boy, after having become a Christian, found himself in the midst of a truly demonic attack in the early weeks of his new walk. Allah had been put behind him, the occult things that had been woven together with Muslim faith had been turned from, but the stability and certainty were wobbly as a tiny child's first steps. A fall is an easy thing, even in the first walk across a room in the presence of a loving family. This boy went through demon activity which he had experienced before in his life, and his call went forth to God, "Oh, God, help me." However, there was no immediate, visible, *feel*-able change, and he fell into Satan's trap set to trip up his feet. "It isn't working; it isn't working!" was the next cry of his heart, and his old reaction pattern came forth: "I'll try this—and this." And so he called, "Allah be praised!" and used some other "magic" Arabic words in a formula handed down for generations. In those brief few minutes, this baby Christian had called—but *not* in truth, not feeling that "there is none upon earth that I desire beside thee." Not acting upon the reality that "I have no good beyond thee." He had acted in a relative way. He had placed God on a sliding scale of possibilities among the spectrum of relative possibilities. The very crossing-of-fingers-behind-the-back attitude—"If this doesn't work, I'll try something else!"—cancelled out the true call. The attitude of the "call in truth" must be Job's attitude: "Though he slay me, yet will I trust in him" (Job 13:15). That boy was later to learn the joy and freedom of trusting the power of the Lord alone.

Now we are ready to consider the promises of God's responses to our calls. Now we can meditate upon the wonder of the contrast of His response to people's calls, so different from the response of people to His call.

> And it shall come to pass, that before they call, I will answer; and while they are yet speaking, I will hear.
>
> Isaiah 65:24

> Thus saith the Lord the maker thereof, the Lord that formed it, to establish it; the Lord is his name; Call unto me, and I will answer thee, and shew thee great and mighty things, which thou knowest not.
>
> Jeremiah 33:2, 3

> Hold up my goings in thy paths, that my footsteps slip not. I have called upon thee, for thou wilt hear me, O God: incline thine ear unto me, and hear my speech.
>
> Psalms 17:5, 6

> I will call upon the Lord, who is worthy to be praised: so shall I be saved from mine enemies . . . . In my distress I called upon the Lord, and cried unto my God: he heard my voice out of his temple, and my cry came before him, even unto his ears.
>
> Psalms 18:3, 6

The world is in a serious condition. We live in a moment of extreme need. Our time may be very short before the Lord's return or before freedoms are removed from us in areas of speech and action. God is asking us a question as Christians, "When I called, was there none to answer?" What is His call to us? Part of it certainly is to call upon *Him*. We are to call in truth. We are to call—with no other solution to pull out of our reserve of ideas. The knowledge we have of the agonizing need of the world's lost people should give seriousness to our responsibility to help them to hear God's call and respond. Our response affects us, but also affects others. How am I, how are you, responding to His call?

"As for me, I will call upon God; and the Lord shall save me. Evening, and morning, and at noon, will I pray, and cry aloud: and he shall hear my voice" (Psalms 55:16, 17). Oh, God, make this an honest resolve for an increasing number of Thy people in this dark period of history.

27

Barren Reform

Two blue-jeaned girls sat beside their huge backpacks, stormily discussing their philosophy of life. Cigarettes filled the room with smoke; a stack of stubs silently told a story of nervousness. Ideas flowed out, along with smoke from one set pair of lips, twisting and turning in the minds of those listening. What is being listened to? Does it make any sense? Does it fit in with what is true?

"The whole trouble with the world is *men*. Men are all wicked. Men have caused all the problems that exist. Men are horrible. Women should never love men. Women should only love women. Women should love women physically and in every other way. A relationship between two women is what can be really beautiful. If you had only women loving women, the world would be all right."

With one rush of sentences the solution set forth would change the world, all right! The suggested reform would bring such barren results that an empty world—empty of a new generation, empty of both boy and girl babies—would grind to a close with the end of civilization. Exaggerated? An exaggerated position, yes, but a position actually held by far-out, lesbian Women's Lib girls who are twisting and filling with fog the minds of other girls until they become dizzy with uncertainty.

Equality of men and women, shifting ideas turning to unisex, then "superiority" of women to the degree that there can be no equality at all, and suddenly a cry for the pushing aside of men altogether. And then the strange result of placing great emphasis on the "difference" between men and women, which the first scream of equality was trying to stamp out. What a maze of twisting, turning paths—leading to a barren solution.

Isaiah 5:20, 21 gives warning: "Woe unto them that call evil good, and good evil; that put darkness for light, and light for darkness; that put bitter for sweet, and sweet for bitter! Woe unto them that are wise in their own eyes, and prudent in their own sight!"

This is a description of reversing truth with false declarations, of

putting an individual human being's wisdom in the center, of substituting the darkness of Satan's twisting lies for the light of God's truth. Eve
fell for this twisting of God's truth, and Adam fell for it later. The results
of pitting human beings' wisdom against God's truth is devastating at
every level—all through the centuries. Today's reversed standards can
have no other results than the barren ones which immediately come to
mind when one realizes that some so-called modern "marriages"
would take place with no bridegroom.

Isaiah goes on to picture vividly the result of living on the basis of
calling evil good, and good evil, of putting darkness for light, and light
for darkness, of putting bitterness for sweetness and sweetness for
bitterness.

> Therefore as the fire devoureth the stubble, and the flame
> consumeth the chaff, so their root shall be as rottenness, and
> their blossom shall go up as dust: because they have cast away
> the law of the Lord of hosts, and despised the word of the Holy
> One of Israel.
>
> Isaiah 5:24

The picture is of plants without roots—roots so rotten that the plant
withers—and of flowers that dry up and become dust, as a fire then
finishes off all fruitfulness by destroying even the stubble. A desert
remains. Life and hope for growth are ended. The picture is bleak and
barren. Making a "new world" built on a twisted base, where all of
God's laws are backwards, will result in only barrenness of every sort.
The very things being screamed for the loudest will die like plants with
no roots! "Be not wise in your own conceits," as we are told in Romans
12:16.

But we may say, "I am not twisted in my views on men and women. I
do believe God has made brides and bridegrooms to be one in an
amazing way—physically, spiritually, and intellectually—with the
wonder of fruitfulness as a result, tangible fruitfulness as new baby
humans come into being. I have no barren reform in mind for the
world's ills. I'm fitting into the real world. I have no fantastically
strange or twisted changes to set forth. I do realize that men and women
are different, and that the *difference* is what God made in the first place,
so that wiping out the differences is starting out in the wrong direction."

There is, however, a danger of putting bitter for sweet and calling evil
good (or good evil) in spiritual areas. There are more subtle areas where

people are being twisted and turned with even more dangerous propaganda than that concerning human relationships. Satan never stops his attempts to put salt in the sugar bowl or sugar in the saltshaker wherever he can. If he can succeed in making people believe that they have some more exciting and "sweet" relationship that feels "more spiritual"—yet without being a relationship with the true Bridegroom who is Jesus Christ—then he continues to blow a stream of confusing "smoke" into people's "eyes of understanding," until they become dizzy with the uncertainty about what is true and what is false.

This is an age of confusion, and there is a plan behind the confusion. Satan's drive is to wipe out truth with scribbles of lies which reverse everything. Paul warns in 2 Timothy 3:5, 7: "Having a form of godliness, but denying the power thereof: from such turn away . . . . Ever learning, and never able to come to the knowledge of the truth." We are not to be fooled with "a form of godliness" which is a false form of the true godliness. The only true godliness comes through being *one with the Bridegroom* who is Christ. There is no other source of being filled with the Holy Spirit than oneness with Christ—through accepting His death on the cross as the death of the Second Person of the Trinity, His death in our place. There is no other name, no other person by whom we can be saved, nor by whom we can have spiritual life and true spiritual fruit or results. We are to be part of His flesh and of His body, as Ephesians 5:30 tells us. Many people who are "ever learning," yet "never able to come to the knowledge of truth" sound like those who either study and study and continue to get farther from the truth of the Bible all the time—or like those who search for spiritual feeling and try out a mixture of possibilities, getting farther and farther from the true Bridegroom and into more and more barren spiritual relationships.

If we are to have the true fruit of the Spirit—love, joy, long-suffering, gentleness, meekness, kindness—and if we are to know something of the power of the Spirit as we read the Word of God and pray, there is a need for being a faithful Bride. As such a Bride, one would not fall into the trap of listening to the confusion of false ideas—fogging the air with smoke (as people want spiritual reform on the wrong base) or shouting out ideas of spiritual excitement—thus leaving out the Bridegroom. There cannot be poison mixed with the milk. There cannot be bitterness added to the sweet water of life. We are told that light does not mix with darkness. There is danger surrounding us spiritually, even as there is danger surrounding girls who sit around discussing possible ways of reforming evil by setting forth reversed values. The resulting spiritual barrenness will have far-reaching effects from one generation to another.

Who is included in the marvelous wedding preparations? "Let us be glad and rejoice, and give honour to him: for the marriage of the Lamb is come, and his wife hath made herself ready" (Revelation 19:7). Oh, wonderful moment yet to come! Future history which will be lived in space and time! The moment *will* arrive. It will matter then whether we have been *literal* in the "now." We cannot change the literalness of the future, but we are responsible for living now on the basis of His literal Word to us. We are now a part of that Bride, and we are now to make ourselves ready—but not by getting on the bandwagon of some false reform. Such false ideas pay more attention to the Bride than to the Bridegroom—concentrating on spiritual excitement or peace of a wrong sort *now* for the human beings making up the Bride, rather than on pleasing the Bridegroom *now*. "Blessed are they which are called unto the marriage supper of the Lamb" (*see* v. 9).

We must not get mixed up with the wrong reform group, as we will then not only sadden the Bridegroom, but we will be specifically neglecting a tremendous task He has given us to do with the help of the Spirit—a task which has been given only to the Bride: "And the Spirit and the bride say, Come . . ." (Revelation 22:17). We are in danger of being turned away from our terrific task which is to have all too short a time in which to be accomplished.

28

One God—One People

My husband and I were recently eating in a restaurant, by windows which looked out at the majestic Canadian Rockies. The impressive thing about such a sight is the solidity of the rocks and firmly rooted trees, the ever-increasing discoveries of depths and heights, as shapes are outlined in sunset colors or highlighted with white snow. Mountain deer ventured close to our windows, letting us realize something of the beauty of creature life in its natural wild habitat, as they gracefully loped across the open space and back into the woods. How *real* are real mountains! No need to dig and analyze and try to prove the reality of mountains being mountains. No need to race out with glue or cement to stick together the Canadian Rockies, the Swiss Alps, or any other mountains, to give a greater appearance of unity to their existence. It is obvious that there is substance to what is being described as one waves an arm and declares, "These are real mountains—" and one's companion replies in fervent agreement, "Yes, they are. No mistake about that."

We turned our heads as we took another spoonful of soup, bit into toast, or lifted our glasses for the next drink of water. "Look! I can't believe it. Why would anyone make imitation mountains *here?*" What a devastating sight—how distracting to turn to the left and see the overpowering reality, and to the right to see a papier-mâché or plastic mess of mountains, shoulder-height and running the length of the room to divide one side from the other. Plastic flowers filled nooks and hollows in the plastic mountains, and gilt paint substituted for the shine of sunrise or sunset—never moving, never changing, never lighting the way to fresh discovery. Why an imitation to merge together in one's view, confusing the pleasure of the reality, detracting from the concentration and appreciation of the real thing? What a work—gluing together the fragile, unconvincing copies to stand in a place where even the mirrors were reflecting the glory of the real thing. "If someone had made these to decorate a room where no real mountains were in sight and where most of the people had never had anything to compare them with, it might accomplish something. But *here* the clash with reality wastes time and emotion which would be better spent involved with the real mountains in some way."

Ever since that time, I have been "seeing" in my memory—the Rockies out of one eye and the papier-mâché or plastic mountains out of the other eye—and over and over again I have seen in my imagination the frantic wasted efforts of men and women trying to paste together a miniature of the real magnificence which exists and is solid and everlasting.

Consider for a moment, with deep thrill, God's description of a future time of undeniable and almost indescribable unity—no need for glue of any kind, no need for human efforts to make the group stick together or to give solidity to the community:

> And I saw a new heaven and a new earth: for the first heaven
> and the first earth were passed away . . . . And I heard a great

voice out of heaven saying, Behold, the tabernacle of God is
with men, and he will dwell with them, and they shall be his
people, and God himself shall be with them, and be their God.
And God shall wipe away all tears from their eyes . . . .

Revelation 21:1, 3, 4

And they shall be His people: God's people. Here are people who are
one people with God, needing no long sessions of arguing fine points to
see whether one or another belongs. The oneness of the entire grouping of people is magnificently solid and real. All of these in the new
heaven and the new earth are tearless, joyful people with a oneness that
is real and will be everlasting. Is there some special baptism which
makes them one people after they get there? Is there an ingredient
which makes the oneness a fact in history which takes place at that
future moment? Do the resurrected and changed bodies create the
oneness?

When has the oneness of God's people become a factual happening
in space and time? What is the *real* adhesive that cements human
beings into the reality of being the people of God, with the certainty of
actually being together in the new heaven and the new earth? Those
who come to God in His given way—bringing the Passover lamb,
looking forward to the coming Messiah, the Lamb of God—*were* His
people right then, at whatever point in history their believing took
place. It was the "circumcision of the heart" that counted, we are told in
Romans 2:29, and those who truly believed did not have to wait to
become God's people till some far-off moment of history; they were His
people *then.*

> . . . Thus saith the Lord God; Repent, and turn yourselves
> from your idols; and turn away your faces from all your abomi-
> nations . . . . That the house of Israel may go no more astray
> from me, neither be polluted any more with all their transgres-
> sions; but that they may be my people, and I may be their God,
> saith the Lord God.

Ezekiel 14:6, 11

> So we thy people and sheep of thy pasture will give thee
> thanks for ever: we will shew forth thy praise to all genera-
> tions.

Psalms 79:13

People who believed could sing Psalm 79 with honesty and truth as
well as with melody. They could truly mean this expression as a fact of

history that it was possible to show forth praise *as* the people of God, as the sheep of the Shepherd, in such a way that the following generations would be affected and would also be drawn to believe.

New Testament believers and you and I who believe today are called upon with just as specific a statement of the fact that we are now the people of God. First Peter 1:18, 19 speaks of our not being redeemed with silver and gold, but with the precious blood of Christ, as a Lamb without spot or blemish. Then we have a statement of fact concerning those who have believed: "But ye are a chosen generation, a royal priesthood, an holy nation, a peculiar *people;* that ye should shew forth the praises of him who hath called you out of darkness into his marvellous light" (1 Peter 2:9). Peter goes on to speak of a new factor, showing that "the people of God" now include those who were heathen nations before, the Gentiles. Now, however, there is a *oneness*. In John 10:16, we hear Jesus speaking, right after He has spoken of His laying down His life for the sheep: "And other sheep I have, which are not of this fold: them also I must bring, and they shall hear my voice; and there shall be *one* fold, and *one* shepherd."

We are called upon to show forth praise to God and to have compassion enough for all the world. Day by day, as He leads and guides us, He will show us which ones of the "great multitude" (*see* Revelation 7:9) are to be our special responsibility. At least *some* of the "great multitude, which no man could number, of all nations, and kindreds, and people, and tongues"—who will be standing together as one people before the Lamb—are to be given the truth by you or me. The cementing of the people into truly *one people* is accomplished by the historical fact that the Holy Spirit indwells each believer, and that God will gather His people together when the great moment arrives when all history and space will no longer separate us in our finiteness, but will melt away to enable us to be together.

What feeble glue, what pasty plastic—if the cementing together of people were to be accomplished by organizational achievements and committees' deliberations! How frequently do the long hours of attempting to stick together a unity result in each person's attempt ending with the glue sticking hands together—diverting energy and strength, time and compassion, and appreciation and understanding away from the *real* and factual solidity of what God *is* doing, *has* done, and *is going to do*. We despair over breaks and fresh splits, short-lived unity in hopeful new combinations. Is it wrong to band together in such human groupings as churches and missions in different localities? A thousand

times *no,* but—and the "but" is so important—we need to take a long
satisfying look out of the windows of past history and present events
and drink in the beauty of the solid, lasting magnificence of what God
has put, is putting, and will put together and which was not, is not, and
will not be a failure.

So we thy people and sheep of thy pasture will give thee
thanks for ever: we will shew forth thy praise to all generations.

                                                                    Psalms 79:13

And I heard a great voice out of heaven saying, Behold, the
tabernacle of God is with men, and he will dwell with them,
and they shall be his people, and God himself shall be with
them, and be their God. And God shall wipe away all tears
from their eyes; and there shall be no more death, neither
sorrow, not crying, neither shall there be any more pain: for the
former things are passed away.

                                                                    Revelation 21:3, 4

No more sorrow individually—or as groups in painful blindness to
the reality of God's power and ability to form together one people,
indwelt by one Spirit at the time of the "new birth."

29

~~~

Poured-In Protection

I craned my neck to get a better view of the building as the car slowly
turned to go up the hill. The angles were terrific as they soared skyward
in beautiful dark brown symmetry. "The Steel Triangle—what a fantastic building, fitting into the three rivers and the rest of Pittsburgh and
enhancing rather than dominating it," I thought. "What a lovely brown
that steel is—my favorite shade," I remarked. Our friend, who knew
well the details of what made up this United States Steel Building,
began to tell us some of what could not be seen by merely looking at the

outside of the structure. "See those columns? They rise to a height of over eight hundred feet, and there are eighteen of them. Each column is made up of hollow box sections containing a total of about four hundred thousand gallons of water plus antifreeze." He went on to say that the water was to maintain the strength of the building during any possible outbreak of fire. Without the water, the columns would lose their strength, buckle, and collapse.

Poured-in protection! Observable beauty, strength, and purpose were easy to see in looking at this especially fine modern building. But a *hidden protection* was poured in to stay—ready for a sudden attack of fire from any side.

What a titanic illustration of the marvel of the "water" with which God has promised to fill those who are a part of His "building"—His people.

> Jesus answered and said unto her . . . whosoever drinketh of the water that I shall give him shall never thirst; but the water that I shall give him shall be in him a well of water springing up into everlasting life.
>
>   John 4:13, 14

> In the last day, that great day of the feast, Jesus stood and cried, saying, If any man thirst, let him come unto me, and drink. He that believeth on me, as the scripture hath said, out of his belly [his innermost being] shall flow rivers of living water. (But this spake he of the Spirit, which they that believe on him should receive: for the Holy Ghost was not yet given; because that Jesus was not yet glorified.)
>
>   John 7:37–39

Water! Life-protecting water is to be poured in and will flow out of the ones who believe on Jesus. The Holy Spirit is to be given, after Jesus is glorified, to *everyone* who becomes a Christian. Each Christian is then promised to be given the water of the Spirit—and in addition to refreshing us, the Holy Spirit is to be a protection to us in times of special "heat or fire." Ephesians 6:16 speaks of our quenching the fiery darts of the evil one by using the "shield of faith." But as I looked at those silent brown columns filled with water, I felt a special comfort in knowing that the Holy Spirit was also filling each of us as a protection against those fiery darts. Satan's fiery darts come from unexpected angles, but the water of the Spirit is there. We have His cooling system as we feel the heat of the attack.

We're also told in 1 Peter 4:12: "Beloved, think it not strange concerning the fiery trial which is to try you, as though some strange thing happened unto you." Sufferings, tribulations, trials, and disappointments are spoken of here as fiery-hot, something which could cause us to buckle and collapse if we had no help. But we have been given help at the very beginning of our becoming a "building"—the water was poured in when we became that building. "Know ye not that ye are the temple of God, and that the Spirit of God dwelleth in you?" (1 Corinthians 3:16). Each one of us who is a Christian is a special building, the temple of God, filled with the water of the Spirit. It is an amazing thought! A protected building which Satan would very much want to destroy! Individual buildings—not, however, a product of technology, no matter how wonderful some machine productions can be—but *personal* buildings. These buildings represent personalities, and the infilling, poured-in water is a Person—the Third Person of the Trinity—the Holy Spirit.

Although the United States Steel Corporation certainly did not construct a building to illustrate a spiritual truth, it *can* give us a special aspect of fresh understanding. However, as with other illustrations, it cannot be carried to the *nth* degree. We individual buildings can communicate with the Architect, God the Father, who has sent His Son to enable us to become His temple and has sent the Holy Spirit to be poured into us. We can communicate as individual persons with the Triune One and ask for special help in times of fire and heat. In this we have something beyond the protection of the United States Steel Building. We can *choose* to call out when alarmed—not automatically, but as God's people.

The Steel Triangle stands unique in Pittsburgh as a building protected by water-filled columns. But each of us as a Christian temple or building has another kind of strength, that of being together with other individual structures, forming a complex. Such a unit is supposed to stand out as fantastic—not in just one city or one country or even in the whole world at any one given moment of history, but in both space and time throughout all geographic space and all history.

> For through him we both have access by one Spirit unto the Father. Now therefore ye are no more strangers and foreigners, but fellowcitizens with the saints, and of the household of God; And are built upon the foundation of the apostles and prophets, Jesus Christ himself being the chief corner stone; In whom *all* the building fitly framed together groweth unto an

holy temple in the Lord: In whom ye also are builded together
for an habitation of God through the Spirit.

Ephesians 2:18–22

The whole company of believers, no longer "strangers and foreign-
ers," belonging to the same country and the same family, are also
described as a building, with Jesus as the cornerstone, a building where
God dwells "through the Spirit." The Holy Spirit indwells each believer, but there is also a special feature of His indwelling—the *whole*
building, all of us "fitly framed together" in a special oneness of construction. The Holy Spirit, whom Jesus called "rivers of living water"
in John 7, is to fill the entire body of believers and protect them against
the fiery attacks that *have* broken out, *are* breaking out, and *will continue* to break out in all history.

Martyrs are not failures. Martyrs are not like twisted, buckled pieces
of steel, destroyed by the fire. Martyrs are those who have withstood the
fiery darts, have stood straight, with the "steam escaping" because the
cooling system of the "living water" worked. This building of God—the
body of believers—has been and ever will be protected against destruction by fire. The river of living water *is* effective in protecting God's
people. At times we may fail in our response. We may not ask for help
when we should. We may disappoint our Architect by not sending forth
an alarm or not using what He has given us for keeping constant
communication open. But one thing is sure—when the living water is
"poured in the column" that is you or me, and when it fills the "building
fitly framed together" which is the entire combination of believers, it is
very special water.

"Fear not, O Jacob," God says in Isaiah. "For I will pour water upon
him that is thirsty, and floods upon the dry ground: I will pour my spirit
upon thy seed, and my blessing upon thine offspring" (*see* 44:2, 3).
After Jesus died as the Lamb of Atonement, the Temple was
destroyed—but only the physical building. God's building continues
through the ages. All hell cannot prevail over it. There is a poured-in
protection in its columns—*living water.* A new way of putting it to
ourselves, if we are considering bowing before God and accepting
Christ's death as our atonement, could be, "Am I fireproof? Have I been
filled with water?" For each of us who knows that we *do* believe and
have bowed, take comfort when the heat is turned on in some area of our
lives. We have a water-cooling system within! Thank God for the truth
of His promises.

30

{ornament}

Flavored Sawdust

The churches were full. My imagination carried me to many of them, and in each the same thing was taking place. People with cheerful smiles and satisfied nods at each other sat as if munching food in time to the strains of the organ music. Bite—bite—bite. Munch—munch—munch.

"Such a lovely roast-beef flavor!"

"Mine is turkey with herbs."

"This one is fresh tomato and lettuce, though the texture is strange."

"Mine is honey-and-peanut-butter flavored."

Hungry people being filled? No. Then what *is* taking place in each of these locations I'm gazing at in this flight of fancy? A closer look analyzes the content of those sandwiches. Cleverly disguised sawdust is being chewed, mixed with saliva, and swallowed—filling people's stomachs with a comfortably full feeling. Cleverly prepared imitation bread, imitation meat, imitation vegetables, and imitation honey have been arranged and have been eagerly accepted, eaten without careful examination, swallowed completely. People walk out—assured of being fed. "Wasn't that a lovely repast? So tasty and satisfying!"—"I did enjoy the flavor so much this morning."

It is impossible to talk to people in a dream, in an imaginative scene, in a flight of fancy. If only I could call out: "Stop! Stop! You are eating sawdust. Don't be fooled; you haven't any vitamins, proteins, or carbohydrates in your systems. You haven't been fed at all. What terrible results are taking place in your bodies if you keep on eating sawdust—if you fill yourselves with less than husks, time after time. Oh, examine the food. Recognize it for what it is, a clever substitute for the real thing. Insist on having *food* in your diet. Refuse the sawdust."

What disastrous results would take place in our physical bodies, if sawdust were substituted for food—if well-flavored imitation foods with no content or element of nutritious value were always placed on the plates of hungry people. Physical illness would soon take place, and death would result. "What a fiendish plot!" someone would say, if enemy nations succeeded in fooling the majority of their opponents by luring them into "eating" to their own destruction, without any resistance.

What is more important: physical health—or spiritual health? What is more important: the length of life on this earth—or eternal life? What is more dangerous: sawdust sandwiches munched by physically hungry people—or spiritual sawdust munched by people hungrily expecting to be spiritually fed? When is it more important to examine the content of the food being handed to us: when it is a silver platter of real sandwiches—or a silver platter of eloquence serving spiritual food from the pulpits of full church after full church? Is it important to analyze the spiritual food to see whether the content is the food which the Word of God describes to us? Are we meant to simply open our mouths and swallow anything that is being served? Or has the food already been carefully described, so that we have a base from which to judge, a sample with which to compare it? How long do we have to fulfill our responsibilities to our own spiritual health and the health of our children and our children's children? Only the span of a very few short years. Are we only interested in flavor and some kind of full feeling?

It was in the midst of hearing a discussion about what was considered "most important" by some board which was examining candidates for the ministry, that my mind became filled with this picture of thousands of people eating sawdust sandwiches, Sunday after Sunday. The discussion was about an article which told of two young men who were refused ordination because they would not say that they would take part in services ordaining women as pastors. A strong statement was made by one pastor to the effect that it did not matter whether a pastor believed in the Virgin Birth of Christ (or other such things!), as it would not hurt another person if one did not believe these things. However, according to this pastor, not believing in the ordination of women was dispossessing and hurting other people. What a substitute! What an emphasis on reversed values! What an attempt to flavor sawdust with artificial roast beef! It is mind-boggling to toss away the importance of the Virgin Birth as an essential belief for pastors who are to feed the lambs, especially when the introduction of women pastors is set up as a more central issue.

Hungry people with heads tilted up, eyes on the pastors—the undershepherds—eating what is being given them. "And Jesus, when he came out, saw much people, and was moved with compassion toward them, because they were as sheep not having a shepherd: and he began to teach them many things" (Mark 6:34). Jesus, the Second Person of the Trinity, the virgin-born Son of God, had *always* been, as John writes: "The same was in the beginning with God. All things were made by him; and without him was not any thing made that was made" (John 1:2, 3). Jesus was moved with compassion because of the spiritually hungry people who needed to be taught truth, who needed to be given spiritual food which would nourish and bring lasting health.

The moment came when physical food was needed, and the command came in Mark 6:37: "Give ye them to eat." The undershepherds were to give food to the hungry, but where was it to come from? ". . . he looked up to heaven, and blessed, and brake the loaves, and gave them to his disciples to set before them; and the two fishes divided he among them all. And they did all eat, and were filled" (Mark 6:41, 42). The same powerful God who was able to feed the Israelites with manna, day after day in the wilderness, multiplied the bread and fish so that thousands were fed properly with the nourishment of the bread and the protein of the fish. The physical food was not false, nor was it a mystical or fanciful food. It was made by the Creator of all things, who had come in the flesh through the promised Virgin Birth, and the food was passed out in real baskets by the disciples who were commissioned to distribute what Jesus had prepared. Jesus carefully instructed His disciples what to pass out and prepared it for them, so that the nourishment given would be equal and fair. This same Jesus spoke later to Peter—and to the many "Peters" who are the true undershepherds or pastors—"Feed My lambs." This feeding was also to take place with what was given: a precious basket of food, fantastic silver platters piled high with the nourishing abundance of life-giving bread.

The Pharisees—who did not believe in the Virgin Birth, who did not believe that Jesus was truly the Messiah, Son of God, the Second Person of the Trinity—accosted Him with questions. The disciples were seeking answers that they might know more about this One in whom they were coming to trust. Jesus spoke clearly and strongly:

> Labour not for the meat which perisheth, but for that meat which endureth unto everlasting life, which the Son of man shall give unto you: for him hath God the Father sealed. Then said they unto him, What shall we *do*, that we might work the *works* of God? Jesus answered and said unto them, This is the *work* of God, that ye believe on him whom he hath sent. They said therefore unto him, What sign shewest thou then, that we

may see, and believe thee? . . . Our fathers did eat manna in
the desert . . . . Then Jesus said unto them, Verily, verily, I
say unto you, Moses gave you not that bread from heaven; but
my Father giveth you the true bread from heaven . . . . Then
said they unto him, Lord, evermore give us this bread. And
Jesus said unto them, I am the bread of life: he that cometh to
me shall never hunger; and he that believeth on me shall never
thirst. But I said unto you, That ye also have seen me, and
believe not.

John 6:27–32, 34–36

[And again He said:] Verily, verily, I say unto you, He that
believeth on me hath everlasting life . . . . I am the living
bread which came down from heaven: if any man eat of this
bread, he shall live for ever: and the bread that I will give is my
flesh, which I will give for the life of the world.

John 6:47, 51

Bread is to be given to the hungry. That bread is the flesh of the Son of
God who became Son of Man that He might have this flesh through the
Virgin Birth.

. . . the angel Gabriel was sent from God . . . To a virgin
espoused to a man whose name was Joseph, of the house of
David; and the virgin's name was Mary . . . . And the angel
said unto her, Fear not, Mary: for . . . . thou shalt conceive
in thy womb, and bring forth a son, and shalt call his name
JESUS . . . . Then said Mary unto the angel, How shall this
be, seeing I know not a man?

Luke 1:26, 27, 30, 31, 34

Mary had a perfect right to find it difficult to believe in the Virgin
Birth when she first heard it predicted. She was a virgin, and no one
needed to prove to her that this was a fact; she knew it to be so. The
angel gently answered her question and made it clear to her, to whom it
mattered very much, just how this was to take place: "And the angel
answered and said unto her, The Holy Ghost shall come upon thee, and
the power of the Highest shall overshadow thee: therefore also that
holy thing which shall be born of thee shall be called the Son of God"
(v. 35).

The angel went on to tell Mary with what person she could share her
news—another woman, her own dear cousin Elizabeth who also car-

ried a miracle within her body, in that in her old age she had become
pregnant with John the Baptist. Elizabeth was prepared to believe that
". . . with God nothing shall be impossible" (Luke 1:37).

To "dispossess" Mary is pretty horrible treatment of a dear young
woman who deserves to be believed; and to dispossess Elizabeth, the
mother of John who called Mary "the mother of my Lord," is also a very
real insult to a mature and wise old woman. To dispossess the angel
Gabriel—who explained how a virgin, the unique mother of the Messiah, could bear a son without knowing a man—is a terribly crass way to
place oneself as higher in knowledge than an angel and to segregate
oneself into a proud, superior position. The worst form of dispossession
is to dispossess the Son of God, the Second Person of the Trinity—to say
that He is a liar when He says He existed before Abraham, and to say
that He was, instead, the son of Joseph or another man. Yes, being
dispossessed hurts people. Being dispossessed also hurts God. Some
believed Jesus when He spoke to them face-to-face, and others fell into
the category of which He said, "Ye have seen me, and believe *not.*" It is
a pretty serious thing to give a man the task of serving bread, when he
cannot distinguish food from sawdust—and a pretty serious matter to
get mixed up in the kind of *dispossession* that is of primary importance
in life and in all eternity.

"Then said Jesus to those Jews which believed on him, If ye *continue
in my word,* then are ye my disciples indeed" (John 8:31).

31

Fear of Fear

The rhythmic swish of gentle waves; the muted voices of parents'
calls to children; sounds of children's laughter interrupted by splashes
of water tossed into their faces; the soundless breeze, too light to cause
even a rustle in the leaves; the quiet sunshine noiselessly baking
upturned faces; a sailboat gliding toward the beach without a ripple of
sound. Human beings of all ages—separated from daily work and wor-

ries in what is called the summer vacation. Whether in Italy or the Great Lakes, the Atlantic shore or the Pacific, or on one of the islands of the seas, there is an attempt for a period of time to relax, to unwind, to put aside worries, to put "fear of fears" away, and to breathe deeply and easily in a place separated from the world for a pathetically short time.

Suddenly the blue of the sky and the green of the water are pierced by two dark shapes accompanied by the shriek of jet sound, as bomber planes and their shadows dive close to the water and turn sharply up again, rising like a streak of lightning and disappearing over the hills. A quick return curve to repeat the practice, and the shattered silence is restored. Heads that were lifted to look in surprise are back contemplating the sand castles, their books, or the need for more suntan lotion, or checking watches to see if it might be lunchtime. Fear? No. No fear where there is confidence. The confidence on the part of each person on this particular beach (and many others at this moment of history) is that there is no war *yet*, in this part of the world, that would make such bombing dives spell anything but "practice." Confidence that one is protected, that one is in a safe place, that danger is far, far off. Confidence nullifies fear! Not a person on this curve of sand today feels fear because of those bombers. Why? There is confidence of one kind or another that there is nothing to fear—not today.

But there are those who have had misplaced confidence. The students studying innocently as part of their university work in Africa had no fear of being kidnapped. They were confident that they were safe because it was a study center of a reputable sort. Their confidence was suddenly shattered when what they had *not* feared came suddenly upon them. Confidence as a quality in itself will not push away the reality of a fearful calamity. There *are* sudden attacks, snipers, assassins, kidnappers, accidents, illnesses, operations, breakdowns, fires, robberies, wars, floods, depressions, losses, earthquakes, death. Telegrams, phone calls, letters, and messengers *do* sometimes bring fearful news. *Confidence* that "no difficulty will ever arrive at my home," that "nothing bad can happen to me or mine," that "everything will be all right, dear. Don't worry!" is so very often just whistling in the dark. The question should be: "In whom is my confidence placed?" Am I being optimistic with no *ground*—no base for my confidence—and free from gnawing, nagging, constant fear, only as a mindless, ignorant creature would have such freedom? Or is there a difference between confidence and *confidence?*

Come to Proverbs for a moment. "Be not afraid of sudden fear, neither of the desolation of the wicked, when it cometh. For the Lord shall be thy confidence, and shall keep thy foot from being taken" (3:25, 26). It seems to me this comes as a command: "Don't be afraid of sudden fear, My child." It seems to me that the Lord is speaking to each of His children—in the dark of the night, during a walk when the wind is moaning in the trees, while we are waiting in a hospital hall, during the long moment before the doctor speaks, even in the midst of a symphony or in the waves on a shore. Midst quiet and beauty or midst shock and confusion, the fear of fear can come as a nibbling thing within, as well as a wild, searing-hot shock from without. Our fear of fear can be ever present, whatever secret thing it is we shrink from.

Our Father in heaven knows us so well. He knows that our energies, time, emotions, conscious thought, and creative possibilities can be nibbled at, wasted, or even destroyed by being "afraid of sudden fear." Don't we see how fantastic is God's understanding, as He shows us how we are so often afraid of fear unknown, unnamed—a nebulous, floating thing we are apt not to recognize, and which therefore eats away at us, spoiling what we could be right now, because of what we fear in the future? The word comes sharply to us—"Don't!" We are not to waste our time being afraid of something, although it may come suddenly and will be real at the moment it does come.

Why not? Because the Lord shall be our confidence! The Creator of the earth, the One who can speak a word and change things in history— this One who is our Father through the reality of the new birth which Jesus explained to Nicodemus—*is now our confidence.* Not at some future date when never again will fear be a reality, but now, before Satan is defeated, before the resurrection of the bodies, before Jesus destroys the last enemy. He is to be our confidence. Our first confidence in His power is to be our certainty that, although "the body they may kill," no one can do anything to remove from us eternal life and the certainty of our new bodies. The dear missionaries recently martyred, along with all the other martyrs, did not have a "misplaced confidence," will receive the martyr's crown as well as their new bodies, and even now are present with the Lord while they are absent from their bodies. They are reassured ten thousand times that their confidence was correctly placed.

Our confidence is also to be in the power of the Living God to act upon history right now to keep us safe in completing the plan He has for our lives. This same chapter of Proverbs speaks of walking in one's way safely, with foot not stumbling, and of not being afraid when one lies down to sleep, as we shall be given "sweet" sleep (*see* 3:23, 24). All this fits in with "For the Lord shall be thy confidence, and shall keep thy foot from being taken." Our Father—our Guide, our Lord, our God—is able to do marvelous things for us in the land of the living. He it is who asks us, who tells us, who commands us: "Be not afraid of sudden fear." Each time a fear of fear nags us within, we should verbalize an apology to the Lord. "Sorry, Lord; I'm doing it again. I'm not thinking; I'm not concentrating on my work; I'm not reading; I'm not full of love and appreciation for You, Father, or even for the people and the things You have given me. I'm in danger of allowing my fear of fear to push out every other emotion and therefore every response You have told me to have. Help me, O God, to push out this fear of fear so that the doubt which is mingled so closely with it may be replaced by confidence." Naturally, it must be our own apology at the time, filled with the reality of our recognition of what we have done wrong.

In Matthew 8, the disciples awakened the Lord, crying, "Lord, save us: we perish" (*see* v. 25). At that moment they were really afraid of fear. They were afraid of the fear they felt they were about to have if they were plunged into the water. They were still in a boat—tossing, to be sure—but their fear was of what was ahead of them. In the next verse, the Lord's word to them was a question: "Why are ye fearful, O ye of little faith?—Oh, My dear disciples," Jesus speaks then to the men and to us now, "where is your confidence? Please tell Me when you are going to show your confidence in Me? Why are you dwelling on your fear of sudden fear, instead of wondering whether there will be very much time left in which to demonstrate your confidence?"

> [O ye of little faith] Be not afraid of sudden fear, neither of the desolation of the wicked when it cometh. For the Lord shall be thy confidence, and shall keep thy foot from being taken.
>
> Proverbs 3:25, 26

And the Lord's own formula needs to be added here. It is not a matter of simply declaring, "I won't ever be afraid again," but of fulfilling, time after time, His clear "how it can be done," as given in Philippians 4:6. Instead of being "anxious" or fearful, we are meant to pray. That prayer is to start with thanksgiving for very real things that have taken place in the past, so that we are filled with an emotion of real thankfulness and confidence in the One who has done all these things we are recounting audibly to Him. After the thanksgiving, we are then ready to ask, request, and supplicate our listening Father concerning the thing which was making us fearful or anxious or worried. This is the *how* of carrying out the command to "be not afraid of sudden fear," in obedience as well as love for Him.

32

Negative Watching or Positive Seeking?

> But if from thence thou shalt seek the Lord thy God, thou shalt find him, if thou seek him with all thy heart and with all thy soul.
>
> Deuteronomy 4:29

> Then shall ye call upon me, and ye shall go and pray unto me, and I will hearken unto you. And ye shall seek me, and find me, when ye shall search for me with all your heart. And I will be found of you, saith the Lord: and I will turn away your captivity, and I will gather you from all the nations . . . .
>
> Jeremiah 29:12–14

> Blessed is the man that heareth me, watching daily at my gates, waiting at the posts of my doors. For whoso findeth me findeth life, and shall obtain favour of the Lord.
>
> Proverbs 8:34, 35

> Seek ye the Lord while he may be found, call ye upon him while he is near.
>
> Isaiah 55:6

Generation after generation and century after century, there were those who truly sought the Lord with sincere, honest seeking and who found Him—without ever seeing Him face-to-face in the land of the living. These found Him to be near them, to never leave them nor forsake them, to listen to them when they called upon Him. They came one by one, through the Lamb—His appointed way—and they came with the motive of wanting to follow Him as soon as they could find Him. Honest seeking turns into honest following when He is found, accompanied by an assurance that He is who He says He is. The "following" is not just a nebulous religious act, a ceremony, a mystical formula. It is an open, frank, honest belief that there is a Person to follow, and that Person is God, a Personal God who responds. The natural reaction to this kind of specific, assured following is a spontaneous telling to others.

"One of the two which heard John speak, and followed him, was Andrew, Simon Peter's brother. He first findeth his own brother Simon, and saith unto him, We have found the Messias, which is, being interpreted, the Christ. And he brought him to Jesus . . ." (John 1:40–42). Remember that old Anna, who had waited and watched for the Messiah for many years in daily praying in the Temple, recognized the One for whom she was watching, even though He was a tiny baby. "And she coming in that instant gave thanks likewise unto the Lord, and spake of him to all them that looked for redemption in Jerusalem" (Luke 2:38). There needs to be no urging those who are convinced that the Second Person of the Trinity, the Son of God, the long-awaited Messiah, has indeed come, to *tell* to others this fact which is so exciting and at the same time so deeply comforting. If people care about other people— brothers, sisters, or friends—the finding of what has been sought for and the "seeing" of what has been watched for brings a burst of response and then a rush of communication in some very real way. The honest, sincere search can be seen inside the heart by God, but the results of that search, when the finding has taken place, can usually be seen by other human beings. People are affected by people! God is affected by what is taking place inside minds and hearts, in the hidden area of our beings where other finite people cannot "see" what is really going on.

Come to the opposite of positive, sincere, honest seeking. "And they *watched* him, whether he would heal him on the sabbath day; that they might accuse him" (Mark 3:2). The motive, the intent, and the desires of the heart were known to God the Son, the Second Person of the Trinity. The motive of these religious men, well trained and proud Pharisees, was to find a flaw, with the expected result of being able to accuse him. Verse 6 of this same chapter shows with what glee and fiendish feelings of success these men pounced on the "evidence" they felt they had found by their negative watching: "And the Pharisees went forth, and straightway took counsel with the Herodians against him, how they might destroy him." The result was one of assurance that they were right in their denial and rejection of the Messiah, in their pouncing upon a flaw, according to their legalistic standards wherein they had put their own relative laws on a par with absolutes. "Now we have

Him!" was their feverish reaction to the healing of the man with the withered hand. They planned now to destroy Him and held a meeting to discuss how it might be done.

Face-to-face with the Son of God, face-to-face with the Messiah, these men heard His voice in their ears, looked into His eyes, watched Him gently restore a man's withered hand with compassion, *but they did not find Him.* One can be close enough to the Living God, as they were, to feel His breath upon one's face, to have one's ears ring with His voice—and yet *not* find Him. The finding is not a matter of having sufficient opportunity for proof. The finding is something which God tells us depends upon the deep sincerity described as "seeking with all thine heart." Unseeing eyes and unhearing ears can stand in the presence of the Living God without believing what is being seen and heard. What a frightening picture of "hard hearts" and their effect on the senses. How ineffectual is "clear proof" to those who are watching with only a desire to disprove and conjure up new ways of destroying the proof. And how staggering a picture we are given when we realize that the Pharisees, the religious rulers, are not confined to one moment of history. Religious men watching—watching—only to be able to find new and brilliant ways of "accusing Him" of not being who He says He is, that they might destroy Him.

We are meant to watch. We are commanded to watch. Watching is one of our central occupations. But the watching is to be the natural result of having come to Him truly, having found Him, having bowed and then followed Him. We are then told to be aware of the rapid passing of time and of the increasing signs of His coming, and we are to watch with loving, eager assurance that He will keep His promises to come back again and restore that which has been spoiled. We are to watch with loving faith, not suspicion. We are to watch with awe and admiration, not scorn and superiority.

> Watch therefore: for ye know not what hour your Lord doth come . . . . Therefore be ye also ready: for in such an hour as ye think not the Son of man cometh . . . . Blessed is that servant, whom his lord when he cometh shall find so doing.
> Matthew 24:42, 44, 46

The motive of this kind of watching is a desire to acclaim His fulfillment of His promises, on the basis of believing He is all He claims to be—just the opposite of watching in order to accuse and destroy. The "evil servant" in this parable is pictured as being cut off and sent out with the hypocrites. What a warning! There *are* hypocrites. It is a sobering thought, and meant to help us ask the Lord to cleanse us and help us to be honest and sincere in our watching.

"Blessed are those servants, whom the lord when he cometh shall find watching: verily I say unto you, that he shall gird himself, and make them to sit down to meat, and will come forth and serve them" (Luke 12:37). If we read the previous verses, we will see that this kind of watching takes place on the part of those who are "seeking first the kingdom of God"—to whom all things are added. This kind of watching takes place by those who have provided themselves with "bags which wax not old, a treasure in the heavens that faileth not, where no thief approacheth, neither moth corrupteth" (v. 33). In the next verse is given a key as to how to be watching with the right motives: "For where your treasure is, there will your heart be also." We can do something about the reality of what is going on in our hearts, where the Lord can see and others cannot. We can examine our "treasures" from time to time and determine whether we are putting them all in the dangerous bank—or the safe bank—from the viewpoint of its effect upon our hearts. What a great thing to have our hearts in the right place—to insure that we are watching with the right motive.

Jesus spoke sharply to the disciples about watching with Him in the Garden of Gethsemane; ". . . What, could ye not watch with me one hour? Watch and pray, that ye enter not into temptation: the spirit indeed is willing, but the flesh is weak" (Matthew 26:40, 41). Added to the key of putting our treasures in heaven is the command to pray with our watching, in order to ward off the power of temptations. "Watch and pray" is Jesus' combination given for us to follow actively, not simply to read as a devotional word. Watch for His coming, but watch also that Satan's subtle temptations don't twist and turn us aside. The watching must be accompanied by our keeping in close communication with our Heavenly Father through talking to Him. If the disciples needed to watch and pray at that time, how much more *we* now need to watch and pray, day by day. Not only is there the danger of being tempted in some way by Satanic influences that people recognize as "evil," but Pharisees with other names can also tempt us. Satan uses whatever would be most tempting. "Watch and pray that ye enter not into temptation."

Ye are all the children of light, and the children of the day: we are not of the night, nor of darkness. Therefore let us not sleep, as do others; but let us watch and be sober.

1 Thessalonians 5:5, 6

But the end of all things is at hand: be ye therefore sober, and watch unto prayer.

1 Peter 4:7

But watch thou in all things, endure afflictions, do the work of an evangelist, make full proof of thy ministry.

2 Timothy 4:5

Here *watching* is coupled with enduring afflictions—not with being removed from all difficulties, but having difficulties which can be called afflictions. And the admonition is to "endure" them—while watching. "Behold, I come as a thief. Blessed is he that watcheth, and keepeth his garments, lest he walk naked, and they see his shame" (Revelation 16:15). The *watch* we are to be concerned with is something that helps us to consider our readiness for His coming and our preparation to be in His presence. Negative watching caused the Pharisees to be filled only with critical desires and thoughts of how to cut down the Lord. What opposites can be described with the one word *watch!* God help us to be among the blessed ones who have the garments of the righteousness of Christ, because we have bowed and accepted what He has done for us, rather than sitting in judgment upon Him with suspicious, accusing eyes.

Let us then: "Be watchful, and strengthen the things which remain . . ." (Revelation 3:2).

33

❧ ❧

Seeking for Life or for Death?

With what different emotions we respond to the words *seek . . . seeking . . . sought* and the words *find . . . finding . . . found.* There is the eager seeking for one whom we love, the joyous finding with all the resultant responses and expressions of love. There is the fearful search by the harsh dictator's forces, the terror-filled sound of the knock on the door, indicating that the search has ended in successful finding—with the intent of harming the one or ones found, even killing him, her, or them. The motives for seeking and the carrying out of the purpose of the "found one" when that one is found, can be totally opposite, as opposite as the words *evil* and *good.*

The statement "I am seeking Jesus" or the statement "I have found Jesus" cannot stand alone without definition at any point in history. God alone knows the heart, and so only God can know the real motive behind the words. We cannot judge each other from a place of perfect understanding and knowledge, because we are sinful, limited, and finite. However, we do have a responsibility to examine ourselves, each one of us, and to discuss with others—remembering that words in themselves are not sufficient. We also need to be careful not to help anyone "seek" or "find" or lead others in a search with the wrong motive! This is not an academic game, but a practical reality in our own moment of history, even as it has been in other periods of time.

Come to the time when the Wise Men were searching for the new-born baby Jesus in order to worship Him. Their search was with the true motive of recognizing Him as having come from heaven, no ordinary man but the One to be worshiped. When they found Him, they fell down and worshiped Him (*see* Matthew 2:11). Then it was God who directed them supernaturally by warning them that someone else who had asked to be shown where this baby was did *not* have the right motive for his search. Not only did God warn the Wise Men not to return the way they had come, but God sent the angel of the Lord to Joseph in a dream, telling him directly, ". . . Arise, and take the young child and his mother, and flee into Egypt, and be thou there until I bring thee word: for Herod will *seek* the young child *to destroy him*" (v. 13). Here God, who knows the motives of men's hearts, defines the motive and the purpose of Herod's search.

But what had Herod said as he mouthed the words into the ears of the Wise Men? "And he sent them to Bethlehem, and said, Go and *search* diligently for the young child; and when ye have found him, bring me word again, that I may come and worship him also" (Matthew 2:8). Herod's words at face value sounded honest and beautiful. He *said* he wanted to find Jesus to worship Him, but his motive and purpose were exactly opposite. He wanted to destroy Him, to smash any possibility of His leadership, to stamp out the worship of other people for this One, to demolish the true search of other people like the Wise Men, by wiping out the Person for whom they might search. He wanted to keep humanistic man in the place of honor—himself, yes, but I believe a deeper meaning can be seen here.

Come to another moment when, in another geographic place and another exact time in history, God pulls back the flesh and bone of men's minds and hearts and lets us see what is behind mere spoken words. "And they sought to lay hold on him, but feared the people . . . . And they send unto him certain of the Pharisees and of the Herodians, to *catch* him in his *words*" (Mark 12:12, 13). And place with this, Matthew 22:15: "Then went the Pharisees, and took counsel how they might entangle him in his talk." Add Luke 20:20 to these two statements of fact: "And they watched him, and sent forth spies, which should *feign* themselves just men, that they might take hold of his words, that so they might deliver him unto the power and authority of the governor." God lets us see an historic record of what was going on in men's minds and private conversations—the wicked intent of a "search for Jesus," so that with dishonest questions with no desire for an honest answer there might be success in twisting and turning what Jesus said into something else. We have clearly a warning here that some seekers do not really want to find anything except opportunities to point out loopholes, to twist words into double meanings, to leap upon Jesus with accusations, and to finally succeed in killing Him for whom they were searching. The result these men wanted was an undisturbed continuance of their own leadership after rejecting the Messiah. As religious leaders they wanted to maintain their following and their leadership—at any cost.

Slip back again into history, the most central period of all history, as the Lamb of God approaches the moment when He will be once and for all the Sacrifice, the Atonement, the Substitute. Hold your breath as we imagine ourselves in the Garden of Gethsemane and listen to the words of Jesus as He asks, "Whom seek ye?" (John 18:7). What is the meaning of their answer—"Jesus of Nazareth"? There is a quietness on a lake before the wild lightning streaks the sky and the thunder crashes down and the waves whip up into whitecaps. One sees, feels, senses the quietness as the water goes into flat patches of gray and darker gray. In this moment of quietness in the Garden: "Jesus answered, I have told you that I am he: if therefore ye seek me, let these go their way" (v. 8). Ah, yes; they have found Him! He has made Himself known to them. Can they go on in their motive and purpose without recoiling in fear? They do fall backwards to the ground, but it doesn't last long. They brush themselves off, strain their stomach muscles or leg muscles in hastening to get up and go about their appointed task. If you have a vivid imagination, even now, centuries later, you feel like putting out a hand, shaking one of them, and urgently whispering in his ear, "Don't.

Oh, don't take part in this. Stop. Don't you know this is the virgin-born son of Mary—the Son of God, the promised Messiah! Don't take part in finding Him with this evil motive. Change now, seek Him for your own life, find Him as your Messiah. Oh, soldier—whatever your background has been—open your eyes before it is too late." But we aren't there. It is history. These men either believed later, or they didn't. We'll meet them in heaven, or we will never see them because of the gulf between the lost and the found people. They went on with their seizing of Him whom they had found, to deliver Him up to be spit upon, scourged, placed on a cross to die. They had been seeking Him in unbelief, to try to stop anyone—who had sought Him in the belief that He was God— from having Him ever near them again. Both in Herod's case and in the case of the Pharisees and those religious leaders and other men who put the Son of God on the cross, the desire was to eliminate Him.

We do live in our own little sixty-, seventy-, ninety-, or hundred-year span. Our spot in history is the place where our motives and purpose will make a difference and where our warnings and explanations will help to pull a "soldier" of Herod's (or a soldier of any other group which seeks with the intent to destroy Him) out of the wrong search and into the honest search. There are individuals today who only seek Jesus in order to prove that He is *not* who He claims to be, who spend a lifetime seeking to prove Jesus to be just a good man—not God, not the Second Person of the Trinity. There are seminaries which train men and women to seek Jesus with skill—to demolish His place in the Trinity, to destroy the truth of the Virgin Birth, to reduce His Resurrection to an airy, spiritual happening with no body involved. There are whole churches or groups within churches who use the words *seek* and *find* in relationship to Jesus, but who cast away His Word, who reduce the Bible to simple myths and fables with a variety of applications that change with the shifting winds. There really is no difference between Herod's search with his mealy-mouthed promise to worship, the search in the catch questions of the Pharisees, the search in the Garden, and the search today by those who have many followers in their attempt to destroy this One about whom we are told: "In the beginning was the Word, and the Word was with God, and the Word was God. The same was in the beginning with God. *All things were made by him;* and without him was not any thing made that was made" (John 1:1–3).

It isn't just that those who "seek" and "find" with false intent destroy in one way or another, but the final result is that each one of them is destroyed. It is a matter of life or death to the one seeking, whether the meaning of the search is for tearing apart, judging, criticizing, and destroying the Word of God, or whether the final meaning or intent of the search is to bow before the Living God and allow Him to do the "finding" of that lost one. Jesus came to seek and to save the lost people, and He so clearly reveals Himself to the ones who are lost and truly want to be found. He came to bring eternal life. But those who seek with the wrong motive—to destroy Him—find only death if they persist. The sad thing is that, as with Herod, the Pharisees, and all the false seekers or false prophets, they influence others into following them.

For each of us there is a very short time during which we can use our words, our influence, or our prayer times to help others to be in the right place or to have the true motive for their search. It was not long after the soldiers in the Garden had found Jesus, only a long weekend later, that Mary weepingly sought Him. He had been hung on the cross. He had died. Her weeping was with desolate loneliness and disappointment and fear. She was seeking her Lord's dead body with sorrow, love, honesty, but also with depression. No thought of life in her words to the gardener. "[Then] Jesus saith unto her, Woman, why weepest thou? whom *seekest* thou? . . ." (John 20:15). She supposed He was a gardener and wanted to know where her Lord's body was, and then the living, resurrected Jesus spoke in accent and tone that she recognized with a sharp remembrance. "Mary . . ." and her reply was "Master." She had found Him. She had found her risen Lord in a body which she would be able to touch after He ascended to His Father, and her Father, His God and her God. And she believed. She went to the others to tell them that she had seen the Lord. He was alive. One day—if we have found Him as our Saviour and Lord, our Atonement and our God—we will talk to Mary—alive forevermore in her resurrected body, as we are in ours.

There is a seeking and finding which results in everlasting *life*. There is also a seeking and finding which ends in everlasting *death*. There is no neutral position.

34

Abased or Abounding—Interchangeably

The big truck wound its way up the steep curves of the mountain road, a red car filled with a variety of people, close behind but not trying to pass. The driver of the truck waved happily at the driver and passengers in the car. Then, as another curve was rounded, the passenger in the truck waved vigorously at the red car. A bit behind, another car was following, heading toward the same destination. In fact, it was a little caravan of cars—perhaps separated by some distance, but together. This is a "crew," a gathering of people, a group, a number of human beings placed together for a period of time to produce something which couldn't be done if they weren't together. A documentary film is being made. A film which we pray may say something strong in the midst of a world which has turned its back on true truth, a world in which children are being born into homes where truth has never been known. In the process of months of daily travel and work in that which is very new to some of us, a basic demonstration of an old biblical truth is being enacted in a practical way, day by day and over and over again. I have discovered in the organizational setup of this particular filming that there is an amazing unfolding of what Christian life is all about.

The producer is the top man in the undertaking. Yet the producer is also the truck driver and at times he is under the truck trying to find out why the oil is leaking. When the cameraman has set up his equipment in a strategic spot and it is time for "action," it is the director who barks out the orders to be followed by the soundman and his assistants, the script girl, and the cameraman. At that moment the producer must suddenly be willing to dash off at a run to stop noisy people from walking by, to ask a farmer to stop running his tractor for a few minutes, or to get something forgotten by someone and left behind in the truck. Later the director sits at a meeting where the producer is making decisions and giving orders. That day, as I sat in the red car watching the producer wave, knowing it was a perspiring job of sheer hard (and often dangerous) work—safely getting up the mountain with that truck

full of equipment, props of various kinds, scaffoldings, clothing, camera
gear, and an amazing assortment of other things—it struck me that the
days ahead of us and the days behind us were a tremendously realistic,
living demonstration of what it means in some measure to be abased
and to abound—interchangeably.

Is it beneath the dignity of a producer to be treated as an errand boy?
Is it beneath the dignity of a director to go back up a mountain to get the
truck when it had to be left behind because of a sudden storm? Is it
beneath the line of responsibility to ask the narrator to get up at 5:45
A.M. along with the rest of the crew to get somewhere during the best
morning light? In the light of Christian teaching about our place in life,
the stress is on willingness to accept sudden changes and interchange-
able positions—taking leadership or taking direction, being served or
serving, sitting at the table or washing floors. The primary willingness
is knowing how to change places gracefully—by His grace! There is so
much talk of "roles" today. "What is my role?" people ask. God asks us
to be ready for anything He has in His plan for us and He does not give
us the plan far ahead.

"Sufficient unto the day is the evil thereof," He tells us in Matthew
6:34. In the project of making a film of this sort, one learns that more
changes are made in the schedule than had been originally lined up.
Why? Because weather and other unpredictable ingredients are things
no human being can anticipate. God *knows* what is ahead (though a
human producer does not), but He doesn't promise to hand His children a blueprint, a set schedule. Day by day we are to be ready for His
changes, His sudden orders to go somewhere else, to do another thing.
Our role is to be ready for His direction, which includes the constant
changing of role.

Paul is speaking to the Philippian church people when he rejoices in
their good care of him, but acknowledges that they did not have the
opportunity to do all they had hoped to do for him. Then he goes on:

> Not that I speak in respect of want: for I have learned, in
> whatsoever state I am, therewith to be content. I know both
> how to be abased, and I know how to abound: every where and
> in all things I am instructed both to be full and to be hungry,
> both to abound and to suffer need. I can do all things through
> Christ which strengtheneth me.
>
> Philippians 4:11–13

We know something of the extent of Paul's abasement when we read 2
Corinthians 11. We know that he knew real hunger and shipwreck,

prison life for two years, and cold and nakedness—dangers in cities as well as in the wilderness. Paul knew what he was talking about when he said he had learned to be abased. However, he tells the secret of being able to live through such excruciating experiences when he declares, "I can do all things through Christ which strengtheneth me." Only because of His strength made perfect in our weakness is it possible to live through the sufferings, persecutions, attacks of Satan, afflictions of all kinds. Also, however, only through having some reality of the need for Christ's strength and grace can we ever *experience* the fact that "My strength is sufficient for thee."

It is just as important to notice, however, that when Paul says, "I can do all things through Christ which strengtheneth me," it also applies to what he has just said when he indicated that he has learned to *abound* as well as to *be abased*. It takes the help of the Lord's strength to abound, to be the director or the producer in moments of being in charge, as well as the Lord's strength to be willing to be treated as a servant. There is a marvelous promise which God gives us here through Paul, of having a fantastically delicate "adjuster" within us—as delicate as the shock absorbers in shockproof watches.

We who are apt to be thrown around—tossed back and forth between abasement and abounding if we are willing to do what the Lord has in His plan for us—have, by the power of the indwelling Holy Spirit and the help of the strength of Christ, the most sensitive adjuster which is meant to make us in a certain sense "waterproof and shockproof." Thus, we don't drown in the midst of difficulties, nor do we drown in another sense in the midst of the honors or responsibilities given to us. We are meant to be prepared for changes: sudden events, storms, shipwrecks, famines, pestilences, dangers in cities and in the care of the churches! We are meant to be abased and to abound with whatever rapidity the interchange is to take place in God's plan for us.

This same Paul speaks to the Corinthians with great strength as he tells them what God gave him to say for our present needs, too. In 1 Corinthians 4:7, he asks who made us to differ from one another and in what we have that we did not receive from the Lord. The warning in this is to take not glory ourselves, but to give the glory to the Lord who made us in the first place.

> For I think that God hath set forth us the apostles last, as it were appointed to death: for we are made a spectacle unto the world, and to angels, and to men. We are fools for Christ's sake . . . . Even unto this present hour we both hunger, and

> thirst, and are naked, and are buffeted, and have no certain
> dwellingplace; And labour, working with our own hands:
> being reviled, we bless; being persecuted, we suffer it . . . .
> I write not these things to shame you, but as my beloved sons *I*
> *warn you.*
> 1 Corinthians 4:9–12, 14

What is the warning? It seems to me that we are being told over and over again that we must be ready for a quick interchange—to be abased and to abound, to be received by people wanting to listen to what the Lord has for us to say or to be "fools for Christ's sake." Paul as an apostle was a leader, yet undoubtedly he suffered and was also willing to work with his hands interchangeably with speaking and teaching. There is to be no set role whereby people can become puffed up. The very picture of interchangeability makes the position of the apostles one in which the men did not risk being in danger of losing their walk of humbleness before the Lord. They did not refuse to be apostles because they might find it too tempting to be egotistic, nor did they refuse to work with their hands, as was often required of them as apostles.

Jesus—our Lord and Master, our Director, Counselor, King, and Saviour—Himself showed us what quick changes we are to be ready for, as He left the table where he had commenced the marvelous succession of times which will continue until He comes back again— eating the bread and drinking the wine as a remembrance of His death for us. He had been teaching, leading, and beginning a New Testament in this central moment of history as He led the disciples in the first Lord's Supper or Communion Service. Yet it was *at this moment* that He girded Himself with a towel and poured water into a basin and began to wash the disciples' feet and to wipe them with the towel wherewith He was girded. It was after this example that Jesus put His command into words:

> If I then, your Lord and Master, have washed your feet; ye
> also ought to wash one another's feet. For I have given you an
> example, that ye should do as I have done to you. Verily, verily,
> I say unto you, The servant is not greater than his Lord; neither
> he that is sent greater than he that sent him. If ye know these
> things, happy are ye if ye do them.
> John 13:14–17

In what practical ways are we showing the Lord and the angels, demons, and people watching us that we are willing to be abased or to abound—interchangeably?

35

No Hiding Place?

Loud protests and screams of "Unfair!" have been made through the centuries when human beings have spied upon human beings by uncovering what has been said and done in supposedly well-hidden places. Now a recent *Newsweek* has had an article declaring that there is *"no hiding place,"* as it goes on to tell of the advances in technology which make it possible for anyone having the right equipment to "pick up" telegrams sent all over the world and all telephone calls sent by microwave. Nation can spy upon nation, and dictator upon individuals, as electronic devices "open" telegrams and "listen in" to phone conversations and record them to be studied at leisure. Never before have there been such possibilities of discovering the secrets "hidden" in men's private communication.

Electronic "arms" stick up in the desert, and square pieces of equipment, which to the uneducated eye look innocently like metal shapes, protrude above buildings, directed to catch the information which is flying through the atmosphere unseen by casual glance. Codes can be recorded and unscrambled with amazing rapidity. Satellites circle the globe like gigantic brooms sweeping up all the dusty bits of information. "No place to hide," states this article—for the readers and the readers' nation—from personal enemies or enemy nations! Added to this is a projection into future results of research dealing with the possibility of "reading" brain waves. Terrifying is the thought of the imperfect, sinful men controlling the machines which in a certain sense are being improved to control the men! Place beside this article a certain box in *Newsweek* which reported on and gave pictures of the results of a photographer—standing on his balcony in Helsinki and taking pictures with a telescopic lens so advanced that it could "see" and "record" a privately handwritten note scribbled by the President to someone sitting near him at a table. The camera could zoom down and look over the shoulders of men, opening up to the readers of newspapers and magazines what was meant only for the eyes of a person across the table!

How can one put into words the exclamations of dismay, which are really waves of emotion, when one thinks what could take place with all the technological advances placed one day into the hands of a world dictator? There will be *no place to hide* from the Antichrist. No place to hide the communications and no place to hide from the results of the discoveries of what has been said and written. How staggering it is to think of how specifically human beings are preparing their own present and future misery and terror.

The Bible makes it clear that there has *never* been a hiding place from God. Adam and Eve were the first to discover this: ". . . and Adam and his wife hid themselves from the presenc one Lord God amongst the trees of the garden" (Genesis 3:8). Adam and Eve were soon to find how useless was that leafy barrier. Not only does God not need an electronic device to see behind the bushes and trees or a satellite to discover what has been said into phone or teletype, He has *always* been able to "read the brain waves," to see into men's minds and hearts. David knew this well as he wrote in Psalms 69:5: "O God, thou knowest my foolishness; and my sins are not hid from thee." Every foolish and sinful thought and act has always been known to God. This is made strong and clear to us in Psalms 139:1–12:

> O Lord, thou hast searched me, and known me. Thou knowest my downsitting and mine uprising, thou understandest my thought afar off. Thou compassest my path and my lying down, and art acquainted with all my ways. For there is not a word in my tongue, but, lo, O Lord, thou knowest it altogether. Thou hast beset me behind and before, and laid thine hand upon me. Such knowledge is too wonderful for me; it is high, I cannot attain unto it. Whither shall I go from thy spirit? or whither shall I flee from thy presence? If I ascend up into heaven, thou art there: if I make my bed in hell, behold, thou art there. If I take the wings of the morning, and dwell in the uttermost parts of the sea; Even there shall thy hand lead me, and thy right hand shall hold me. If I say, Surely the darkness shall cover me; even the night shall be light about me. Yea, the darkness hideth not from thee; but the night shineth as the day: the darkness and the light are both alike to thee.

Job underlines what has been given us in Psalms. "For his eyes are upon the ways of man, and he seeth all his goings. There is no darkness, nor shadow of death, where the workers of iniquity may hide themselves" (Job 34:21, 22).

From Adam and Eve's time on down through the centuries, no man has been able to hide from God. No man can hide his communications, his acts, or even his thoughts from the Living God. We mustn't forget that Satan's temptation to Eve was that if they would eat of the tree, they would become "like gods." Adam and Eve were tempted to want to be like gods, and the temptation that has driven men through the centuries has been the same. Egocentric, self-sufficient, autonomous, and rebellious human beings have always been trying to put themselves at the center of all things. They have tried to be "like gods" in a diverse number of ways. In the days of the prince of Tyrus, we read that Ezekiel was told by God that Tyrus was trying to sit in the seat of God, to declare that there was no secret that people could hide from him (*see* Ezekiel 28:1–3). Today men are already "sitting in the seat of God" by peering into other men's secrets and are determined to be able to do this more completely as technology advances.

The warning came to the prince of Tyrus: "Wilt thou yet say before him that slayeth thee, I am God? but thou shalt be a man, and no God, in the hand of him that slayeth thee" (Ezekiel 28:9). The warning is given to men who search for more and more power to be able to know all the secrets of other men and to govern the machines *and* the men: God is still God! God alone is God. Even as the magicians of Egypt—by the mystical powers which Satan had given them—were able to reproduce some of the miracles which Moses did through God's power, so through the ages, whether by occult powers or by discovering some of the marvels of the universe which science has uncovered, men have been able to begin to do some of the things which God does. But—only God is God. Only God is infinite. Only God is unlimited. And only God is able to have power and knowledge which will not "backfire." Men are so often destroyed by their own inventions. It is a case of the present fear of the machines' controlling of the very men who made the machines! Is there no place to hide from men?

Come to Isaiah 1:10–16. Read it for yourself. We are commanded to *hear* the Word of the Lord—we today who are in a time of Sodom and Gomorrah. Today we read newspaper reports of congresses and conventions of devil worshipers, occult groups, of mystical cults all dancing before a huge pre-Columbian statue of the devil. It is to today that this passage applies. What is it God is saying? He is sick of sacrifices and offerings. Religious meetings, spiritual happenings, the keeping of holy days, solemn meetings—all these things are an abomination. God says, "Your new moons and your appointed feasts my soul hateth: they are a trouble unto me; I am weary to bear them. And when ye spread forth your hands, I will hide mine eyes from you: yea, when ye make many prayers, I will not hear: your hands are full of blood" (vv. 14, 15). God is declaring that He is not interested in religious things being done, in worship being enacted mechanically, in words being used with no honesty. Men and women cannot hide from God. But God declares that He will hide His eyes and ears from the false worship of people. Sodom and Gomorrah live, and outward but empty acts of worship are an abomination to God. People cannot hide in worship, any more than they can hide in the bushes. Perfume cannot mask filthy odors. Powder cannot cover up a dirty face. Food cannot be sprinkled on top of garbage. It is an abomination to God when such attempts are made. This is when He hides from people. People who say, "It doesn't matter how you worship, as long as you worship in some way; it is all the same . . ." are ignorant of the fact that God has said, "Bring no more vain oblations; incense is an abomination unto me . . ." (v. 13). We cannot hide from God—but He can hide from us.

"Wash you, make you clean; put away the evil of your doings from before mine eyes; cease to do evil." Verse 16 is a transition in Isaiah 1 which lets us know the compassion of this one true Holy God. Unlike men who are preparing to make the world free from hiding places, this God, perfect in His holiness as well as knowledge, has prepared *one* hiding place. "One Hiding Place," which follows, will be the second part to this study.

36

One Hiding Place

As children we have played hide-and-seek and known the nervous stillness of hiding in silence, almost afraid of breathing lest we be found. If we have lived through the terror of war and search parties by enemies or bandits, we have known further breathlessness of a more serious nature, the silence of hoping our hiding place would not be discovered. The usual good hiding place has to be very hidden indeed, from both sight and sound! But the God who sees all we do, knows all we think, hears all we say, and from whom we cannot hide, has prepared *one hiding place* which is so safe we need not keep quiet when there—we can sing and shout! What a unique hiding place is safe from the enemy even when we are singing loudly, "Here I am!" Safe from electronic spying, even in the midst of our open communication.

Psalms 32:6, 7 speaks to us and for us, even as it expresses the truth which David understood in his time of need: "For this shall every one that is godly pray unto thee in a time when thou mayest be found: surely in the floods of great waters they shall not come nigh unto him. Thou art my hiding place; thou shalt preserve me from trouble; thou shalt compass me about with songs of deliverance . . . ." The One from whom we cannot hide has made it possible for us to hide *in* Him. He Himself is our hiding place. What a miracle. How fantastic. Impossible to hide from Him, but we may hide *in* Him! A song of deliverance indeed. Imagine you had never heard this before. What shivers it would send up your spine.

Prayer is on David's lips as he cries, ". . . O Lord, attend unto my cry, give ear unto my prayer . . ." (Psalms 17:1), and he pleads in verse 13 that Satan will be disappointed. As we read and also pray with verse 8: "Keep me as the apple of the eye, hide me under the shadow of thy wings," Satan will indeed be disappointed at the results. Satan will be furious when we, who cannot hide from God, take our place *under His wings*, a secure, prepared hiding place.

"Rock of Ages, cleft for me, Let me hide myself in thee," we sing.

How wonderful that it is not just romantic poetry or a fanciful song, but *truth* with meaning that is applicable to each one of us. It is possible to find our hiding place *in* God. The Second Person of the Trinity made it possible for us to hide *in* Him, by coming to prepare that hiding place in His death on the Cross. The "splitting" of the Rock, opened up the "cleft place" in which to hide.

Think of it in another way for a moment. Come to Psalms 27:5: "For in the time of trouble he shall hide me in his pavilion: in the secret of his tabernacle shall he hide me; he shall set me up upon a rock." This is a certainty. God is able to provide a hiding place. It is not impossible for God to provide a hiding place for the ones whose sins and imperfections and open rebellions and secret complainings are known to Him. But in order to provide the hiding place, the Second Person of the Trinity had to be exposed Himself, be without a hiding place. As Jesus hung on the cross, naked, taunted, and reviled, He was exposed to everyone who looked. In Psalms 27:9, David cries out, "Hide not thy face far from me; put not thy servant away in anger: thou hast been my help; leave me not, neither forsake me, O God of my salvation." David's prayer was answered and our cry to the Lord is answered, as we call on Him to accept us—on one basis only. What is the basis upon which we can find a hiding place, and upon which we can know God will not hide His face from us? The basis of an exchange. Jesus was exposed, with no hiding place when He was on the cross, so that we might have the absolute assurance of having a hiding place. He became sin for us, He who knew no sin, but also He who was exposed for us, He who had always throughout all eternity been Himself One with *the* hiding place. They mocked Him, those who were able to gaze upon Him in His agony and shame, and He cried, "My God, my God, why hast thou forsaken me?" (Matthew 27:46). He was willing to be without a hiding place, so that He could become *our* hiding place. The long-looked-forward-to Messiah, David's hiding place, had to actually take the place of all who were to hide *in* Him, by historically living through that time of knowing the stark reality of being without a hiding place. He experienced the awfulness of that moment, that we might experience the security of an impenetrable hiding place for all eternity.

We are told in Colossians 1:26, 27 that for ages the full understanding of all this wonder was not known. After Christ came to fulfill all the prophecies, to be the awaited Lamb of God who died and also became our High Priest, the full understanding was no longer "hidden" from anyone who would listen with "ears of understanding"—"Even the mystery which hath been hid from ages and from generations, but now is made manifest to his saints: To whom God would make known what is the riches of the glory of this mystery among the Gentiles; which is Christ in you, the hope of glory." No longer is the wonder of *truth* to be hidden in any way. Now Gentiles as well as Jews are to see the pieces fitting together like the pieces of a jigsaw puzzle. Paul goes on in verse 28 to say we are to warn every man as well as to teach people "in all wisdom." By warning and by teaching, by preaching and by discussing, the *truth* is to be not hidden but made clear, so that people can first find their need of *a* hiding place—and then find the One Hiding Place.

The fact that we have accepted what Christ has done in our place when He died is not one which leads us to settle back passively into the Hiding Place, as if we had nothing to do but hide! In Colossians 3:2, 3 we are prodded to do certain things. "Set your affection on things above, not on things on the earth. For ye are dead, and your life is hid with Christ in God." How is our life "hid"? It seems to me this is explained to us in Romans 6 as a need for us to recognize that we are to have changed lives. We are not to continue in the sin which Christ died to free us from. Do we become perfect? No. A thousand times no. There is a struggle, a battle to the very end. Constantly we are told that we are to confess our sin, and that He will be faithful to forgive us and cleanse us from all unrighteousness. *But there is to be a change.* And part of that change involves another kind of "hiding"—hiding under the ground in a kind of death.

We need to be buried as a seed, a grain, a kernel of corn, before we can bring forth any kind of result while we are in the land of the living. Yes, the seed is sown in us, and we ourselves are the ground, good ground or thorny ground. But then again *we* are the seed—and we are to be active in commitment, willingness, and declaration in prayer to the Lord of our desire to be "buried in the ground," dead to self, dead to pride, dead to a desire to be thought of as humble, dead to ambition to succeed, dead to wishing to be a failure as a self-inflicted punishment, dead to everything that would hinder us from God's plan to use us. In this picture of being willing to be buried as a seed, there is a "hiding" which is in the hands of the Master Gardener who is able to care for us and bring forth the green shoots, the leaves, buds, blossoms, and harvest. There is to be a time when we are not as seeds apparently rotting under the ground, but are gathered as in Mark 4:20 and "bring forth fruit, some thirtyfold, some sixty, and some an hundred." We do not stay in a static place in this matter of first having the Hiding Place which is the Lord Himself, where we are safe from His wrath, as well as from Satan's final victory. Nor do we stay in a static place when we are willing to be buried as a "corn of wheat" (*see* John 12:24).

In Revelation 6:14–17 a strong and important prophecy is given. We are not to hide our eyes and thoughts from this truth of what is coming in the future.

> And the heaven departed as a scroll when it is rolled together; and every mountain and island were moved out of their places. And the kings of the earth, and the great men, and the rich men, and the chief captains, and the mighty men, and every bondman, and every free man, hid themselves in the dens and the rocks of the mountains; And said to the mountains and rocks, Fall on us, and hide us from the face of him that sitteth on the throne and from the wrath of the Lamb: For the great day of his wrath is come; and who shall be able to stand?

The day is coming when no person will be rejecting the existence of the Living God. In that day there will be only two divisions of people— the ones who will be loudly verbalizing their belief in God's existence by crying out for the rocks to hide them *from* Him whom they neither acknowledged before nor came to in His given way—and the ones who did hide *in* Him during their lifetime, and are secure in this everlasting Hiding Place. We are to pray for each other that a "door of utterance" (*see* Colossians 4:3) may be given, so that *the* Hiding Place will not remain hidden to men.

37

Walled In or Walled Out?

It was still dark, and the city was silent with the deep sleep of the before-dawn hour. An occasional swish of tires and a roaring of a motor were the only noises to be added to the bark of a dog. We were waiting for the crack of dawn, the first gray light in which to see the Berlin Wall.

Guards in the watchtowers were wide-awake, as they scanned the strip of dirt filled with barbed-wire traps and sharp spikes set at any likely spot for jumping. Well-trained police dogs, caged like lions in the strip, kept their noses and ears alert. As the sky suddenly lightened, and shapes emerged out of the darkness, a milk wagon could be seen with a tired woman delivering her morning burden, and a man on a bicycle started for whatever was his destination, while lights appeared in first one window and then another—on the *other* side of the wall.

A wall? A wall in name and in fact, but strange in construction indeed! Pathetic remains of houses—only the first floors now, and uninhabited because of the many who jumped out of windows trying to escape—and pathetic remains of stores with bricked or boarded-up windows, which for a space of time had been open for business on the East side of the "wall" which they themselves formed. Houses and stores *were* the wall, inhabited for a time by occupants who were walled in and walled out by their own precious walls which had been purchased by their owners for life and livelihood some years before. Human beings trapped by the choices and decisions of other human beings. Human beings without freedom, without gates that open by choice. Crosses and placards on the sidewalk of the West side marked spots where people had died. One eighty-seven-year-old woman had jumped in desperation to escape—out to the other side of the wall which had shut her in the home which had suddenly become a prison. Her curtains still fluttered in the movement of air after her jump—the inanimate cloth still to be seen.

The Berlin Wall. What a constant demonstration of man's inability in all his pride and power to bring about freedom and justice in what people have so long spoken of as the civilized world. Man cannot even tear down a wall of feeble bricks and mortar, once certain choices have made them permanent. What powerful evidence of man's bungling when he uses an assorted number of bases for his decisions! Walled in *and* walled out—and incapable of doing anything about it. Years go by . . . .

If one stands and looks at the ruins of Pompeii, the number of years blurs the acuteness of the reality of the people's suffering and also tends to blur the facts and evidence that these people by choice had allowed Satan to wall them *in* to heathen religions and *away* from the truth of God. One can look at crumbling walls with grass in the cracks and feel far removed because of *time*. But in Berlin there is no soothing syrup of time to take off the edge of our feeling as we now stand in full morning light and watch the armed guards with binoculars, constantly alert to keeping people in places they want to be out of—keeping people in thinking, ideas, and philosophies from which they want relief. Walls shutting people *in*.

Isaiah speaks with prophetic wonder of a time ahead about which we need to tell the walled-in people, whatever their walls may consist of and wherever in the world's geography they may be:

> Violence shall no more be heard in thy land, wasting nor destruction within thy borders; but thou shalt call thy walls Salvation, and thy gates Praise. The sun shall be no more thy light by day; neither for brightness shall the moon give light unto thee: but the Lord shall be unto thee an everlasting light, and thy God thy glory. Thy sun shall no more go down; neither shall thy moon withdraw itself: for the Lord shall be thine everlasting light, and the days of thy mourning shall be ended. Thy people also shall be all righteous: they shall inherit the land for ever, the branch of my planting, the work of my hands, that I may be glorified.

> Isaiah 60:18–21

There is coming a time and a place where we need not wait for the dawn to break. Dawn need never be awaited again, because the Lord will be the everlasting Light of that place. In this time and place there will be no more violence or destruction, whether by armies or by volcanoes. There will be walls—marvelous walls called *salvation*, a word which itself speaks of freedom that is everlasting. These walls will have gates—gates that are open—called *praise*. At this time all mourning, all weeping, and all desire to jump out of a window will be over.

For whom? Who will inherit a place in this land of freedom and wonder? John 10:1, 2 speaks of the need to come in by the door, rather than by trying to climb the wall and get over in this other way. There is a door, an access, a way to get in—and in verse 9 it is given. Jesus says clearly, "I am the door: by me if any man enter in, he shall be saved, and shall go in and out, and find pasture."

The Door Himself is the One who has gone to prepare a place for us. He Himself is our way into the place He has gone to prepare. But the place is a place that is real enough, and though He is the Door, our salvation, our way into that city, when He lets John have a glimpse of the heavenly city, the New Jerusalem, it is not given as a mere figure of speech, a way of making truth clear in picture language. It is a comforting, exciting pulling back of a curtain so as to have a small glimpse of a tiny part of what is ahead for us if we have understood something of what Jesus did for us to become the Door—and have accepted what He did in our place.

Read Revelation 21 and rejoice with thanksgiving for what is ahead if you are a believer and pray for people caught behind walls of men's or Satan's design, that they might find the eternal way *out*. As you read, notice the very different kind of wall described:

> And had a wall great and high, and had twelve gates, and at the gates twelve angels, and names written thereon, which are the names of the twelve tribes of the children of Israel . . . . And the wall of the city had twelve foundations, and in them the names of the twelve apostles of the Lamb.
>
> Revelation 21:12, 14

Here is a wall which has gates—three on each side—gates to come in and out of, gates through which one passes to behold the wonder of all that the city contains. A wall to protect and yet to be opened. No prisoners here—only people who have believed the *true truth* and who have become free indeed. In verse 27, you find that the walls are to keep out anything that would defile the city; but all who "are written in the Lamb's book of life" may enter. Am I not one who would defile the place if I had come in my own goodness? Oh, yes—tattered and torn garments of "self" can't be mended. But we can come, cleansed by the blood of the Lamb and dressed in the white linen of His righteousness. So we can know we will be there, safe inside but also with the gates open in both directions.

What a wall! This wall is not of ugly broken brick, mortar, and barbed wire, but: ". . . the building of the wall of it was of jasper: and the city was pure gold, like unto clear glass" (v. 18). Beauty in every detail is here prepared for us—beauty that cannot be described so that we can take it in, but which leaves us breathless in the amount we *are* given. Here are gorgeous walls on firm foundations, garnished with precious stones. Behind these walls trudge no weary prisoners delivering food and drink. Crystal-clear waters gush forth, and hanging on trees are fruits of a variety and flavor we can look forward to but cannot yet experience.

"And God shall wipe away all tears from their eyes; and there shall be no more death, neither sorrow, nor crying, neither shall there be any more pain: for the former things are passed away" (Revelation 21:4). Oh, glorious walls! How different from any walls of men's making—whether philosophic or of ugly brick and stone, crumbling or strong and guarded by violence. As we stand by the Berlin Wall in gray daybreak, in imagination or in reality, let us feel the certainty of the wall we look forward to—and consider very soberly whether we are looking forward to the literal wonder of what God has given us in His Word. There is a sense of needing to be sure we are "walled in" and not "walled out" of all that is ahead for the children of the Living God. But there is also a sense in which we need to be excruciatingly conscious of the building of Satan's walls which is going on in our own period of history—physical walls and intellectual walls. We need to be careful that we are not by our own "choices" bending down to pick up a trowel to add a little mortar between the stones and bricks which keep other people away from true truth and freedom.

Is there any decision of ours—"to do" or "not to do"—which will help to "wall in" or "wall out" other people from the possibility of ever hearing of the fantastic future wall—and how to get in?

38

What Harvest?

Harvesttime in so many parts of the world brings the golden glow of changing leaves, balanced beauty of grapes thick in triangular clusters, heavy branches of red, yellow, or green-streaked apples, rows of brown-tasseled corn with hidden yellow kernels popping with juice, curling spirals of sweet-smelling smoke from burning leaf mounds, or the rich odor of charcoal-roasted chestnuts. What are the crops? Terraced vineyards—climbing old stone-pillared arbors on Italian hillsides or wrapped around individual wood or iron sticks in Swiss fashion—bring forth grapes. Neat garden patches in suburban gardens produce peas, beans, beets, or broccoli for thrifty homemakers to prepare for their freezers. Orchards in the Northwest fill endless boxes

with individually wrapped pears or apples or plums for distant custom-
ers, while people in southern climes are packing crates of tangerines
and grapefruits from their groves. The universal answer to "What are
you harvesting?" is "What I planted." A harvest consists of what at one
time or another was carefully—or carelessly—planted.

The time to pore over seed catalogs or fruit-tree descriptions is *before*
the proper planting time. It is too late when harvesttime arrives to
change one's mind and say, "I really wanted blackberries, not raspber-
ries." Or, "I don't like spinach; what I really wanted was a variety of
cabbage—red and green." Or, "Why aren't we having any lima beans
and sweet potatoes?" Harvesttime is so often synonymous in our minds
with Thanksgiving time. It is right that we are meant to gather crops
with thankfulness and enjoy the eating of them with an understanding
of all that has gone into the beauty and sufficiency of what has been
gathered after months of growing time. However, harvesttime can be a
time of disappointment also. It is good not to brush aside the disap-
pointing aspects of the harvest—and just go out and buy sufficient
things to load the table for a "harvest festival" or "Thanksgiving
dinner"—without remembering that God intends for the yearly time of
harvesting or reaping to jog us into consciousness of the solemn reality
and awareness that there is a specific connection between planting and
harvesting. Harvesttime is the time to examine ourselves, alone before
God, and to remind each other that God has warned us vividly in
language that is understandable and with an illustration that is universal.

God has warned us, "Be not deceived; God is not mocked: for whatsoever a man soweth, that shall he also reap" (Galatians 6:7). *Don't let
Satan deceive you,* God says to us. Don't let your own foolish optimism
fool you. What you choose to do with your days and years and the
decisions you make are like the planting of seeds—a reaping time
specifically and definitely will follow, the harvest will be seen by you
and others. As you act daily in the history of your life, the result of what
you are "sowing" will be the arrival of a moment of time when the
"reaping" will take place. It would be good to stop and read the whole
Book of Proverbs in this context. "My son, forget not my law . . . .
Trust in the Lord with all thine heart: and lean not unto thine own
understanding. In all thy ways acknowledge him, and he shall direct
thy paths" (Proverbs 3:1, 5, 6). Much has been given us as warning, as
direction, as fair road signs of the dangers we can so easily tumble into
through our own weaknesses or Satan's carefully placed traps. What are

we sowing? Are we looking daily into the "catalog" of God's Word, so to speak, to find the variety of precious seed to be given us personally in the context of our immediate need for decision? Are we faced with a pressing problem, a titanic decision, a strong temptation, an impossible situation? Our decision in this moment's need—our choice of the alternatives which come into our minds—will affect the reaping time in a definite way. We can't "put off planting time," because in our lives as the Lord's children in the land of the living, we plant right up to the end!

Going back to Galatians, let us think soberly for a few moments: "For he that soweth to his flesh shall of the flesh reap corruption; but he that soweth to the Spirit shall of the Spirit reap life everlasting" (Galatians 6:8). This passage faces us with the basic and central decision of choosing to accept what Christ has done for those who accept Him as Saviour, being born into God's family with the assurance of being indwelt by the Holy Spirit, and the possibility of living by His direction. But it also faces us with the fact that it is possible for us, as children of the Living God, to *sow to the flesh* and *reap corruption*, as we deliberately put self and selfish decisions first. An angry Christian can burst forth and create much destruction or corruption for the space of some minutes or hours or days. A Christian who gives in to the lust of pride or of eyes or malicious gossip can be sowing corruption of the flesh which will result in a corrupted harvest. A Christian who says inside himself or herself, "I don't care what God wants me to do, I *will* do thus and so. Later I can do the Lord's will when I finish what I am determined to do first!" is sowing seeds of corruption, no matter how "good" the thing being done seems to be.

As Paul begins this sixth chapter of Galatians, he says very carefully that if we find a brother (and that would be true of a sister, too) who has been overtaken by a fault—and alcohol, sex, and drugs are not the only "faults" that are serious—we who are spiritual are to "restore such an one in the spirit of meekness; considering thyself, lest thou also be tempted . . . . For if a man think himself to be something, when he is nothing, he deceiveth himself" (vv. 1, 3). We should note that no one is spiritual except through the blood of Christ's cleansing and the strength of God made perfect in weakness. The Word of God to us as individual Christians is very strong here. Not *one* of us is "above" doing the very thing we are to meekly point out in another person who has been making choices of sowing very corrupt seed. What is told us is that "spiritual Christians" *can* fall. We are told to watch out that we don't get filled with a blinding kind of spiritual pride which will make us miss the trap Satan will set before our own feet. To feel that we can *not* fall—that we can *not* ever sow the wrong seed as Christians—is the first wrong move. We are not heeding God's warning if we shrug it off with the attitude of applying it to someone else, but not to ourselves.

"And let us not be weary in well doing: for in due season we shall reap, if we faint not" (Galatians 6:9) can be coupled with 2 Thessalonians 3:13: "But ye, brethren, be not weary in well doing." In verse 11, disorderly and lazy, nonworking people have been spoken of, but the danger to those who are making good choices in the Lord's will and who are working hard is of becoming "weary in well doing." There is the danger of saying, "Why bother to do this hard thing, to put in double the working hours of anyone else, to care about the burdens of other people, to try to live according to the Word of God?" when one is surrounded by others who are tearing off to do their own thing. There is the danger of turning way from the real absolutes of the Word of God and making up a list of rules by which to live which fit into the modern scene of the hedonistic think-of-yourself-first pattern.

In Hebrews we find: "For ye have need of patience, that, after ye have done the will of God, ye might receive the promise. For yet a little while, and he that shall come will come, and will not tarry. Now the just shall live by faith: but if any man draw back, my soul shall have no pleasure in him" (Hebrews 10:36–38). It takes patience to go on and not "draw back," to be not weary in well-doing. It takes patience to go on with a desire and willingness to do the Lord's will, no matter what He unfolds it to be in our individual cases. It takes patience to wait for the promise to be fulfilled of the Lord's coming.

But the illustration which God gives us and which we can understand year by year is the harvest. Each harvest ought to remind us that we *will* reap what we are sowing. It is both a promise and a warning. The yearly patience of waiting for crops of apples is a tiny example of the patience needed for awaiting the final reaping of what we have sown. However, in *this* life there is reaping that results in changed history for each one of us, depending on what we have sown. We don't have to wait until the coming of the Lord to be affected by the sowing and the reaping. He has warned us. Our own lives will be different in the future because of what we are sowing today. The beauty of this sowing is that we don't need to wait until next spring, nor even the time for winter wheat's sowing. Read 2 Corinthians 9:6: "But this I say, He which soweth sparingly shall reap also sparingly; and he which soweth bountifully shall reap

also bountifully." *This is true in this life.* Today we can bow before the
Lord and ask Him to help us in today's sowing, and tomorrow's, that the
harvest might be changed.

This is true of universities, towns, states, and nations. There is going
on a reaping of what has been sown, as we can read in the newspapers
each day. What will be tomorrow's harvest? What responsibility do we
have in our personal decisions for the wider *reaping*—locally, nation-
ally, and internationally?

39

God's Greatest Creation

Stand in front of Masaccio's mural in an old cathedral in Florence,
take a deep breath and look. The faces of people living centuries ago are
alive. You pick out strength, imagine personality and character, feel you
could talk to various ones, sense their emotions. How old was this
Masaccio when he stood with brush and paint he had mixed himself,
shivering in the cold of stone and plaster walls, carefully standing back
to look, continuing to put on a flat gray surface that which would bring a
depth of reality, people talking to each other, taking part in a moment of
history—but preserved in a way that no changes of time and situation
could touch? One moment preserved in paint by an artist who had to be
younger than twenty-seven, because he died at twenty-seven before
the whole fresco was complete. How did his hands have such skill?
How could his mind conceive of new delicate ways to bring out
perspective, to mix his paints? How *could* he place on a cold, hard wall
the features and personalities of people he knew or had seen—and
make them alive for so many centuries? Inherited? From whom? Who
first had such skillful hands, such workable ideas?

Come to Ghent and walk in the little room to carefully look at the
well-lighted van Eyck altarpiece. Sit and look and wonder. Walk up
close and find the detail of delicate flowers in the grass, birds flying, the

fine hairs of men's beards so real that one feels one could brush them, the pearls embroidered on robes standing out with a roundness and luster that take one's breath away. Sit and contemplate as you look at the marvel of the subject matter—the Mystic Lamb, standing on the altar, bleeding yet standing, and speaking of the Messiah who would come as the Lamb to die and rise again. Contemplate not just this for a time, but think of the fantastic colors as you take in the bright greens, scarlets, blues, yellows—mixed by a "secret formula" devised, invented, thought of and discovered by van Eyck himself. Where did it come from?—His skill? His ideas? He was a "first" to do certain things never done before. How? Let your eyes move down to the date at the bottom of the frame: "van Eyck 1432." Feel it! Marvel! Be *moved* with your realization that this man had skill that was not taught. No art school produced him. Where did it come from?

Walk into the Leonardo da Vinci section of the National Science Museum in Milan and walk slowly by the models of his inventions. Remember his paintings, think of him as an artist, but look now at his models and sketches which show something of the fabulous diversity of this man's ideas. Here is a finely proportioned wing made as he projected the thought that one day men could make flying machines. There is a wonderful device to distill water, one to refrigerate, and here is a model of how to produce steam and then how to use it in never-before-thought-of ways. See the model of a furnace for melting metals, cranes and levers for lifting weights, hydraulic power harnessed in his mind and made in a model men could copy. Look at the walls covered with sketches of muscles, veins, the heart, lungs, the nervous system— complete anatomy understood in an amazing way in this man's mind, yet also sketched with beauty and detail that cannot be described. Study for a moment his maps of cities and regions, his botanical studies of flowers and plants, his architectural plans that include a whole model city. See the weapons: a cannon, boats with contraptions to drag rivers or lakes, barges to drag the sea, paddle wheels and devices to turn them—no need to row. Look at the drawings of musical instruments and those that show his understanding of acoustics, his geometric studies, the movement of the moon, stars, planets, and his applied geometry and algebra. Spend time to think, wonder, and feel the fact that this was a man who had come from *where?* Where had the ideas come from? The skill—was it inherited? From whom? How can any human being have such creativity as demonstrated in the work of artists, the genius of scientists, and in such combination as in Leonardo?

And God said, Let us make man in our image, after our likeness . . . .
                                                                            Genesis 1:26

I will praise thee; for I am fearfully and wonderfully made: marvellous are thy works; and that my soul knoweth right well.
                                                                            Psalms 139:14

O give thanks unto the Lord; call upon his name: make known his deeds among the people. Sing unto him, sing psalms unto him: talk ye of all his wondrous works.
                                                                            Psalms 105:1, 2

Thus saith the Lord, thy redeemer, and he that formed thee from the womb, I am the Lord that maketh all things; that stretcheth forth the heavens alone; that spreadeth abroad the earth by myself.
                                                                            Isaiah 44:24

I have made the earth, and created man upon it: I, even my hands, have stretched out the heavens . . . . For thus saith the Lord that created the heavens; God himself that formed the earth and made it; he hath established it, he created it not in vain, he formed it *to be inhabited:* I am the Lord; and there is none else . . . . Woe unto him that striveth with his Maker! Let the potsherd strive with the potsherds of the earth. Shall the clay say to him that fashioneth it, What makest thou? or thy work, He hath no hands?
                                                                            Isaiah 45:12, 18, 9

Thus saith God the Lord, he that created the heavens, and stretched them out; he that spread forth the earth, and that which cometh out of it; he that giveth breath unto the people upon it, and spirit to them that walk therein: I the Lord have called thee in righteousness, and will hold thine hand . . . .
                                                                            Isaiah 42:5, 6

All things were made by him; and without him was not any thing made that was made. In him was life; and the life was the light of men.
                                                                            John 1:3, 4

. . . him declare I unto you. God that made the world and all things therein, seeing that he is Lord of heaven and earth, dwelleth not in temples made with hands . . . seeing he giveth to all life, and breath, and all things; And hath made of one blood all nations of men for to dwell on all the face of the earth . . . .

Acts 17:23–26

Because that which may be known of God is manifest in them [even in unrighteous men]; for God hath shewed it unto them. For the invisible things of him from the creation of the world are clearly seen, being understood by the things that are made . . . .

Romans 1:19, 20

Surely your turning of things upside down shall be esteemed as the potter's clay: for shall the work say of him that made it, He made me not? or shall the thing framed say of him that framed it, He had no understanding?

Isaiah 29:16

Forty years long was I grieved with this generation, and said, It is a people that do err in their heart, and they have not known my ways . . . . O come, let us worship and bow down: let us kneel before the Lord our *maker*. For *he* is our God; and we are the people of *his* pasture, and the sheep of *his* hand. To day if ye will hear his voice, Harden not your heart, as in the provocation, and as in the day of temptation in the wilderness.

Psalms 95:10, 6–8

We are to worship God, the only Living Eternal God who is the Creator and who made man in His image. Man is wonderful, though fallen and sinful, spoiled and warped, far less by far than he could be. But man *is* wonderful and glimpses of the original wonder of God's most marvelous Creation show through in people through the centuries. The glimpses of the wonder of *people* created in the image of the Creator can be seen in the artists who seemed to come out of nowhere in past centuries. The very existence of artworks speaks of the existence of the Creator-Artist God who made men in His own image. Stand before great works of art and weep for the spoiled Creation, as Satan tempted and twisted Eve's and Adam's minds into believing him rather than God. Weep today for those who are twice twisted, as they claim to be following God, yet do what Isaiah 29:16 calls "turning of things upside down" by saying, "He made me not." Everyone who turns away from the literal creation of Adam and Eve (and therefore the marvelous, literal design of human beings made so fearfully and wonderfully down to the tiniest detail—which Leonardo could so magnificently draw as he sketched heart, lungs, eyes, ears, nervous system, and bones) is actually turning away from the personal design in God's mind—brought out by His hands in the reality of living beings made in His image—and is saying in essence, "He made me not." This is what grieves God.

Forget theological discussions for a minute. It is Christmastime. Sweet music, soft lights, and emotional thoughts of the baby Jesus bring a rush of "spiritual feeling," but what is it all worth if the pastors, theological students, or church members are being drawn by Satan's clever lies into "grieving God!" This God is the One who emptied Himself to take upon Himself the form of man, the form which He had created, but now to be assumed in reality for a lifetime of thirty-three years—without sin's spoiling! God who made man in His image is thus being born in the image He created, to live with finite men, not in a body that evolved, but in the very same kind of body He made when He made Adam. Oh, staggering thought! What a blow Satan wants to strike as he whispers, "Don't believe it," again and again in this moment of history. Don't do what Eve did. Don't believe him.

"O come, let us adore Him, O come, let us adore Him, O come, let us adore Him, Christ, the Lord!" This is the Creator of all things—the One who made man in His image and then came in the image of man to enable man, all people, to become the sheep of His pasture, the people of His own flock forever—never to be spoiled again.

40

Conformed Nonconformists or Transformed Conformists?

A strange stream of circumstances put me in a front seat of an ambulance, parked at the corner by Deux Magots, the well-known café on the Left Bank in Paris, where Sartre sat and discussed his existential philosophy which changed the thinking of so many of today's people. I sat in this ambulance seat for six hours, watching people walk by, stand on the street corner, go in and sit at the tables in the glassed-in sidewalk section of the café, as well as disappear into the main portion of the café. Six hours of watching people—people—people—hit me with a very striking fact which could be observed from the view of one's own eyes as one watches thousands of people walk, run, stand, stop, sit, frown, laugh, gesture, talk, or be silent. The striking observation was the amazing conformity of people in this spot of the world where nonconformists speak in the loudest tones!

I saw humanity conforming by the thousands. Yes, there were the *Vogue*-look people in the new straight-cut boots wrinkled properly under the whirl of flared, mid-length skirts, capes swirling above them, hats of the twenties back again. There were the shades of purple matched in boots, bags, stockings and hats, and even people whose clothing matched their expensive dogs' coloring. One could see a parade of *haute couture,* as obvious models were meeting the right people at the right place at the right hour, conforming to a pattern in every detail. There were blue jeans in another stream of conformists walking by—blue jeans with fur jackets, blue jeans with cashmere sweaters, blue jeans with matching jackets and old shirts, blue jeans with expensive silk shirts and tweed jackets, blue jeans with the newest of capes, blue jeans with soft suede jackets—all conforming to the absolute "must" of blue jeans. Scattered in between were the obvious nonconformists—conforming to a pattern of nonconforming! There were the longer-than-long-haired men with strange clothing which matched others who looked just the same, and the girls whose combination of found-in-the-attic or secondhand-store clothing also looked just the same as others dressed in the same type of assortment. Nonconformists—conforming in detail!

People conforming proudly, haughtily, diligently, vainly, snobbishly, and others conforming rebelliously, stubbornly, angrily! Some conformed with fierce humbleness, others with simple pleasure in "fitting in" to today's scene, brushing shoulders with those who think they are not conforming at all, but whose "originality" is immediately recognizable as fitting in with still another grouping of people, easily categorized!

It wouldn't matter whether you were sitting on this particular street corner in Paris, beside the café where flowed forth ideas which affected even the churches in your town (if your pastors preach existential theology) or whether you were sitting on a corner in midwestern

America, Hong Kong, Vancouver, or Miami. Observing human beings for a time, just from the outside, one sees that conforming to other human beings—and thus seeking their good opinion, interest, or approval—is almost universal. Everyone knows what it feels like, as well as what it means practically, to want to or try to conform to some way of dressing or living.

When God speaks to us in Romans 12:1, 2 as members of His family, after we have become His children through the new birth, He is speaking in an area we can all recognize and understand as part of our own experiences since childhood. We all know by experience what it means to want to conform "to this world" in some way. It is not a foreign concept for us to conform. We have no problem in knowing what it means to conform in dress to the kind of clothing and looks which please us or to conform in gardening to the kind of plant cultivation which fits in with that of others whose gardens are the way we would like ours to be. To conform in some way is something which even the greatest rebels have experienced in their very conforming to other rebels. All the world knows by experience what it means to conform.

The admonition comes to us to experience and understand something very different now as children of the Living God. We are given a dash of cold water in our faces as we read these verses in Romans and realize we cannot suddenly copy someone else and be all right in God's eyes. We cannot copy the person we think to be the "best Christian" and in that way "fit in" to the Christian family or group—in the way we have copied or conformed and adjusted to other things, other patterns, other groupings of people in this world. The dash of ice water is this:

> I beseech you therefore, brethren, by the mercies of God, that ye present your bodies a living sacrifice, holy, acceptable unto God, which is your reasonable service. And be not conformed to this world: but be ye transformed by the renewing of your mind, that ye may prove what is that good, and acceptable, and perfect, will of God.

These first two verses of Romans 12 are followed by the admonition that we are not to think more highly of ourselves than we ought. On the background of all this, we come to the fact that we have *not* all the same office, but that we are a "body." That is, some are to be feet, some hands, some eyes, some ears, some knees, some elbows. We have diverse things to do and be, as diverse as the parts of the body. We are not to conform to the world, but something *is* to happen which is just the opposite of a sheeplike conforming. It is a *transformation*—human beings transformed into willingness to be different, diverse, and to accept the part God gives them to do and to be in *His body*. This is really a quite different, sober, revolutionary concept from the usual conforming of human beings. This is a call to come directly before God and to be ready to do and be what He plans for us. To be able to act in this fashion necessitates a real transformation.

Our minds are renewed and made different, as we are transformed. Our minds are involved in this transformation, not just our feelings and emotions. We are to have different attitudes, but also a different set of mental "sieves" from the ones we were given to judge by in our education from books and lectures presented from the world's standards. Our renewed, transformed minds come not by hard work, as Titus 3:5 tells us: "Not by works of righteousness which we have done, but according to his mercy he saved us, by the washing of regeneration, and the renewing of the Holy Ghost." This chapter of Titus starts out by speaking of how we were sometimes foolish, disobedient, serving a variety of lusts "in malice and envy," in other words conforming to the world's emotions and motives in the past. Now as Christians, transformed, there should be not only a new set of emotions, but also a new set of the mind. How? Well, the *how* is the transformation which takes place immediately at salvation, when the regenerational washing away of sins occurs and the renewing or transformation by the entrance of the Holy Spirit starts. The Holy Spirit dwells in us, and He alone can transform us, moment by moment, when everything of the "old man" that remains in us screams out to conform.

Romans 12 goes on to tell of some of the things which will demonstrate the reality of our being transformed by the renewing of our minds, rather than being conformed to the world. So often Christians think that being *conformed* is a matter of dress and kinds of houses and gardens and that being *transformed* and willing to sacrifice their bodies is a matter of dressing in some way that stands out as strange, ugly, plain, or different, and living in houses that are in some way uncomfortable or unattractive to anyone else in the world. God speaks very clearly to show what the willingness to sacrifice and the transformed mind will do. Let us rethink soberly as we read some of these things:

> Be kindly affectioned one to another with brotherly love; in honour preferring one another; Not slothful in business; fervent in spirit; serving the Lord; Rejoicing in hope; patient in

tribulation; continuing instant in prayer; Distributing to the
necessity of saints; given to hospitality. Bless them which
persecute you: bless, and curse not. Rejoice with them that do
rejoice, and weep with them that weep. Be of the same mind
one toward another. Mind not high things, but condescend to
men of low estate. Be not wise in your own conceits. Recom-
pense to no man evil for evil . . . . Dearly beloved, avenge
not yourselves, but rather give place unto wrath: for it is written, Vengeance is mine; I will repay, saith the Lord. Therefore
if thine enemy hunger, feed him; if he thirst, give him drink:
for in so doing thou shalt heap coals of fire on his head. Be not
overcome of evil, but overcome evil with good.

Romans 12:10–17, 19–21

It takes a "living sacrifice" to act even in a small measure this way,
day by day. It takes a changed, renewed mind—and transformed people
with attitudes that do not conform to the world's attitudes—to live
according to these verses. It also takes willingness to stand directly
before God—in day-by-day, moment-by-moment practice—to not be
simply conforming to the triteness of many Christians' ideas of noncon-
formity. Are you and I conformed nonconformists or transformed conformists in our practical lives?

41

~~~~~ ~~~~~

Destination—Possible or Sure?

Green lights blink in double eye-catching announcement. The name
beside the lights can be read easily with eyes searching for confirma-
tion of a specific destination—Beirut, Rome, Ankara, Tokyo, New York,
London, Zürich, Chicago, Hong Kong, São Paulo, San Francisco, Hous-
ton, Amsterdam, Frankfurt. What can be read with the watchful, seeing
eyes is suddenly further confirmed as a deep throaty voice speaks in
accents affected by the mother tongue, announcing in two or three

languages the departure gate and the need for immediately proceeding to that gate if this city or that one is your destination. I observed this for some hours recently, on a day that we were filming in an airport, and since my job was just to guard the crew's coats and extra equipment, I had plenty of time to watch and think. Blink-blink, blink-blink— warning people that the time has come to go. Blink-blink, blink-blink—green signals drawing eyes to check the accuracy of plane number and seat assignments. People—people—people of all nationalities, all races, all ages, all sizes and sorts, and all with one thing in common, as their passports have been checked and are found in order, their baggage has gone through the controls and has passed inspection, and their bodies have walked through the arch with the electric test, declaring that they are not taking any forbidden weapons. The thing they have in common is a basic fulfillment of the requirements for the passage from where they are to another destination. They are each quite sure of their destination—well, pretty sure; it is a very real probability or at least a possibility. But could each one know with absolute assurance that he or she will reach that destination?

There are such things as storms, faulty motors, sabotage, and hijacking. Machines can fail, human beings can fail, and enemies can succeed in destroying what they set out to destroy, so that the expected destinations are never reached. People walk, run, or stand waiting for a door to open—holding boarding cards, confident of leaving, minds full of what they are leaving behind or with what lies ahead. But is there any reason to believe that each one is absolutely sure of reaching his destination in order to discover what there lies ahead? Are there doubts, fears, apprehensive feelings, or uncertainties as to what those twin blinking lights beside the "right names" are really announcing? The certainty of having a destination with a name, a ticket, and the official permission to board a plane is not a guarantee of arrival. The life jackets under the seats and the oxygen masks being demonstrated a few minutes after takeoff give an added emphasis to the fact that there is no absolute guarantee possible when one is depending upon man and machine to care for one's voyage and arrival. Percentages may be very high on the side of probable arrival in a safe and sound condition, but the percentage of those who do not arrive includes real people who have walked, run, stood, watched the green lights, been full of thoughts of what they were leaving and what was ahead. The destination has *not* been certain for them. They did not arrive!

People have troubled feelings about destinations as they travel for pleasure or business or in flight from wars or earthquake regions. People have uneasiness about the uncertainties of travel, wherever they are going in the world. However, far more universal is the recognition by some—children, young people, middle-aged people, and even more people growing older—that there is another kind of "going" that everyone has to face, whether or not they pack a suitcase, buy a ticket, make a plan. A five-year-old recently was in the bedroom with her little brother when he died at three and a half, choking with croup. "Mother, Mother. He has gone. I'm alone. Philippe has gone." Although she had never seen death before, this little girl recognized that Philippe had left—had gone away, was no longer there in that location anymore. Gone where? What destination is ahead when people go in this way? Is there a specific destination? Is there a place? Can one be absolutely sure of arriving when the time comes to go out of the body, to somewhere else?

The Lord Jesus was speaking directly to that haunting fear when He said so clearly, "Let not your heart be troubled: ye believe in God, believe also in me. In my Father's house are many mansions [or rooms]: if it were not so, I would have told you. I go to prepare a place for you. And if I go and prepare a place for you, I will come again, and receive you unto myself; that where I am, there ye may be also" (John 14:1–3). Don't be fearful about the journey ahead; don't worry about where you are going or how you are going to get there. If you believe in the First Person of the Trinity, God the Father, also believe in the Second Person of the Trinity, the One who came as the Light of the World, not only to die for people, but to light up the way to a certain destination. This One, Jesus Christ, the Lamb of God, provides the ticket, is Himself the Light, will guide the footsteps along the way, and is even now preparing a specific, definite mansion or room as a place for us who are on our way. He not only promises with the absolute, certain promise of God that He is preparing the place, but states that He Himself will one day return to take us there in resurrected bodies (the dead in Christ will rise first, and then the living ones will be changed in a moment, in a twinkling of an eye, when He returns).

Hebrews 11 speaks of those who have believed and who are a part of the family of the Living God and of the desire of these people for a better country, a heavenly country. Is their desire a fanciful idea or wishful thinking? God states to them and to us: ". . . . wherefore God is not ashamed to be called their God: for he hath prepared for them a city" (v. 16). There is a certain destination ahead for all who have come through the Lamb into the family of the Living God. That destination is a very real city, a place, a goal so real and definite that God indicates clearly and with infinite force that, because of the existence of this place which He has created and prepared, He is neither ashamed to be called the God of those who are expecting to go there, nor to be called the God of those who are suffering tribulations, persecutions, hardships, afflictions, weariness, and pain. He is not ashamed to be called the God of those who are having a hard journey, because the destination is perfect and it is also *sure*.

". . . the testimony of the Lord is sure, making wise the simple" (Psalms 19:7). When God makes a promise and declares a prophecy, even a simple person may be sure of the fulfillment of that promise or prophecy. God has what no human being has: the absolute power to fulfill his promises. When God states that there is a destination that is *real* and also *perfect*, there is no doubt about its existence. When God explains the requirements for getting there, and they are fulfilled, there is no storm or enemy that can intervene and "hijack" or "kidnap." God the Son is able to say:

> My sheep hear my voice, and I know them, and they follow me: And I give unto them eternal life; and they shall *never perish*, neither shall any man [any created being] pluck them out of my hand. My Father, which gave them me, is greater than all; and no man [no created being] is able to pluck them out of my Father's hand.
>
> John 10:27–29

God who spoke to the Israelites concerning a land of brooks of water, a land of wheat and barley and vines, a land of oil olives and honey, a land where they would eat bread without scarceness (*see* Deuteronomy 8:7–9), also spoke of the destination ahead of us with just as much certainty: "But ye are come unto mount Sion, and unto the city of the living God, the heavenly Jerusalem, and to an innumerable company of angels" (Hebrews 12:22). There is a specific destination where . . .

> They shall hunger no more, neither thirst any more; neither shall the sun light on them, nor any heat. For the Lamb which is in the midst of the throne shall feed them, and shall lead them unto living fountains of waters: and God shall wipe away all tears from their eyes.
>
> Revelation 7:16

John was taken to see a real destination and he reports: "And I John saw the holy city, new Jerusalem, coming down from God out of heaven, prepared as a bride adorned for her husband . . . . Having the glory of God: and her light was like unto a stone most precious, even like a jasper stone, clear as crystal" (Revelation 21:2, 11). Those who are on their way, with the "passport of salvation" through Christ's work, need not fear that mechanical hindrances, human intervention, or Satan's attacks will cut off the journey partway and cause those waiting to receive them to weep in agony. This is an absolute destination, based on the absolute promises of an absolute God. The Light is absolute, pointing to the Way which is sure.

And what about *before* the "final journey" which little Philippe took so recently to his sure destination? What comfort is there for those of us who have a longer period of waiting? What about the temporary "destinations" on the shorter day-by-day, moment-by-moment journey through time and space in present history? Is there any assurance of the *now* being protected? Isaiah gives comfort as we step into the "next thing," whatever that is for you or for me. The Lord who is preparing the future destination cares about the details of the *now:* "For ye shall not go out with haste, nor go by flight: for the Lord will go before you; and the God of Israel will be your rereward" (Isaiah 52:12).

He will go before and be our rear guard, this One of whom we can say, "For this God is our God for ever and ever: he will be our guide even unto death" (Psalms 48:14).

42

Fractured Understanding

The plane had taken off, and I was settled by a window with a determination to use my time alone, with no interruptions. A small clock was on my tray with a pile of typed sheets of paper beside it, and with pencil in hand and glasses firmly on my nose, my intent was to look neither to the right nor the left until my work was accomplished! The task in front of me was to coordinate the number of lines on the sheets of paper to the time it took to read a line, that is, to shorten a forty-five-minute lecture to a half hour, and I had decided that the time space between Rome and Saint Louis would see the job done, if I concentrated. It wasn't just a matter of cutting out lines, of course, but of keeping the content and continuity intact.

"Will you have earphones for the movie? Two dollars and fifty cents." The hostess was passing with the usual armful of earphones in plastic bags, for hearing words and music. "No, thank you; I'm concentrating." It was a struggle to shut out everything and really concentrate, but I was getting on. However, time and space were flowing past rapidly, and I needed my little corner of self-made privacy. Lights went out, but individual lights could spotlight the tray for reading, as the movie started in the darkened plane. "Never mind," I thought. "I simply won't look up, and since I can't hear anything, I won't be distracted." Suddenly shrieks came from the other passengers, and my eyes were drawn to the screen. Time after time, squeals and shrieks broke into my thoughts and my eyes shifted from paper to the front. *Jaws* was being shown, and my eyes caught glimpses of waves splashing on a beach where people were running, evidently in fear of the wide-open jaws and teeth of a shark as it demolished a human being out in the deep, next what looked like a hospital, and then some sort of committee meeting.

What was I doing? Seeing fractured bits and pieces of the whole and hearing no verbalized explanation of the movie *Jaws*. What a garbled account I would give of what was being shown, if I depended on the impressions my eyes were giving me without the words. Yes, I was actually seeing some things with my eyes from time to time, but my seeing was disconnected with the actuality of what was being set forth, because the verbalization was missing. Human beings need a continuity of words—words which explain what cannot be understood through the eyes alone. *Mis*interpretation takes place in so many situations when people see bits and pieces and come to their own false conclusions. "But I saw it with my own eyes!" can be a very tragic statement when a judgment has been falsely made. What agonies have occurred in human relationships when one or another person has jumped to false conclusions because of seeing partially and because of not hearing the verbalized connecting links.

People who see the world, the stars and planets, and the history of their own lifetime with their eyes, and who make whole world views and explanations of where it all came from and what it is all about—from the observation of their eyes—cannot ever have a full and balanced and complete understanding of what was, what is, and what is to be. People who declare that they will only take what they *see*, as a basis for judgment and for making decisions, have a very fractured and partial base for daily decisions, let alone for the great explanations of life and the universe. Knowledge is gained by being given a verbalized explanation of what is being seen with the eyes, as well as of the things one cannot see.

"Thy word is a lamp unto my feet, and a light unto my path" (Psalms 119:105) is not only true for guidance but in our understanding of what is *true* in interpreting the things we see in the universe. Later in the same psalm comes the declaration: "Thy word is true from the beginning . . ." (v. 160). So we realize that this verbalized Word of God, that which is written for us so carefully and preserved for our children and grandchildren, is not only a light in the midst of the darkness of men's foggy understanding, but is *true* in the midst of the garbled half-truths which people set forth in the way of explanation.

Jesus is speaking, verbalizing, talking, and praying to God His Father in John 17:8 when He so clearly says, "For I have given unto them the words which thou gavest me . . . ." How fantastic! God the Son, Jesus Christ, the Second Person of the Trinity, is saying that God the Father, the First Person of the Trinity, verbalized to Him, using words which could then be passed on to human beings, words which were *not* some language that could not be understood with the mind and related to life, but words that had present meaning—then and now. How exciting to think that the Father gave words to the Son which the Son could give to people and which would be sufficient to give understanding. Listen to the next phrase: ". . . and they have received them, and have known surely that I came out from thee . . . ." The Lord Jesus is saying that people heard with their ears but also accepted, made a judgment on the basis of the content of what was given them, and came to *know* in their minds, to understand that it was an historic fact that He, Jesus, had come from God the Father to the place where these people were. This was a "known" fact to them, because they had listened to the words of explanation which God the Father sent along with the Son. The *presence* of the Son of God, without the words of explanation as to who He was and what He had come for, was not considered by God the Father as sufficient to make truth clear. Then: ". . . and they have believed that thou didst send me."

Jesus is telling the Father that people have believed the words which He, the Father, gave Jesus to tell. What a happy report! The truth of

God—believed in its verbalized form. There were those who did not believe the words which were clearly given and who hated those who *did* believe the words which gave truth. "I have given them thy word; and the world hath hated them, because they are not of the world, even as I am not of the world" (John 17:14). The world's "explanation" of all things comes from seeing bits and pieces and refusing the putting-together-in-verbalized-form explanation which God has given. The world prefers *not* to know, in this sense, and takes off the earphones, preferring to guess and jump to conclusions.

Romans 10:16 quotes Isaiah 53:1: ". . . who hath believed our report?" Who has believed Isaiah 53—written so long ago and giving the clear prophecy of what the death of the Messiah would accomplish and how it would take place. Who has believed at any point of history? Romans 10 goes on in the next verse "So then faith cometh by hearing, and hearing by the word of God." The hearing which brings understanding, so that believing or faith can result, is the hearing of the *Word* of God.

Isaiah 55:8–11 is a beautiful message from God directly to us:

> For my thoughts are not your thoughts, neither are your ways my ways, saith the Lord. For as the heavens are higher than the earth, so are my ways higher than your ways, and my thoughts than your thoughts. For as the rain cometh down, and the snow from heaven, and returneth not thither, but watereth the earth, and maketh it bring forth and bud, that it may give seed to the sower, and bread to the eater: So shall my word be that goeth forth out of my mouth: it shall not return unto me void, but it shall accomplish that which I please, and it shall prosper in the thing whereto I sent it.

Although God's thoughts are so very much higher than ours, and although He is beyond us in His infiniteness and His perfection, *He speaks to us in words we can understand,* not in some religious formula that needs a translation but in understandable verbalization. How absolutely marvelous! Do we stop to be in awe about this fact, and to thank God that it is true? God's Word to us will not only be something we can understand, but it will accomplish, complete, and fulfill the thing He has given it to do. It will not be an empty, resultless failure. God's Word will *not* fail. How reassuring this is. There are those who hear, who believe, who are affected to the extent that in and through their lives there is the accomplishment of that which God's Word was sent to do in them and through them.

When Satan tempted Eve, he tried to get her to deny the Word of God. When Satan tempted Jesus Christ, he also tried to get Jesus to deny the written Word of God, as he misquoted, twisted, and took God's Word out of context. Jesus answered by quoting without hesitation: ". . . Man shall not live by bread alone, but by every word that proceedeth out of the mouth of God" (Matthew 4:4). It is on the basis of a clear understanding as given in words—in language that brings sequence of thoughts in the mind and response in action—that people are to live. When Jesus continues to answer Satan it is with this: "It is written . . . it is written . . . it is written . . . ." Words—verbalized explanation of what exists, who made it all, who we are, how we came to be spoiled and not perfect, and what can be done about it—all has come to us in words. Words make up the Word of God.

We do not have to rely on fractured bits and pieces of truth from our short experience of living a few years and seeing flashes of the world and its meaning on a "screen." We are not left to our own resources to "patch in" to some meaning. Thank God for His Word.

"For the Lord is good; his mercy is everlasting; and his truth endureth to all generations" (Psalms 100:5). He is so merciful that He has given a fully understandable explanation in His Word. Our part is to reach out and put on the earphones!

43

Truth Translated

Circle the earth in imagination for a few brief moments. Walk down the streets of Hong Kong and look up at the apartment houses crowded with more people living in one room than you would think possible. What strikes you as we look from the outside? Drying clothes—lines strung from window to window, or sticks poking out of one window and hung with shirts, socks, dresses, underwear. Washed clothing, drying. Make your way through Bombay streets by lurching taxi, avoiding the cows, goats, and heavy man-drawn carts. See people living on the sidewalks in a little pile of rags or under a few makeshift bits of cardboard or tin. What strikes you? Even with water so scarce that there is a line of hundreds waiting at one outdoor water tap, saris are being washed in buckets right on the street. *Slosh, slosh*—a certain amount of dirt is coming out, and soon this sari will join the splash of colors draped over the rails which separate the sidewalk from the railroad line or on any bit of available fence, where those without four walls to make a home still dry their washed garments.

Look out of train windows as you speed along through Switzerland, Germany, Holland. Whether you are passing poor sections or wealthier ones, the view often consists of lines of clothing from window to window, on rooftops, or above little railroad stations from the station-master's apartment upper windows—five blue shirts, six sizes of children's pajamas, babies' diapers, sheets, towels, socks—dirty clothing now clean. Come to the impressive art museum, the Academy in Florence, and walk away from Michelangelo's *David* down a wing to suddenly look out of a window left open by a guard and find that the next-door neighbor of the museum has the family's weekly wash flapping in a slight breeze, to be seen with the ancient artworks in one glance. Even as you marvel over the Roman ruins in Aosta, Italy, it is impossible not to notice the underwear of the people living in humble nearby houses, drying in the hot sun so close to centuries-old columns.

Americans may tumble-dry their clothes in machines, but this clothing, too, has been washed with detergents to remove the dirt. Country houses, whether in America or Australia, still have clotheslines strung between trees or between posts in a garden, drying clothes with sweet, blossom-filled air and sunshine. The English finish off their outdoor drying in inside "drying cupboards," but one still travels through the English countryside conscious of washed and drying clothes.

East, west, north, south—on great continents and the islands of the seas—people everywhere know what it means to have dirty clothing and then to have clothing with the dirt removed. Whether one changes twice a day or twice a year, once a week or once a year, there is an understanding of what it means to have dirty clothing and clean clothing. Poets have written about washing, and artists have painted every aspect of washing. I sat thinking about the universal understanding of the meaning of "clean," as I stood looking at a painting in the Boston Museum of Fine Arts this week. A small painting—*The Washerwomen* by Eugène Boudin of the French School (1824–1898)—centers on the community scene of a few women washing clothing in a river, bending over, undoubtedly talking together. The view beyond them is of horses and wagons, fields, trees, and sky on the other side of the river. Whatever their conversation was about, they were understanding each other's need for washing their clothing. No explanation is needed. In every moment of history and in every geographic location, the washing of dirty clothing means *something*. This painting can be understood.

People plunge into the ocean, lakes, ponds, rivers, streams. For pleasure? Yes, but also to get clean. Some people have bathtubs and showers, others have saunas. Some have buckets of rainwater or mere puddles, and others have only the rain itself. But the washing of bodies, of hands and feet, is something that does not need a university education to understand. "To wash" and "to be dirty" are not terms that are mystical, hidden to understanding, religious, out of reach of the uninitiated. "I am dirty; I need to wash!"—"My clothes are covered with mud; I must wash them." These are not meaningless sentences. These words do not need translation and explanation.

Time after time, God has used understandable illustrations. The difference between the Bible and other religious books is that the important, central teaching is so understandable. It does not need to be translated from a hidden meaning into everyday concepts, because God Himself translated truth into understandable everyday concepts. In His gentleness and compassion, God translated truth into terms anyone can comprehend with the mind, because of daily experience and because of the historic and geographic universality of the basic illustrations He uses.

David understood the "dirt" of his sin when he cried out in Psalms 51:2, "Wash me thoroughly from mine iniquity, and cleanse me from my sin." God speaks understandably to Israel through Isaiah as He likens them to Sodom and Gomorrah and states that their sacrifices are making Him weary because of the insincerity of it all. He goes on to say that He will hide His eyes from them and not hear their prayers because their hands are "full of blood." Then comes this:

> Wash you, make you clean; put away the evil of your doings from before mine eyes; cease to do evil; Learn to do well; seek judgment, relieve the oppressed, judge the fatherless, plead for the widow. Come now, and let us reason together, saith the Lord: though your sins be as scarlet, they shall be white as snow; though they be red like crimson, they shall be as wool.
>
> Isaiah 1:16–18

Washing dirty things to make them clean is understandable. That God could promise that His washing is special, so special that crimson could become as white as wool, is not hard to understand when one has come to accept the power of God the Creator who is able to do all things. *His* washing power would of course be above man's washing power—but the concept of making dirty things clean by washing is an everyday piece of knowledge.

God speaks to Israel through Jeremiah: "O Jerusalem, wash thine heart from wickedness, that thou mayest be saved. How long shall thy vain thoughts lodge within thee?" (4:14). It is very clear for people to understand that this particular "washing of dirty things" is to deal with getting rid of false ideas, vain thoughts, ideas that are contrary to God's truth. *How long shall thy vain thoughts lodge within thee?* is a beautiful and understandable question, calling for people to come and be washed in God's special and powerful way for getting rid of the sin of false thinking and ideas.

In 1 Corinthians 6:11, after defining the sins of people (idolators, adulterers, thieves, the covetous, drunkards, revilers, and so on), God speaks through Paul to say to us, "And such were some of you: but ye are washed, but ye are sanctified, but ye are justified in the name of the Lord Jesus, and by the Spirit of our God." The sins have been washed away. The long list of things mentioned before is of faults which *can* be washed away. People *can* become clean. The washing by God is not a temporary thing but a cleansing that lasts, a cleansing that justifies the washed person in the sight of God because of what Jesus did on the cross. It is a different kind of washing from the daily or weekly washing of clothing or of skin, but it is meant to be understandable.

It is crystal-clear in the last book of the Bible, as if God were gathering together all that is said throughout the Bible and emphasizing it in a last burst of trumpet music, so that no ears could be deaf to the wonder of its meaning. Here is truth translated with no possible shadow of misunderstanding. John is speaking:

> . . . Grace be unto you, and peace, *from him which is, and which was, and which is to come* . . . And from Jesus Christ, who is the faithful witness, the first begotten of the dead, and the prince of the kings of the earth. Unto him that loved us, and washed us from our sins in his own blood, And hath made us kings and priests unto God and his Father; to him be glory and dominion for ever and ever. Amen.
>
> Revelation 1:4–6

Revelation 7:13, 14 adds to these verses, as a question is asked by John and answered, that we, too, might know absolutely just how effective this washing is: "And one of the elders answered, saying unto me, What are these which are arrayed in white robes? and whence came they? And I said unto him, Sir, thou knowest. And he said to me, These are they which came out of great tribulation, and have washed their robes, and made them white in the blood of the Lamb."

And in case you think you won't be included in those who "came out of the great tribulation," so that maybe you won't have a white robe, come on to Revelation 19:7, 8: "Let us be glad and rejoice, and give honour to him: for the marriage of the Lamb is come, and his wife hath made herself ready. And to her was granted that she should be arrayed in fine linen, clean and white: for the fine linen is the righteousness of saints." This is the Bride of Christ, made up of all believers, dressed for the occasion in His righteousness, cleansed completely—within and without.

We are told that some from every tribe and nation and kindred and tongue shall be there in that marvelous gathering of people forever and ever. All these have *understood* what it means to be made clean by God's washing and have been actually cleansed by the blood of the Lamb. God so effectively translated truth that it has been, is now, and will be until the end of history understandable and understood by some from every nation, from every culture, and every language group. God is able to place His Word in a readable and understandable form for all. The central truths are *not* reserved for some highly educated theologians to translate.

44

Illusion or Reality?

It was the perfect moment of a perfect sunset hour, as our car sped on toward the Golden Gate Bridge which so identifies the location as San Francisco. "Look, the portion of that structure at the left of the approach really looks as if it were made of gold. That sunset lighting effect must have given the Golden Gate its name. What a fantastic sight! An illusion of real gold." The appreciation of the skill of design and engineering and the sheer wonder of the effect continued as we drove over the bridge itself. Then, as we gained altitude on the road on the other side, the view of the city, seemingly hung between sky and bay water, glistening with the light of the setting sun in myriads of windows in the superstructures, gave the illusion of a golden city as high as it is wide, floating in space. After the evening filming was over in a nearby town, the drive back brought us to the same spot in moonlight—with thousands of twinkling lights again causing that city on a hill to give the illusion of being hung in space, almost a cube, breathtakingly beautiful and sparkling, hung among stars and moon and reflected in water. Perfection? Dream's end? Paradise found?

> And he carried me away in the spirit to a great and high mountain, and shewed me that great city, the holy Jerusalem, descending out of heaven from God, Having the glory of God: and her light was like unto a stone most precious, even like a jasper stone, clear as crystal . . . . And the city lieth four-square, and the length is as large as the breadth: and he measured the city with the reed, twelve thousand furlongs. The length and the breadth and the height of it are equal. And he measured the wall thereof, an hundred and forty and four cubits, according to the measure of a man, that is, of the angel. And the building of the wall of it was of jasper: and the city was pure gold, like unto clear glass. And the foundations of the wall of the city were garnished with all manner of precious stones . . . .
>
> Revelation 21:10, 11, 16–19

Is this heavenly city a real place? Do you believe our eyes will see it, our hands touch the material it is composed of, our nostrils become filled with the air we can breathe there? What is *real?* What is an illusion?

Jesus says in John 14:1–3, "Let not your heart be troubled: ye believe in God, believe also in me. In my Father's house are many mansions: if it were not so, I would have told you. I go to prepare a place for you. And if I go and prepare a place for you, I will come again, and receive you unto myself; that where I am, there ye may be also." Hebrews 11:16 adds to this promise of Jesus to prepare a place a strong statement from God the Father: "But now they desire a better country, that is, an heavenly: wherefore God is not ashamed to be called their God: for he hath prepared for them a city." God here is telling us that the very real existence of the city, which we are going to come to know by experience in the future, is one very valid reason that He, God the Creator, can state that He is "not ashamed to be called their God." Whose God? It is clear later in the chapter that the God who is the God of miracles—who stopped lions' jaws and caused fire to burn not even the clothes of the men in the fiery furnace—is not ashamed to be called the God of those martyrs who were sawed in half or were otherwise terribly persecuted and afflicted, *because that which is ahead is reality.* There is to be a city prepared by God. Jesus has gone to prepare a place. John was taken to see that city and to write some measure of description for us, with down-to-earth measurements and facts which put it into time and space for us. The time is future, but it is not in any way an illusion. It is a city, foursquare.

"But with my own eyes I saw San Francisco as a golden, glistening city of fairylike beauty floating in space." Was what I saw with my eyes real? Was it not painted with sunlight, moonlight, and imagination? What is more trustworthy—our eyes as we watch a magician, as we add and subtract with our own imagination, or God's clearly stated factual promises? God is trustworthy. God's Word can be depended upon. He is not ashamed of His promises, and we do not need to be afraid of ever being ashamed of believing Him.

Drive into San Francisco now. Hear the screaming police sirens as men risk their lives answering a call; listen to ambulances with their own peculiar shrieks; see the fire engines swerving around corners to get to an accidental (or planned) fire before it is too late to pull out burning people alive. Remember that this is where the drug cult had its beginning. Look, as you remember the sixties, at the porno advertisements hanging from buildings out into the streets. The shifting, changing morality doesn't need to be guessed at. Smog is not only a matter of polluted air which hurts human lungs. There is the intellectual, emotional, psychological, spiritual smog which pours forth from so many mediums in all the cities of the world—not leaving out San Francisco. The golden beauty and twinkling lights do not spell perfection—this is Paradise Lost! Here are lost dreams, agony, depression, ugliness. Here are all the marks of the spoiled Creation, spoiled at the time of the Fall. This golden city has so much that mars or defiles it. The golden perfection was only an illusion.

Come back to Revelation 21 and read the last verse: "And there shall in no wise enter into it any thing that defileth, neither whatsoever worketh abomination, or maketh a lie: but they which are written in the Lamb's book of life." Nothing is going to mar, spoil, or pollute in any way *this* city. No person who is not perfect will even be there; only those whose names are written in the Lamb's book of life will be present. And when are these names recorded? The names are recorded at the same moment that Jesus gives eternal life and guarantees that a person will never perish—at the moment of being born again, through accepting the substitutionary work of Jesus Christ as the Second Person of the Trinity who died in place of each one who believes in Him. This city of people will remain unspoiled and untarnished forever. No mere illusion of sparkle here. The beauty will never be scratched or wiped out by bomb, fire, flood, famine, or pollution of any kind. A shining city of reality!

> And God shall wipe away all tears from their eyes; and there shall be no more death, neither sorrow, nor crying, neither shall there be any more pain: for the former things are passed away. And he that sat upon the throne said, Behold, I make all things new. And he said unto me, Write: for these words are true and faithful.
>
> Revelation 21:4, 5

These words, these descriptions, these promises are reality. This is true. Heaven is a place. There is a city we are going to see and walk in. Neither the place, the singing instead of sighing, nor the pleasure instead of pain is an illusion. We await that which is real.

"The fool hath said in his heart, There is no God . . ." (Psalms 14:1). This is the fool who will not be there to err or to spoil that perfection. The warning is given at the end of the Bible that no man is to take away from or add anything to the Word of God: "And if any man shall take away from the words of the book of this prophecy, God shall take away his part out of the book of life, and out of the holy city, and from the things which are written in this book" (Revelation 22:19). This warning is also a strong affirmation that the Bible is to be taken as true truth in things pertaining to history and the universe. This also includes future history.

Are you sitting by the bed of someone struggling for breath in a painful death? Have you just had a shattering telegram concerning a plane crash? Do you have hidden fears about the moment of leaving your body? Is there an anguish as to whether there is a home for your baby who died in infancy? Do you long for beauty and perfection as you look at sunrise or sunset and fear that you will never find it? Has your life been one series of disappointments and depressions? Do the spoiled universe and the abnormal world—since the Fall brought about the devastating changes in what God originally created—cause you to doubt that He can keep His promises and restore all things, bringing beauty from ashes?

Take comfort in remembering that, although we can doubt our own eyes and ears, there *is* an absolute. Let no one take away from you any of the truth of God so strongly given in His Word. Remember with Isaiah that God spoke centuries ago to reassure His children:

> For the mountains shall depart, and the hills be removed; but my kindness shall not depart from thee, neither shall the covenant of my peace be removed, saith the Lord that hath mercy on thee. O thou afflicted, tossed with tempest, and not comforted, behold, I will lay thy stones with fair colours, and lay thy foundations with sapphires. And I will make thy windows of agates, and thy gates of carbuncles, and all thy borders of pleasant stones.
>
> Isaiah 54:10–12

This already hints at the shining, golden, gleaming beauty which God is preparing for His children. Take heart, you who are in the hospital or nursing home or in the position of nursing and doctoring others. Keep your heart and mind fixed on the place of hope where Abraham stayed. As Abraham demonstrated his faith by leaving his home and going out into the wilderness where God led him, it was with the certainty that there was coming a complete fulfillment of His promises. "For he looked for a city which hath foundations, whose builder and maker is God" (Hebrews 11:10).

With Abraham let us look forward with a firm assurance to *reality*, not illusion. Enjoy the distant view of San Francisco at sunset, but thank God, while you look, for the city which will fulfill all His promises of perfection with no letdown!

45

〜〜 〜〜

Trustworthy Analyzing

A few days ago my husband and I were in the demonstration room of an electronics plant belonging to a friend in Menlo Park, California. There we marveled over the new inventions for analyzing air pollution by counting particles in water and other liquids. Fantastic that it is now possible to put on one's belt a small box (about five inches square and a couple of inches thick) which can then assess the air pollution with an accurate measurement, giving one fair warning of a dangerous situation. This is marvelous in mines, for instance, where in years gone by the only indication that the air was dangerous to breathe was the discovery that the "test" canary—taken down into the place where the men were working—had died! Now no canary must die to show that the air is too polluted to breathe, but a trustworthy device can go right along with the men to make a moment-by-moment test. This company is also putting out an amazingly compact machine which will throw a laser beam through a bottle of water or other liquid and count the particles in that liquid. As if by magic, numbers appear on a screen, rapidly changing as the count takes place, until the total number is reached and then stays without a flicker of change until that liquid is removed and some other liquid is put in its place to go under the same scrutiny. What a great help to people in various positions in communities or in different industries, in hospitals or in research laboratories! Here are quick and accurate devices for analysis of air and liquid—which may mean life or death for people for whom these organizations are responsible.

It is a good thing to be able to measure pollution in air, water, food, and environment, but there is something that must not be neglected in the midst of recognizing and doing something about these physical dangers. There is a greater danger which is changing the atmosphere in our countries, with the resulting possibility of death—an eternal death. Jesus gives a warning in Matthew 10:28: "And fear not them which kill the body, but are not able to kill the soul: but rather fear him which is able to destroy both soul and body in hell." This one who is so dangerous has many prophets or teachers who spread a pollution that fills not only books, magazines, and other media for spreading ideas, but the conversation of many people, ignorant of the "saturation point" of harm! People are "breathing" and "swallowing" *ideas,* and are trying out and plunging into practices which are dangerously full of the false teaching which is multiplying like germs. As we become thankful for the possibility of analyzing our air and water—so that warnings may come in time to do something about it all—we need to use the measuring device which God has put into our hands, and which is as effective today as it was centuries ago. There is a warning signal for us as we read, listen, discuss, look, or make a decision. Jesus also warns in Matthew 7:15, 16: "Beware of false prophets, which come to you in sheep's clothing, but inwardly they are ravening wolves. Ye shall know them by their fruits. Do men gather grapes of thorns, or figs of thistles?" The Bible is our accurate "laser beam," throwing light that penetrates and giving us warning signals before we get immersed in that which is false.

A new book points up the fact that America and other Western countries are being flooded with Eastern thinking and practices. *TM* [Transcendental Meditation]: *Discovering Inner Energy and Overcoming Stress* is a best-seller and is sweeping our countries with a smooth-sounding solution to everyone's need of rest and repose in the midst of the stresses of life, which are certainly on the increase. What a tempting way for a nervous, uptight person to find repose. "Neither a religion, or a philosophy, nor a way of life . . ." is the claim at the beginning of the book. So, if a young Christian feels free to go ahead and try out what follows, what difference does it make? With the Word of God as our laser beam—penetrating the flowing mass of material with its light—and with the Word of God as our sieve—straining the mixture of ideas which are floating in the mental and spiritual atmosphere—we can come up with some measure of warning to protect us from dangers from which we otherwise might not be immune, as we are immersed in the poisoned "atmosphere" or drink from the flood of dangerous words.

It is important not only to believe that the Bible is true, but to live by what it teaches. It is important in Christian growth to show forth one's faith by one's life, as James says so strongly. This means showing by actions as well as words the meaning of the reality of God's teaching. This reality of living by the Word of God includes the active use of the Bible by which to test other "prophets." We are not to follow false prophets in any way. We are to beware of them, to keep our distance from the poison of their falseness. There is real danger indicated, not only by the word *beware* but by the word *fear*—and it is Jesus' warning in Matthew.

"It [TM] was first introduced into the Unied States in 1959 by the Indian teacher Maharishi Mahesh Yogi . . . . Maharishi's technique for achieving this state is effortless . . . . Maharishi has explained . . . . Maharishi has indicated . . . . Maharishi describes . . . . Maharishi has suggested . . . ." As one reads on, it becomes completely clear that there is a "prophet" and that he is an Indian mystic. It is this man's teaching that is being taught by others in this whole process of TM.

"Maharishi and the thousands of trained teachers of TM rely on an ancient tradition through which many generations have fathomed the full depth of the mind. This tradition provides a systematic procedure for selecting the most suitable sounds for use in TM by particular individuals. Such procedure has been maintained since 5000 B.C. or earlier . . . the Vedas . . . . To insure correctness in every aspect of these fundamentals, personal instruction in the technique by a qualified teacher is necessary. The technique cannot be learned second-hand, from a book or from another meditator . . . . The thought-sounds used in TM are called 'mantras.' 'Mantra' is a Sanskrit term which designates 'a thought the effects of which are known' not on the level of meaning—in fact, the mantras taught for use in TM have no denotative meaning—but on the level of vibratory effect . . . . Once learned, the mantra is confidential and is used for only one purpose, to effect the spontaneous process of reducing mental activity during the practice of TM . . . . Teachers of meditation invariably reply that anyone can master TM because it involves no control of any kind but only sitting back and letting whatever happens naturally during the practice simply happen."

These scattered quotes from *TM* by Bloomfield, Cain, and Jaffe show first of all that this whole new practice is one that is taught. There is a primary "teacher" or "prophet" who is making proclamations and teaching a way to have rest and repose and an oft-repeated claim of "awareness." Does he come from the true Living God? The answer is that his teaching is based on Eastern thinking. It is related to the Hindu stream of thinking. It has nothing to do with the teaching of the Bible, but it is *not* just a set of relaxation exercises. It is a means of turning thoughts inward, of emptying oneself of thoughts, of becoming "aware"—not aware of true truth and of God but of some mystical feeling of depth inside one's self. This is where the "rest" is supposed to come from.

What does the Bible say? Jeremiah warned people back in those days: "Thus saith the Lord, Stand ye in the ways, and see, and ask for the old paths, where is the good way, and walk therein, and ye shall find rest for your souls. But they said, We will not walk therein" (6:16). In Jeremiah's moment of history, the majority of people were turning away from God's teaching of how to have rest. In Matthew 11:28–30, Jesus, the Second Person of the Trinity, stands and declares the way to have rest in the midst of stress: "Come unto me, all ye that labour and are heavy laden, and I will give you rest. Take my yoke upon you, and learn of me; for I am meek and lowly in heart: and ye shall find rest unto your souls. For my yoke is easy, and my burden is light."

The Son of God is to be our Teacher, our Prophet, as well as our King. The Word of God tells us to meditate day and night—not with an emptying of our minds, but a filling of our minds with His teaching, His Word. "This book of the law shall not depart out of thy mouth; but thou shalt meditate therein day and night, that thou mayest observe to do according to all that is written therein: for then thou shalt make thy way prosperous, and then thou shalt have good success" (Joshua 1:8). We cannot meditate according to God's instructions and TM's instructions at one and the same period of time. It is a question of Joshua's choice: "Choose you this day whom ye will serve" (*see* 24:15). "Blessed is the man . . . . [whose] delight is in the law of the Lord; and in his law doth he meditate day and night" (Psalms 1:1, 2).

"But," you may say, "I want instant rest. I want instant relief from stress." True, God's Word does not promise us perfection now. Micah 2:10 says clearly, ". . . for this is not your rest: because it is polluted . . . ." And in Hebrews 4:9 we are told: "There remaineth therefore a rest to the people of God," pointing to a future rest which will be perfect and unspoiled. Whose rest are we going to trust? Listen again to the next verses in Hebrews: "For he that is entered into his rest, he also hath ceased from his own works, as God did from his. Let us labour therefore to enter into that rest, lest any man fall after the same example of unbelief. For the word of God is quick, and powerful, and sharper than any twoedged sword, piercing even to the dividing asunder of soul and spirit, and of the joints and marrow, and is a discerner of the thoughts and intents of the heart" (4:10–12). This is His Word, described by Him, which is to be our "laser beam" and keep us from the polluted ideas of the twentieth century. Use it. Trust it. Don't let it be watered down. Search it. Live by it.

46

❧ ☙

Doors

Nothing hurts quite so much as being shut out. Have you ever approached a lovely gate, leading to an avenue of trees toward a mansion you longed to enter out of sight around a curve? The dignified little sign—PRIVATE PROPERTY—stopped you short, because you weren't a person to force your way in. Have you looked hopefully toward a marvelous wood door, waiting to see if it would swing open to welcome you in for tea? Has the most beautiful cottage you have ever seen—with a brass knocker on its door and flagstones leading from the beach to the steps—displayed a NO ADMITTANCE sign right in the grass where the sand stops and the green begins? Have you ever knocked at the door of acquaintances who you expected to be glad to get to know you better— and been sure the curtains moved slightly and eyes were observing you, but the door stayed shut? Have you ever had a door open a crack after you had knocked, and then had it suddenly close again with a slam in your face? Surely, sometime between your earliest childhood and now, you have experienced rebuff in the form of shut doors keeping you outside when you wanted to be inside with the person on the other side of the door. It wasn't just the desire of sharing the fireside and food with the person with whom you were asking to spend time, but the desire of communication and an acceptance of what you had to offer, which you were certain would be exciting as well as helpful. Just the words—*shut doors, locked doors, barred doors*—bring with them memories of deep disappointment, if the words are connected with remembrances of being on the outside and asking to come in.

Happily, most of us have a long string of memories of open doors, shouts of welcome, and shrieks of joy. "Come in, come in. It is so great to have you here! We have been getting ready for you." We have seen curtains move before we have been halfway up the path, and the door burst open before we could knock, and cries of "Tea is ready; come eat with us. Here is the most comfortable chair." Happily, we can remember doors that opened with the first knock or footsteps approaching after we had knocked but twice. Do you remember the first time you were waited for, expected, welcomed inside, and accepted? Do you remember being thanked for the gift you brought, as it was appreciatively received, and then sitting down to share the meal, to drink the orange juice, milk, or tea, and to communicate with the one you had knocked on the door to see? Do you remember the joy of belonging as an accepted friend and confidant, received by one who was bursting with things to tell you, as well as things to show you inside the house? What a titanic difference it makes to the one knocking—whether the door remains shut or is flung open with a verbalized or demonstrated welcome!

"Behold, I stand at the door, and knock: if any man hear my voice, and open the door, I will come in to him, and will sup with him, and he with me" (Revelation 3:20). An astounding picture! An overwhelming statement of fact. The Everlasting God—the Second Person of the Trinity, the Creator of the universe, the Prince of Peace, the Good Shepherd, the King of kings, the Lord of lords—stands at the door and knocks. What a picture! The mighty One who is able to do all things does not force open the door, but waits for someone on the other side to "open the door." When the door is open, then comes the promise of what will take place: "I will come in to him, and will sup with him, and he with me." What a staggering picture of the validity of human beings as made in the image of God. The reality of thinking, acting, and making choices which affect history, on the part of human beings made to be personalities with importance in the universe, is pictured here in a flash almost too brilliant to look at. God is knocking at the door of an individual person whom He has created, and waiting for the door to open or to remain closed. The person is not a zero, nor is the individual turned into a computer. This is an almost-frightening glimpse of the result of an open or shut door, given in a sudden searchlight of verbalization. The gentle, overwhelming words *I will come in to him, and will sup with him, and he with me* fill our minds with the personal nature of sharing a fireside teatime or an intimate suppertime on a balcony with the One at whose feet John fell, and who replied to John, "Fear not; I am the first and the last: I am he that liveth, and was dead; and, behold, I am alive for evermore" (*see* Revelation 1:17, 18). Amazing thought—we can sup with the One who was the first and is the last and will be forever.

When? Someday—when the time comes for the Marriage Supper of the Lamb and He will serve us the bread and the wine as we remember together His death for us? That is future. This knocking, opening, and eating together seem to be a present possibility, to be our experience when we first hear the knock or when as lost sheep we hear His voice and we "open" in the sense of believing, accepting, and being then born again. However, a "shut door" is an ever-present danger for Christians. It is a temptation Satan would like to dangle continually before us. When calamity hits, when disappointment plunges us into depression, when uncertainty smashes our nerves, when fears about decisions tear at us, when we grow impatient about waiting for the Lord's guidance and are close to lighting our own sparks with a stream of clever ideas, or when we feel an urge to push aside prayer and jump into something *first*, the gentle knock can easily be ignored, without an answering opening. It is easy not to recognize what we are substituting for a time of "supping with the Lord." It is easy never to think of prayer or intimate moments of being with the Lord as a two-sided experience.

It is the worst kind of egoism to fail to think of what God has given us clearly in Revelation 3:20 to shake us into recognition of His waiting outside on our front step or our flagstone walk or our green door with a brass knocker! We picture ourselves as deciding not to knock at His door, not to rush into His presence with our communication, not to call upon Him in our trouble. Indeed, God has given us this set of pictures, too. Of course, we are told to run to Him, cry out to Him. But it has struck me recently that many of us time after time are selfishly ignoring the fact that we have failed to open the door that determines our specific choice and action. Many of us never connect His standing at the door and knocking—His waiting for us to open to His entrance into the room with us, His expectation of supping with us and communicating with us—with *prayer* or with *our* times of desperate need. We forget to take literally the fact that we have a Friend, Counselor, and Guide who is knocking at our door when we need His help. We may think we are too low in faith or even energy to call or to go for His help, but we forget that we are *told* to open the door, sit down, and share a time of refreshment. Things don't have to be sparkling. You don't need to feel ready for a guest. This is the truly understanding Friend who knows you well and is sensitive to your state of mind at the moment, and He is standing at the door.

What makes it more wonderful is to remember that this One who knocks at the door knows what it is to *be* the Door Himself. He Himself *is* the Open Door!

> Then said Jesus unto them again, Verily, verily, I say unto you, I am the door of the sheep. All that ever came before me are thieves and robbers: but the sheep did not hear them. I am the door: by me if any man enter in, he shall be saved, and shall go in and out, and find pasture.
>
> John 10:7–9

There is only *one* Door that opens into the place of eternal salvation, and Jesus Himself is that Door. Others try to point to themselves or to others as doors to eternal life, to peace, to heaven, to God, but Jesus says that any other "doors" would steal the sheep away from the fold for which they are looking. The true Shepherd is Himself the Door to the sheepfold where the sheep will find security and adequate care. People who are trying to entice the sheep to go in a different direction toward another door are classified with thieves. There is no substitute for the Door. "The thief cometh not, but for to steal, and to kill, and to destroy: I am come that they might have life, and that they might have it more abundantly" (v. 10). This One who is Himself our Door takes our hand when we come in through Him: "And I give unto them eternal life; and they shall never perish, neither shall any man pluck them out of my hand" (v. 28). So His *hand* holds us fast. "My Father which gave them me, is greater than all; and no man is able to pluck them out of my Father's hand" (v. 29). His welcome inside the Open Door is forever and ever! His work to prepare this welcome was nothing less than the agony of the cross—His death.

What a preparation for an Open Door! What a consistent Open Door. It is no less than this Person, the Eternal Personal God, who says, "Behold, I stand at the door, and knock: if any man hear my voice, and open the door, I will come in to him, and will sup with him, and he with me." What bitterness, what icy hardness of heart, what sharp disappointment, or what misunderstanding can keep us from opening the door and sharing a meal-for-two atmosphere, as we pour out all that troubles us into His listening and understanding ears. There are many doors upon which He knocks. Don't keep Him standing outside the *only* one we can open.

47

❧ ❧

"Choose You This Day"

Have you ever watched a child stand gazing at a freshly opened box of chocolates—lower lip bitten by upper teeth, a frown of concentration wrinkling that space between dark eyebrows, breath held in fear of making an unchangeable mistake? "Only one, Jessica, no more than one—any one you want. But you may have only one. Choose." Shall it be the biggest one, or might that small round one be the favorite peppermint cream? Then again, the long one could be the honey-and-nut nougat and, with tiny bites, that would last longer. An agony of choice for a mixture of reasons in the next few minutes of time!

Have you pored over pictures and maps, imagined weather conditions, and thought about the alternatives for your precious "only one" vacation? Shall it be mountains or seaside? Will you choose fresh air and exercise or travel and sightseeing? An agony of choice—to obtain the maximum results in refreshment and memories.

Then there are the crisis decisions involving a choice between two job offers, of saying *yes* or *no* to a marriage proposal, of choosing the farm to live on, or the city apartment. Choice always brings subsequent results, and the factor of time is involved on every level. Minutes, hours, days, weeks, months, years, or a lifetime can be different, depending on the direct result of a choice. This is one of the earliest lessons a child needs to learn. If you choose to go swimming, then you can't go to the circus; if you choose to go to the playground, then you won't be here when Daddy gets home; if you choose to take that puppy home, then you'll have to take care of it and do the work that will use up time. Choice always turns out to be negative as well as positive, as it affects a portion of time which soon becomes past history. What we do in one piece of time rules out ever using that segment of time again.

Elementary? Simple? Perhaps, but it is a fact which human beings never seem to learn early enough or thoroughly enough. The call of the Word of God as to the importance of choice and the fantastic results of choice should have been ingrained in people from the teaching of

Adam and Eve to their children, and on down through the grandchildren and subsequent generations. It is clear from history that it was not. Isaiah speaks God's warning to His people:

> Woe to them that go down to Egypt for help; and stay on horses, and trust in chariots, because they are many; and in horsemen, because they are very strong; but they look not unto the Holy One of Israel, neither seek the Lord! . . . Now the Egyptians are men, and not God; and their horses flesh, and not spirit. When the Lord shall stretch out his hand, both he that helpeth shall fall, and he that is holpen shall fall down, and they all shall fail together.
>
> Isaiah 31:1, 3

Here is a promise from God. Those who choose to seek help by turning away from Him will fall down in a heap, along with the people to whom they have turned. We are given a picture of twisted arms and legs and fallen horses and men. Turn back to chapter 30 of Isaiah:

> Woe to the rebellious children, saith the Lord, that take counsel, but not of me; and that cover with a covering, but not of my spirit, that they may add sin to sin: That walk to go down into Egypt, and have not asked at my mouth; to strengthen themselves in the strength of Pharaoh, and to trust in the shadow of Egypt! Therefore shall the strength of Pharaoh be your shame, and the trust in the shadow of Egypt your confusion.
>
> Isaiah 30:1–3

If a jumbled heap of bodies, arms, legs, and horses is too far removed from our experience, "confusion" of ideas, atmosphere, emotions, solutions, introspections, identity, purposes, ambitions, or motives are not. The very solutions which are being given in the twentieth century as "counsel"—abortion, denying the framework given for the home, putting self-fulfillment first, seeking happiness through divorce and a new marriage partner—will end in shame and confusion, in a twisted jumble of both the ones giving counsel and the ones acting upon it, instead of taking the counsel of God.

Joshua 24:14–20 makes it very strong and clear that it is not possible to serve God *and* false gods at the same time. "Choose you this day whom ye will serve . . . but as for me and my house, we will serve the Lord" (*see* v. 15). The choice is specific: one—or the other. And the results are specific: God's orderly results—or confusion. The Creator of the orderly universe is the Author of a plan for each of our lives, which "fits" psychologically, emotionally, materially, physically, spiritually. To seek true solutions from the "author of chaos"—Satan and all his false prophets and philosophies—will have a set of results which brings chaos. God makes this a clear and specific promise, and we can surmise the chaotic results by recognizing what the opposite of God would bring.

"And Elijah came unto all the people, and said, How long halt ye between two opinions? if the Lord be God, follow him: but if Baal, then follow him. And the people answered him not a word" (1 Kings 18:21). "Oh," but we say, "I *do* choose the Living God. I *did* long ago. My cry comes with David's in Psalms 18:31: 'For who is God save the Lord? or who is a rock save our God?' I *made the choice* and now I am a child of this Creator God, the God of perfect wisdom and order."

But it is still true for each of us that there are moment-by-moment choices affecting our lives, bringing results in us and in other people because of us. We are affecting other people by our choices, and we bring a chaos of confused and jumbled misunderstandings if our individual choices are not designed to serve this Lord whom we have chosen as Saviour. It is in this context that we need to review Isaiah 50:7, 10, 11:

> For the Lord God will help me; therefore shall I not be confounded: therefore have I set my face like a flint, and I know that I shall not be ashamed . . . . Who is among you that feareth the Lord, that obeyeth the voice of his servant, that walketh in darkness, and hath no light? let him trust in the name of the Lord, and stay upon his God. Behold, all ye that kindle a fire, that compass yourselves about with sparks: walk in the light of your fire, and in the sparks that ye have kindled. This shall ye have of mine hand; ye shall lie down in sorrow.

When we do not know where to turn, and someone gives us a solution which is contrary to the written Word of God, do we *wait* and cling to the Word, with our faces set like flint, asking God to show the practical steps? The "setting of the face like a flint" is not done in a moment when everything is clear and easy in the path ahead, but rather pictures difficulty. When one declares that one will "not be confounded," it is in the dangerous moment of being twisted up by opinions that conflict with the Word of God. When God calls out, "Who is willing to walk in the dark with his hand in Mine?" He is picturing a time when the way is obscure and could be fearful. The lighting-of-one's-own-sparks example is similar to "going to Egypt" for help, and the promised result is similar: ". . . ye shall lie down in sorrow."

There are a lot of voices giving quantities of advice today—promising richer, more fulfilled, quieter, more peaceful, unhampered, stressless, and happier lives! There are a lot of voices promising equality, identity, freedom, liberation. These voices tempt Christians to rationalize and edit the Word of God to fit something else, rather than to set their faces like a flint and judge and edit only from the base of God's Word.

We are told over and over again to *choose*. "Choose you this day." Choose—day after day. Choose to sit in the dark and wait for His guidance. Choose to sit at His feet and accept the completeness of His truth. Choose as Mary did in Luke 10, as she sat at Jesus' feet and concentrated on what He was teaching. It was not that Jesus was saying that housework is unnecessary—He Himself cooked fish for the disciples—but that there was *at that time* a choice to be made. The rushing around the kitchen could be done another time. Right then the conversation came first, and Mary recognized this priority and was sensitive to the fact that there was a choice involved: "But one thing is needful: and Mary hath chosen that good part, which shall not be taken away from her" (Luke 10:42). Mary had not long to sit in her home at Jesus' feet. He would soon be dying and then risen and ascended. She sat and listened during this time that was so quickly passing. We have a slightly different situation. We have a limited time in which to listen and then do what He has planned for us to do—before we go to be with Him. Day by day and moment by moment, choose carefully whom you will listen to and whom you will serve.

48

Reversed Deterioration

In five more days my father will be a century old! He will have his hundredth birthday, marking the fact that he has lived from 1876 to 1976, half as long as America. This rather astounding length of time is a block that bears contemplation. What happens in a hundred years? The phrases *a hundred years ago* and *a hundred years from now* bring with them a torrent of thoughts, ideas, emotions, questions, fears, doubts, or assurances which are as loud and penetrating inside one's head as a cloudburst of rain upon the outside windows and roof. What happens in a hundred years? One harsh, realistic word covers a lot—*deterioration.* Wooden steps which lead up to a house sag and finally rot. The roof begins to leak and plaster falls out of the window frames, as bricks tumble down the chimney and plumbing rusts and clogs. Lands become drained of their richness, lakes and rivers become polluted, and nations lose their basic value systems and ideals. Deterioration.

Human bodies change. What is Father like? Oh, his mind is clear and his memory amazing. He can still speak Chinese, which he learned at the turn of the century as a missionary going out under the China Inland Mission, and he can still read the Bible as well in Greek and Hebrew as in English. He can tell you stories from his school days in Pittsburgh and his football-playing days in Westminster College, as well as discuss recent sports events and the news he reads in the *New York Times'* big-print edition. But—his ears cannot catch all that you say to him. Only a portion comes into his physical ears now, and with one eye blind and the other growing dim, his magnifying glass and big print enable him to read only a tiny fraction of what he would otherwise be reading.

Father looks at his cane and his swollen ankles and shakes his head as he tells you how dizzy he feels at times. "When I think of how I used to run and tackle great big fellows a foot taller than myself, when I played football, it seems impossible that I can scarcely walk across the floor now without feeling that I might fall." He looks at his hands, gnarled now with what happens to human joints, and you know he is remembering the same hands which learned to write at the age of six, to brush Chinese characters at the age of twenty-six, and to respond to his brain's commands through many years—whether browned with the summer sun or whitened by weeks indoors. "The same hands . . ." he thinks and says—and without any more words you feel something of the confusion of his emotions.

Deterioration experienced is more confusing and bewildering than deterioration looked at as an observer. When one walks through an old folks' home or the hospital wards of the world, when one walks through a countryside full of famine-emaciated people or down the streets of a war-torn town, one can categorize the deterioration of human beings by saying, "Oh, yes—old people," or "Oh, yes—post-operative patients," or "Oh, yes—famine wrecked these bodies," or "Oh, yes—an exploding bomb wrecked the flesh and bones as thoroughly as the restaurant they were eating in." The observer can shake off what has been seen as easily as shutting a door or turning a corner and walking in another direction. When suddenly an illness, accident, operation, a breakdown of veins or muscles, or a crippling virus causes the hands to function no more or the eyes to see less clearly—causes a slowness of response or the need to walk instead of running or to be carried instead of being independent—the realization of what deterioration means cannot be shut out, put around a corner, or behind one's back. The mirror shows not someone else, but you. The heavy feet belong not to someone else, but you. "Marvelous that you can still be so ____ at this age!" Whatever the compliment is, it becomes a ridiculous mockery, because the person can't realize that your condition isn't marvelous at all. It is not the *you* that you have always known and that you know is still there— showing through for the other person to see—or communicating for the other person to understand.

The search for a reversal of deterioration is a constant and varied one. There is nothing wrong with searching for a healthier nutrition program, with being careful about physical exercise, with wearing glasses or getting a good hearing aid, with searching for a climate which helps some physical condition, or with trying to do something about polluted air and water. However, the search for a magic and lasting reversal to deterioration is always going on and ends in the same way—with a death notice in the newspaper of the leading advocate of whatever the "exciting solution" was supposed to be. The biblical list of names and life-spans reads like a constant knelling of a village church bell—and he died. . . and he died. . . and she died. . . and she died. A century? A hundred years ago or a hundred years from now—what has been happening to human beings apart from God has been excruciatingly and vividly described in Hosea 13:3—"Therefore they shall be as the morning cloud, and as the early dew that passeth away, as the chaff that is driven with the whirlwind out of the floor, and as the smoke out of the chimney." Deterioration—decay—death in Cambodia, Angola, Rhodesia, Beirut, Northern Ireland. Your daily newspaper headlines tell the story of situations in the United States or whatever part of the world is in your heart. Is there any reversal to deterioration?

Once again be shaken with amazement at the hope we are meant to have in the midst of tribulation and deterioration, the hope which has a solid base. Read again the promises of the Creator of the universe, as if you had never read them before. Hear with ears of wonder and understanding. See with eyes that take in with the freshness of seeing *in focus* what has been blurred. "And I will restore to you the years that the locust hath eaten, the cankerworm, and the caterpiller, and the palmerworm, my great army which I sent among you. And ye shall eat in plenty, and be satisfied, and praise the name of the Lord your God, that hath dealt wondrously with you: and my people shall never be ashamed" (Joel 2:25, 26). "Fear not, O land; be glad and rejoice: for the Lord will do great things" (Joel 2:21). God who promises that He will do great things is capable of *doing* great things. This God is the One who has said that nothing is impossible to Him. When He speaks of restoring *time*, it is something no human being can do. He can restore the ruined, lost years, as well as restoring the beauty of the land and the trees which had been debarked by insects and blights.

> The Spirit of the Lord God is upon me; because the Lord hath anointed me to preach good tidings unto the meek; he hath sent me to bind up the brokenhearted, to proclaim liberty to the captives, and the opening of the prison to them that are bound . . . To appoint unto them that mourn in Zion, to give unto them beauty for ashes, the oil of joy for mourning, the garment of praise for the spirit of heaviness; that they might be called trees of righteousness, the planting of the Lord, that he might be glorified. And they shall build the old wastes, they shall raise up the former desolations, and they shall repair the waste cities, the desolations of many generations.
>
> Isaiah 61:1, 3, 4

What a reverse! What an exchange! "Beauty for ashes" is what only the Living God, who is able to fulfill what He promises, can speak of without it being merely poetry or tricky advertising of some disappointingly empty product.

When? When can there be any reverse in the devastating deterioration of our broken bodies and diminishing energies? "I had fainted, unless I had believed to see the goodness of the Lord in the land of the living. Wait on the Lord: be of good courage, and he shall strengthen thine heart: wait, I say, on the Lord" (Psalms 27:13, 14). "The Lord is my strength and my shield; my heart trusted in him, and I am helped: therefore my heart greatly rejoiceth; and with my song will I praise him. The Lord is their strength, and he is the saving strength of his anointed . . . . The Lord will give strength unto his people; the Lord will bless his people with peace" (Psalms 28:7, 8; 29:11). There is a *present reverse,* for in the very moment of weakness His strength is given. It is in the land of the living that this reverse is to be experienced. It is only while I am really weak that I can know His strength in this amazing way. This is not a reversal of physical deterioration, but a demonstration, in the midst of what is taking place, that He is able to do a supernatural thing—to give a supply of His strength for the immediate task He has for us to do. It is after Paul has been told by God that "my strength is made perfect in weakness" that Paul goes on to say, ". . . for when I am weak, then am I strong" (2 Corinthians 12:10).

The strength which God gives to us—as we cry out to Him for it for the thing He wants us to do—is *His* strength, and it gives a demonstration of a reversal of deterioration for the amount of time and the historical moment during which it is given. Father, at this time, asks strength to make his bed, to walk to the front door to get the mail from the mailman. I ask strength to write this column. Father does not need strength to play football at present. I do not need strength to be working in a Siberian labor camp. It is the strength needed for what God has for us to do at this moment—the present moment of deterioration! The reversal is moment by moment in a marvelous way.

However, that is not all. Our momentary supply of "reverse" is only a tiny reminder that the *total* reversal of deterioration is coming soon, with the Second Coming of the Lord Himself. The One who said, "I am the resurrection and the life," is coming to put a stop to the swiftly moving deterioration, and we are to have *hope,* even as we read our newspapers. "For the Lord himself shall descend from heaven with a shout, and with the voice of the archangel, and with the trump of God: and the dead in Christ shall rise first: Then we which are alive and remain shall be caught up together with them in the clouds, to meet the Lord in the air: and so shall we ever be with the Lord. Wherefore comfort one another with these words" (1 Thessalonians 4:16–18). *Words of true reversal.*

49

Shifting Sand or Solid Rock?

In America and much of the world, there has been a recent topic of discussion which has occupied varying lengths of time and taken place with varying frequency. *Patty Hearst.* "Poor Patty Hearst"—or "Wicked Patty Hearst." "Innocent Patty Hearst"—or "Guilty Patty Hearst." "Weak Patty Hearst"—or "Rebellious Patty Hearst." Mothers and fathers, aunts and uncles, sisters and brothers, grandmothers and grandfathers, and cousins of girls between the ages of sixteen and twenty-one can't help but question, "What would happen if *our* Patty [Susie, Betty, Carol, or Jane] were kidnapped, tortured, taught a whole new set of values, given a whole new base for judgment and totally new goals for which to work?" How much pain, fear, confusion, and barrage of completely new teaching would it take to cause a shift in our former base of values? And if our base—or that of the "Patty" in our lives—is already shifting, then how could that base do anything but slide in any direction, allowing one's feet to be pulled or pushed by some determined force?

As I have picked up *Newsweek, Time,* or various newspapers and read about Patty Hearst or sat silently listening to discussions about her, a children's chorus keeps surging noisily through my head:

> Wise man built his house upon the rock,
> And the rain came tumbling down.
> The rain came down and the floods came up,
> And the house on the rock stood firm.
>
> Foolish man built his house upon the sand,
> And the rain came tumbling down.
> The rain came down and the floods came up,
> And the house on the sand fell flat.

As this verse pounds repeatedly through my head, I can see the faces of myriads of children, singing and emphatically using their arms in motions to go with the song, smacking their hands briskly together to show the total collapse of the foolish man's house. How sad that many of these same children will be later taught that all they learned in Bible classes or Sunday school was, after all, only religious myth, an emotional crutch to help the weak minded, a kind of escape from reality? How many children have gone on to high school, college, university, and graduate school—to be taught that the "reality" is that *truth* does not exist, that there is no absolute, that everything is relative! In other words, how many children, singing heartily about the contrast of bases and the difference it makes in life, are suddenly told by people whose teaching they sit under (and must respond to and take exams for) that there is nothing in the universe but shifting sand? How many young people and older ones, too, have their feet on such shifting sand that they could not even notice, from one step to another, whether it was the same shifting sand or quicksand?

Shifting sand, proposed as a base for life by teachers of history, science, philosophy, literature, political science, and world view, is also unhappily the kind of material given as a base for the new theology. Relativism in every field is exactly what Jesus was talking about when He spoke in Matthew and warned all who "hear" to "do"—to do something different because of having a different base:

> Therefore whosoever heareth these sayings of mine [Jesus is speaking], and doeth them, I will liken him unto a wise man, which built his house upon a rock: And the rain descended, and the floods came, and the winds blew, and beat upon that house; and it fell not: for it was founded upon a rock. And every one that heareth these sayings of mine, and doeth them not, shall be likened unto a foolish man, which built his house upon the sand: And the rain descended, and the floods came, and the winds blew, and beat upon that house; and it fell: and great was the fall of it.
>   Matthew 7:24–27

Jesus is clearly talking about a base of solid rock, as contrasted to one of shifting sand—a solid base which will support a building throughout all the storms of life, as against one which will shift so thoroughly that it will bring about a collapse that is a disaster. Yes, Psalms 18:2 tells us that the Lord *is* our Rock, and Psalms 61:2 comforts us with the specific possibility of crying out: ". . . when my heart is overwhelmed: lead me to the rock that is higher than I." God Himself is our Rock, but in the Matthew verses, Jesus is pointing to "these *sayings* of mine"—or His Word—as a solid rock which does not shift. So that no one can miss the point, Jesus is making very vivid what He says in another way in Matthew 24:35—"Heaven and earth shall pass away, but my words shall not pass away."

His Word is the *unmovable rock* which cannot be shifted. His Word is the absolute which can be counted on to support the lives of generations of His people in shifting, changing circumstances. His Word is the factor which remains constant and can be trusted. His Word is that by which all other things are to be judged. His Word is that by which discernment can grow. Rains of false philosophies can pour down, winds of untrue political ideas can blow, floods of fake ideologies can break out of the river and stream banks, a hailstorm of empty values can beat down mercilessly, the thunder of counterfeit religious doctrines can startle, and streaks of lightning can rip the skies with false miraculous force, but those who keep their feet rooted and grounded in His Word have been given the assurance that they will not collapse.

Come to Psalm 19 and determine with the psalmist to be more than ever immersed in the Word of God, thereby "building the house of your life" on the rock of God's Word in every area daily—spiritually, emotionally, psychologically, and intellectually, in church life, business or profession, and political life—so that the storms may not break up your house because of your shifting to a pragmatic or relativistic base:

> I will meditate in thy precepts, and have respect unto thy ways. I will delight myself in thy statutes: I will not forget thy word . . . . Stablish thy word unto thy servant . . . . And I will walk at liberty: for I seek thy precepts . . . . I thought on my ways, and turned my feet unto thy testimonies . . . . The wicked have waited for me to destroy me: but I will consider thy testimonies . . . . I have more understanding than all my teachers: for thy testimonies are my meditation . . . . Through thy precepts I get understanding: therefore I hate every false way. Thy word is a lamp unto my feet, and a light unto my path . . . . Thou art my hiding place and my shield: I hope in thy word . . . . Mine eyes prevent the night watches, that I might meditate in thy word.
> Psalms 119:15, 16, 38, 45, 59,
> 95, 99, 104, 105, 114, 148

It is the Word of God, the Bible, which is to give us the stability sufficient to carry us through prison camps, kidnappings, blasts of false teachings, brainwashings by the wicked. It is the Word of God which sheds light in the midst of gathering darkness, whether in a stuffy closet where we might be imprisoned or in the discussions of those who would imprison us in another way by trying to put walls of dogmatic denial of truth around our minds. The rock which has strength enough to hold its shape and to remain as a foundation is the Word of God.

Turn the pages of your news magazines or evening paper. Is Patty Hearst the only one who has been tortured, twisted, and turned around so as to act upon a different base from that acted upon before? In this period of history, when the prevalent teaching is one of relativism, we have example after example of individuals, groups, governments, and whole chains of countries where the base is clearly demonstrated—by the unstable actions taking place—to be one of shifting sand. The base changes and varies, as sand shifts and slides in the way it so often does physically, plunging whole apartment buildings into rubble. The shifting sand of relativism is what many are building their lives and basing their actions upon, in the church as well as in government, in teaching children at home as well as in schools and universities. The solid rock of biblical teaching, the unmovable rock of the whole Word of God, is too easily put aside as one substitutes the changing sands of relativistic or existential theology and builds upon the sliding sands of modern morality for a base. If Jesus stood beside Patty Hearst and spoke of the similarity between what took place in her confusion and the shifting, sliding base of many who sit piously discussing her, how many would be left to "cast stones"? What of the other Pattys and Susies and Bettys and Carols and Janes? What teachers, churches, or governments are going to be held responsible for pouring truckloads of sand into their construction areas? Who then could be shocked at the instability and destruction of all that they build?

We are told in Second Timothy:

> But evil men and seducers shall wax worse and worse, deceiving, and being deceived. But continue thou in the things which thou hast learned and hast been assured of, knowing of whom thou hast learned them; And that from a child thou hast known the holy scriptures, which are able to make thee wise unto salvation through faith which is in Christ Jesus. All scripture is given by inspiration of God, and is profitable for doctrine, for reproof, for correction, for instruction in righteousness: That the man of God may be perfect, throughly furnished unto all good works.
>
> 2 Timothy 3:13–17

Yes, the solid rock which Jesus spoke of as the basis for life is formed of His sayings—His Word, Holy Scripture, the Word of God—to be learned, understood, believed, and acted upon as *true*, not simply as "a religion." The diametrically opposite teaching from what is so often taught today must be stressed—to show that a rock base exists and is available for building. This teaching is that true truth does exist and that the Bible is that truth. This is the only base which does not shift through the attacks of the "evil one" and the storms of life.

"Whosoever heareth these sayings of mine, and doeth them, I will liken him unto a wise man, which built his house upon a rock."

50

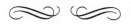

Going Somewhere?

Have you ever watched a dog chasing his tail? Round and round he goes, in dizzy circles that take him nowhere and bring him no nearer his goal, wasting energy, frustrating friends, and amusing foes! "Like a dog chasing his tail" becomes a descriptive phrase that quickly brings understanding as to what has taken place: the same ground has been covered over and over again, with no progress made and all effort wasted. There is no place where this phrase so aptly pictures what has occurred than in some debates or discussion periods among differing human beings. The discussion goes round and round and round, covering the same piece of ground with no starting place, no ending place, no progress being made—while energy and precious time are being wasted, and any onlookers are either frustrated or amused.

There is a sharp difference between an agnostic or unbeliever who is really searching for truth and one who is simply trying to think up new ways of stating the same question—a question which has already been answered as fully as possible, but which, its asker having rejected the answer, is being posed again. The one searching for truth asks a question, seriously considers the answer, and goes on to another question, in the way that a person walking on a winding path through the woods recognizes the yellow pedestrian sign at a branch in the trail and turns in accordance with the directions given, choosing the path which will take him or her to the sought-for destination. The other one is exactly like the dog chasing his tail, making no progress through the woods, but staying in one spot, madly running in a circle, satisfied that he has been very clever in rejecting the path and in choosing the same circle. A one-track circle of thinking about one tiny point (a "sticky" one which has no answer that can be complete in the finite human mind because it is a point that only God has the perfect understanding of) is a mental "chasing of one's tail" which is a useless waste of time and energy.

There are miles to be comered—miles of wonderful trails and fantastic views to be seen around the curves, at the edge of a sudden break in the woods when mountains come into view, or in a fern-filled hollow where violets and mosses are breathtaking. The miles of paths or narrow uphill trails are never to be explored by one who persists in staying in one dusty circle "chasing his tail." There are warm moments of uphill effort that will leave one panting, but also cool, refreshing moments of stopping to have lunch by a stream. None of these varieties are to be experienced by the tail-chasing dog or the mentally tail-chasing atheist or agnostic who refuses to go on the path at all. It is a joy to see the one who "walks" from one question to another, discovering the amazing variety of satisfying, logical steps to be taken along the path that is unfolding in unexpected beauty. Such a one may slip, stub his (or her) toe, fall into a puddle, but he goes on and on, until finally there is the moment of finding the destination.

John Bunyan has so wonderfully pictured this in *The Pilgrim's Progress*. There was progress as the pilgrim went on his journey on the other side of the cross, in his search for the way. "Unto thee will I cry, O Lord my rock; be not silent to me: lest, if thou be silent to me, I become like them that go down into the pit" (Psalms 28:1). David cried this, but it can be the cry of all those who are honestly seeking and are continuing in honest search to go from answer to answer—to walk through the Word of God, not bogging down on one verse or "chasing their mental tails" in one spot. God has not been silent; He has not left an unmarked path. It is possible to say one day, "I sought the Lord, and he heard me, and delivered me from all my fears. They looked unto him, and were lightened: and their faces were not ashamed" (Psalms 34:4, 5). For those who are honestly asking questions and listening to the honest answers, it is possible to be one day in the place of looking back with wonder and recognizing that the intellectual fears of no truth existing and the apprehension of being "ashamed" (ashamed of being considered weak minded to have believed) never resulted at all. Rather there has been an experiencing of the reality of this: "The Lord redeemeth the soul of his servants: and none of them that trust in him shall be desolate" (Psalms 34:22). There *is* a path that will remain undiscovered by those who persist in "chasing their tails"—in going round and round and round. And whoever of us is discussing with such a person needs to pray for the moment of stopping the discussion and walking off on the path alone, hoping to help the cycle to be broken. There comes a point when it no longer is kind or helpful to give audience to an endless chase of the tail.

However, it is not only the non-Christian who is stuck on a single point or who is wasting time on minor or secondary details, rather than considering the basics and moving on into all the wealth there is to be had in what can be understood. Christians often waste time and energy in tail chasing, too. Christians can get into the round-and-round-and-round discussion of secondary points of doctrine and thus never leave that one dusty circle of conversation. Christians can fail to walk the wonderful paths which the Lord has prepared in the land of the living. Christians can live a lifetime and never know what it means to experience the meaning of Psalm 23: "The Lord is my shepherd; I shall not want. He maketh me to lie down in green pastures: he leadeth me beside the still waters. He restoreth my soul: he leadeth me in the paths of righteousness for his name's sake . . . ." Christians who spend hours and hours arguing over hairsplitting points of doctrine can't be spending those hours in another walk which leads somewhere, as described in Psalms 26:6, 7: "I will wash my hands in innocency: so will I compass thine altar, O Lord: That I may publish with the voice of thanksgiving, and tell of all thy wondrous works." Or as in Psalms 9:1, 2: "I will praise thee, O Lord, with my whole heart; I will shew forth all thy marvellous works. I will be glad and rejoice in thee: I will sing praise to thy name, O thou most High."

It takes time to pray in a way that is described as "compassing the altar of God." It takes time to publish the results and the answers—with a voice of thanksgiving—to those who are within hearing range. It takes time to tell of the wondrous works of God to those with whom we have conversation. If theological-seminary students spend all their time in bull sessions, going round and round and round in tail-chasing circles of discussions which are not going anywhere, during *those* hours are pushed aside the "wood paths leading somewhere"—the prayer that brings results, the telling of God's wondrous works. Those hours can never be recalled and lived again. The dry, dusty experience of some who complain about their seminary days might be remedied if a mental, spiritual, or even physical walk were taken, instead of the endless round of continuing on the same points. Learn to say, "We've already had that conversation," and start off on a walk in fresh, "edifying" areas. First Thessalonians 5:11 commands us clearly: "Wherefore comfort yourselves together, and edify one another, even as also ye do." The comfort we are to give each other in conversation is defined in chapter 4, where the Second Coming of Christ is marvelously described, along with the wonder of the moment when we shall hear with our ears the shout and the trumpet as we are caught up in the air in changed bodies. "Wherefore comfort one another with these words" (4:18). The words are to give courage and comfort in the midst of the afflictions and tribulations of this present time. Our conversations are meant to bring each other edification, comfort, and balance along the way.

Theological students, however, are not the only ones who go around in time-wasting circles at certain hours of their lives—like a tail-chasing dog. We all need to be aware of the possibility of doing this same thing and need to examine ourselves and recognize the endless circle when it draws us in with a kind of centrifugal force, causing us to whirl around and around until we stand up to go home or reach up to turn off the lights and go to bed. Ephesians 4:17, 18 admonishes us: "This I say therefore, and testify in the Lord, that ye henceforth walk not as other Gentiles walk, in the vanity of their mind, Having the understanding darkened, being alienated from the life of God through the ignorance that is in them, because of the blindness of their heart." We are not to be walking in circles that lead nowhere in our thought lives, nor in our conversations which, after all, are affecting other people. We who are born again are children of the Living God and are meant to walk in the light, with our understanding now full of light and our lives and our use of time quite changed. Verse 23 describes what we are to have happen to our minds: "And to be renewed in the spirit of your mind." The mind matters. It is not wiped out, but it is to be used to go on. There is to be a "walk," not a static swirl in a circle.

Verse 29 speaks of letting "no corrupt communication" come forth out of our mouths, but rather that which is "edifying," so that it will be helpful to those who are listening. But the edifying conversation is already clearly seen to be more than just *not corrupt;* it is to be a positive thing that helps growth or, as in our picture, helps the "walk" to go someplace. "And grieve not the holy Spirit of God, whereby ye are sealed unto the day of redemption" (v. 30) indicates that not only are we in danger of wasting the time which God would lead us to use in another way and in danger of harming other people's walk or growth, but we are in danger of "grieving the holy Spirit of God."

This is not an isolated thought or little devotional study, but is a part of the warp and woof of the fabric of each of our lives *today*. What am I doing? What are we doing? Chasing our tails—or going somewhere?

51

Watch—Watch—Watch

"Speedily lead the branches of thy favorite Stem, redeemed, to Zion joyously . . . . Next year in Jerusalem! Next year in Jerusalem!" How many have said these words this year as they finished the Seder feast which celebrates the Passover? How many have felt a thrill of expectancy and lived differently—month by month, week by week, day by day, hour by hour—because they truly felt the Messiah might *really* come to fulfill all the years of looking forward, and that indeed there might be a meeting together in Jerusalem within the year?

On a Wednesday Passover night, a very special Seder feast was prepared in *L'Abri* by two Jewish-Christian girls—better described as two fulfilled Jews—who had worked some months to prepare the traditional Passover Service, carefully removing anything that would not fit with Scripture perfectly, and adding (after the meal had been eaten) the Communion Service at the time of the "third cup." For it was after they had eaten the Passover meal that Jesus took the bread and the cup and said, "This is my body, which is broken for you . . . . This cup is the new testament in my blood which is shed for you" (*see* 1 Corinthians 11:24, 25). The girls had spent months carefully preparing the typewritten service and days preparing the traditional meal. Twenty-four people, four fulfilled Jews and twenty Gentile Christians gathered to partake of the Passover together, looking back to the wonders of what

God had done in taking His people out of Egypt—when the angel of death passed over Egypt and spared the firstborn sons in houses where the blood of the lambs had been placed on the doorpost. Then, in the Communion time, we looked back to the Lamb Himself, who came two thousand years ago and made clear that He was the Lamb who would take the sins of those who would come to Him, believing.

It was a special experience to be sitting in a tiny pinpoint of geography in the Swiss Alps, in a tiny moment of history that particular April night in 1976, and know that both the Passover—instituted when Moses led the people of Israel out of Egypt—and the Lord's Supper—instituted when Jesus explained in the middle of the Passover feast what would soon be taking place—have meaning today. The continuity of the people of God is fantastic from the time the first person (Was it Abel? Did Adam and Eve come with the Lamb?) came to God in His commanded way, until now, and until the last one to be born again will one day come to Him.

It became very vivid to me that night that there was a continuity from the very first promise of hope ahead—hope of the restoration from the abnormal state brought about by the Fall. "Why," I thought, "God meant all of His people to partake of the Passover, year by year through the centuries before Jesus came, in order to help them *watch*." The word that is meant to be an unchanged command in both the Old and the New Testament is *watch*. There was to be an expectant watching for the Messiah to come. Simeon was watching. Anna was watching. But every believing Jew was meant to be watching, even as Abraham and Isaac were meant to be watching. The form of reality, meant to be brought about by believing the promises of God which foretold of the coming Messiah, was an attitude of mind and heart—to be expressed in prayer to God Himself and in communication with other believers. This attitude would denote *watching* for the coming Messiah, in action as well as in words. The First Coming of Christ was meant to be hailed by watching believers.

As we met together in the chapel on Good Friday, the reading of Scripture was a wonderful experience of completeness, as we followed the events after the Passover, right through to the death of Jesus. It struck me forcibly, because of my concentration on the importance of watching, that what Jesus asked the disciples to do in the Garden of Gethsemane was to "watch with me" (*see* Matthew 26:38). The watching which Jesus asked the men to do, as He was about to go through His worst period of agony before the cross, was a wakeful, active watching and praying. This watching was to be an involvement with Jesus. It was to be feeling and thinking, and interceding for Him with some measure of understanding of the coming event of His death. They had been told by Him of His death. Now a very concentrated and short period of time of watching was possible for them. This particular request—"watch and pray"—was unique because of the short, crucial, central moment of history they were living through. Yet—*they slept*. They slept in the most dramatic period of time! "How was it possible?" we may ask. "If I had been there, I would have watched and prayed," we may say to ourselves. How sad to have heard the words: "*Sleep on now* . . . ." It seems a realization almost too much to bear to have suddenly recognized that the time was forever over for *watching* in response to the request of the Son of God.

It is easy to long to have had the opportunity given to the disciples in the Garden and to imagine ourselves staying awake and praying, but the really imperative thing for us to be concerned with is our own fulfilling of what the Lord has asked us to do. In the midst of talking about the future and His Second Coming, after speaking about the two in the field and the two grinding at a mill (one taken and one left behind), Jesus says with specific command: "Watch therefore: for ye know not what hour your Lord doth come . . . . Therefore be ye also ready: for in such an hour as ye think not the Son of man cometh" (Matthew 24:42, 44). Again, after the parable of the foolish virgins who did not have enough oil for their lamps at the time of the coming of the bridegroom, Jesus said in Matthew 25:13: "Watch therefore, for ye know neither the day nor the hour wherein the Son of man cometh." A passage in Mark 13 makes it clear that the watching is not a passive matter of gazing off into the horizon with a dreamy look in one's eyes. Jesus has been warning us of false Christs and false prophets which shall arise and shall show "signs and wonders, to seduce, if it were possible, even the elect" (*see* v. 22). After this warning there comes the command to watch, with the same clear force as His word to the disciples in the Garden of Gethsemane:

> But of that day and that hour knoweth no man, no, not the angels which are in heaven, neither the Son, but the Father. Take ye heed, *watch and pray:* for ye know not when the time is. For the Son of man is as a man taking a far journey, who left his house, and gave authority to his servants, and to every man his work and commanded the porter to watch. Watch ye there-

fore: for ye know not when the master of the house cometh, at
even, or at midnight, or at the cockcrowing, or in the morning:
Lest coming suddenly he find you *sleeping.* And what I say
unto you I say unto all, *Watch.*

Mark 13:32–37

We are meant to be specifically and actively watching for the Second
Coming of the Lord, and there is the danger of our sleeping instead of
praying—just as much danger as the disciples faced. Are we in
attitude—but without any reality—in the area of watching for the Lord's
return? Are we in action—but without seriousness—in obeying the
Lord's command to watch? He has given a definite way to demonstrate
that watching—and it is to be prayer. Prayer is to be a demonstration
before angels and demons that we take seriously what God has told us
to do, in expectant belief that He will fulfill His promises to return.
"Continue in prayer, and watch in the same, with thanksgiving; Withal
praying also for us, that God would open unto us a door of utterance, to
speak of the mystery of Christ, for which I am also in bonds: That I may
make it manifest, as I ought to speak" (Colossians 4:2–4). Here, watching and praying are coupled with the "content" of prayer as we look for
the return of the Lord. There is, among other important portions of our
watching and praying, the need to pray for each other, to intercede with
a serious fulfilling of responsibility as we pray for open doors to "utterance," open doors for the making known of the truth of God's Word, as
well as for the help needed by each one of us as we speak. This
intercessory prayer, as we actively watch for the Lord's return at any
time, is to be "without ceasing," as we are given in Ephesians 6:18–20:

> Praying always with all prayer and supplication in the Spirit,
> and watching thereunto with all perseverance and supplica-
> tion for all saints; And for me, that utterance may be given unto
> me, that I may open my mouth boldly, to make known the
> mystery of the gospel, For which I am an ambassador in bonds;
> that therein I may speak boldly, as I ought to speak.

We may feel sad about all the Passover ceremonies through the
centuries, during which people were only saying words, only having a
festive time, not being serious about the coming Messiah. We may feel
sad about the many Jews celebrating the Passover in Jerusalem at the
same time that Jesus was celebrating it, but who did not recognize the
One for whom they were supposed to be watching. We may feel sad

about many who take Communion with no belief in the reality of who Christ was.

What about *our* use of words and phrases in song and in services, without fulfilling the reality of obedience to do what we are verbalizing? Are we really watching and praying—or are we sleeping? "Behold, I come as a thief. Blessed is he that watcheth, and keepeth his garments, lest he walk naked, and they see his shame" (Revelation 16:15).

52

Earthquakes—Release or Destruction?

Tall buildings swayed slightly in Geneca, slight tremors were felt in Lausanne. Aware of that uncertain feeling of the sudden instability of the solid earth, people felt a clutch of apprehension in Yugoslavia. It was in Northern Italy that several hundreds of people went to bed in their homes for the last time, dying under debris, thrown and buried as the earth shifted and buildings fell, while others waited in pain to be released. For some, the earthquake in Europe was simply a map with an interesting pattern of "faults" traced on it—or an interrupted radio program with a minute of news of the tragedy taking the place of music. The report told about villages unknown to the hearer, reducing personalities—who had so short a time before been full of joy, sorrow, agonies, excitement, boredom, weariness, fear, troubles, or hopes—to just a number. "Latest number has risen to two hundred and forty bodies recovered. More expected as the search continues." Music again, as the news voice and its announcement faded out.

Mountains and rocks, earth and trees, seas and shores—such comfortingly stable surroundings are there—day in, day out! We walk along our usual paths and find the familiarity of landmarks a strong continuity in life—reassuring. I wonder how often Elijah had stood on the mount to think, to pray. When the word of the Lord came to tell him to "stand upon the mount," it must have been a familiar mount (*see* 1 Kings

19:9–18). What a terrifying and awesome sight it must have been to stand there alone and feel and see the great strong wind which would have moaned and whistled with terrific force. Elijah must have felt he was going to be blown over, as this wind split the mountains and broke rocks as if gigantic sledge hammers were tearing them apart. After this wind, Elijah felt the earth shift and move, because he stood there through an earthquake which must have changed the scene even further. After the earthquake, a fire swept through the area. Whatever else was happening, Elijah was seeing the power of the Living God in the elements. These were not chance happenings. Elijah had been complaining that he was the only one left in the world who worshiped God, and God was about to speak to Elijah and tell him that there were seven thousand who had not bowed to Baal, the false god, but who were faithful to the true and Living God.

It was with a "still small voice" that God spoke to Elijah. We are told that the Lord did not come in the wind or the earthquake or the fire, but in a "still small voice" after Elijah had observed these things. However, as I read and heard about the earthquakes in Guatemala and in Northern Italy, my imagination brought Elijah as a picture to be watched—a picture of a man *alone*, being given a demonstration of the power of God in the earth which He had created. "Oh, Elijah," I said to myself, "you were being shown something of the marvel of the fact that you were *not really alone*. You had the Living God who was able to command wind and fire and earthquake to be seen, heard, felt, and smelt by you—tangible evidence of His power when you felt alone and deserted."

The earthquake came, and Elijah was able to know that God is to be understood as all-powerful and that nothing is impossible to Him. Then, after the earthquake, Elijah had the fact pointed out to him that not only had he such a God as His Lord and Guide, but that he had seven thousand others who were with him in this worship. In addition, he was immediately to be given Elisha to be his assistant, apprentice, helper, and understudy who would one day follow in his footsteps and continue the line of God's servants. He was not the only one or the last on earth to love and trust the Living God. There was to be an unbroken line of God's children down through the ages.

Other earthquakes in Old Testament times brought destruction. Earthquakes are prophesied as coming "in the time of the end," which will bring destruction. People are meant to look beyond the earthquake to understand something of what God has said concerning truth. The earthquake should do more than interrupt the music on the radio or take the front page of the newspaper. There should be a shaking of minds and hearts to consider what exists that *is* stable, that *does* have continuity, that changes not. If the mountains can fall apart and rocks be split, if men's buildings can crumble like a child's blocks and solid earth turn into a canyon—what *is* lasting? What *is* stable?

How many people who are reading news or taking part in discussions about past, present and future earthquakes are being shaken into a condition, a position, or an attitude of listening to see whether there is a "still small voice" or *any* voice to speak with authority. Men want authority when things fall apart. People want something to hang on to when the familiar things disintegrate. Nations look for leadership not only after a disaster has been officially declared, but when the actions of the masses seem to split apart and disintegrate, and yawning caverns open up in the solid ground of public behavior. "Who will lead us? Where can we find authority?" But among them, how many are really listening or even expecting or hoping that there is any possibility of the existence of a voice which will give true and absolute authority? Even while longings are stirring, those who could preach with authority are giving up their very source of authority by allowing the "ground" upon which they stand to be split—not by God, but by other men.

In the end of the sabbath, as it began to dawn toward the first day of the week, came Mary Magdalene and the other Mary to see the sepulchre. And, behold, there was a great earthquake: for the angel of the Lord descended from heaven, and came and rolled back the stone from the door, and sat upon it. His countenance was like lightning, and his raiment white as snow: And for fear of him the keepers did shake, and became as dead men. And the angel answered and said unto the women, Fear not ye: for I know that ye seek Jesus, which was crucified. He is not here: for he is risen, as he said . . . .
                                                        Matthew 28:1–6

Here stands the angel who saw the earthquake and who rolled the stone from the door. What an earthquake! One that added to all the rest of the frightening happenings which scared the keepers of the tomb into a state that brought on a faint! This earthquake preceded the bursting forth of the risen Jesus from the tomb and announced in a marvelously realistic and graphic way that the "still small voice" of God had not been silenced by death on the cross, but would speak and speak again to many "Elijahs" who would be following one another as His children.

Here was an earthquake which ushered in a release which would affect thousands upon thousands of people bound by death. All who would ever die from that time onward, too, would have their resurrection announced or preceded by this "earthquake." The Second Person of the Trinity became the First Fruit that day—in His resurrected body—of all who would ever be raised from the dead. I like to think of the rumble of the earth announcing this fantastic event, although Jesus Himself was to speak quietly, to individuals and later to small and large groups, of all that had taken place, as well as to give the "great commission" to go and teach all nations the truth. No, Elijah was not the last one to stand in the midst of unbelieving people. There was to be Elisha and Ezekiel and Daniel and then Peter and Paul. Nor are any one of us the last today. The God who is able to shake the earth will do it again.

"And at midnight Paul and Silas prayed, and sang praises unto God: and the prisoners heard them. And suddenly there was a great earthquake, so that the foundations of the prison were shaken: and immediately all the doors were opened, and every one's bands were loosed" (Acts 16:25, 26). Here an earthquake shook the prison so that there was a release for the men of God who were to do more preaching and teaching outside the prison, as well as a way to lead the prison guard and his family to a knowledge of God and of how to be saved. The earthquake released Paul and Silas from the prison bars—but also shook up the guard so specifically that he was ready to listen to the voice of God through Paul and Silas. He and his family were released in a permanent way from bondage to Satan and sin—into the freedom of salvation and light! A special earthquake, indeed, which made a difference in the eternal history of individual people at that time and which has been the means (as the history has been told and retold) of convincing many others of the truth of the God who sent that earthquake.

We are told in Matthew that earthquakes are among the things which will precede the end days and the return of the Lord Jesus Christ. We should never be unmindful of that as we hear of the earthquakes which seem to be on the increase today. However, we should pray for the release of many, many people before He returns—release from the variety of bondages and prisons into which Satan thrusts people in this moment of history. People are bound in a way that needs a special kind of shaking in order to loosen the bonds of intellectual blindness or a willful deafness to the Word of God.

May we earnestly and seriously pray for that which God comforts us with in Haggai 2:5–7: "According to the word that I covenanted with you when ye came out of Egypt, so my spirit remaineth among you: fear ye not. [Thank God we are *not* alone. He is with us today.] For thus saith the Lord of hosts; Yet once, it is a little while, and I will shake the heavens, and the earth, and the sea, and the dry land; And I will shake all nations, and the desire of all nations shall come: and I will fill this house with glory, saith the Lord of hosts."

53

Who Is the Troubler of Israel?

Have you ever been in a storm at sea? Thunder mingles with the roar of waves beating against the side of the boat, lightning zigzags across the sky and seems to pierce the froth of the wild breakers, while passengers slip and slide and clutch at rails at the side of the corridors or collide with furniture as they try to cross a cabin. The world seems suddenly out of perspective, and mixed with the desire to see it right side up again is the feeling that someone should be blamed for the situation. The sailors in the ship, where Jonah was peacefully sleeping below, fought to keep their boat afloat by doing everything else they could do, before they began their search for someone to blame for the storm. (*See* Jonah 1.) It *was* Jonah's fault, as you well remember, because he had turned from the Word of God to him at that time and did an exactly opposite thing. His refusal to believe that God's Word to him was of primary importance, and to act upon it in that moment of history, affected not only himself but other people—the sailors at that dramatic moment, and also the people of Nineveh who were not conscious of the fact that they were being deprived of what God wanted them to hear. Jonah, during his period of pushing aside both what God had spoken to him, and what God had given him to speak to other people, was the *troubler* or the one responsible for a physical storm which affected other people. He was also the troubler responsible for spiritual igno-rance on the part of a whole city.

A *Way of Seeing*

Happily for the sailors and for Nineveh, Jonah confessed his sin and learned a tremendous lesson, as well as had a marvelous change of perspective. Within the great fish's belly, he prayed and cried out, "When my soul fainted within me I remembered the Lord: and my prayer came in unto thee, into thine holy temple" (Jonah 2:7). Jonah had a great change within, and God answered his cry for deliverance and gave him another opportunity to consider the importance of His words to him, and to *act* upon them. Jonah's proclamation of the Word of God to Nineveh affected the people of that city to the extent that they repented, and for at least a time their history was changed.

Storms at sea are nothing compared to the waves of unrest in the world today—among all nations, in the political situation within America, England, Australia, Rhodesia, and other individual countries, in universities, schools, associations, and churches. One can truly say that it is an abnormal world ever since the Fall, and that nothing will ever be perfect until the Lord comes back. Yet we are meant to not only read the Word of God, but to act differently because of fresh insights which help us to evaluate our own immediate situations and responsibilities. We cannot shrug off the history of Jonah as merely true and intensely interesting history. It is of utmost importance for us to remember, as did Jonah, that we need to turn from a running-away response (even if we are running only into silence and shut lips) to an openly courageous declaration and to say with Jonah: ". . . I fear the Lord, the God of heaven, which hath made the sea and the dry land" (1:9).

The taking of a position as one of the people of the Living God— believing Him and intending to act upon that which He has spoken in His Word—affects more people than any one of us can know about. For whom are we in danger of causing trouble? What people are we plunging into a storm at sea? Is the word *compassion* simply a musical-sounding word in our mouths and ears, accompanied by no willingness to pay a costly price to be fulfilled in our own lifetime for those who are affected by us?

There was another man who asked the question: "Art thou he that troubleth Israel?" A drought had brought famine for a long period of time, and the one asking the question was King Ahab who accused Elijah of being the cause of this "trouble." The answer was swift and spoken with the authority of a prophet of the Living God—who was serving God and both believing and acting upon His Word to him. "And he answered, I have not troubled Israel; but thou, and thy father's house, in that ye have forsaken the commandments of the Lord, and thou hast followed Baalim" (1 Kings 18:18). In 1 Kings 16:32, 33 we are told that Ahab had made altars to worship the false god Baal, and had done more to provoke the Lord God of Israel than any other king of Israel. Elijah was saying, "You, King Ahab—because of your leadership of the people, taking them away from the truth of the Living God—you are the one who has troubled Israel. The drought and its consequences are to be traced beyond my being used to pray for the lack of rain. They are the result of your turning away from God. You, King Ahab, are the one who must bear the blame for this." It is not the one pointing out the turning away from the commandments and Word of the Living God who causes trouble, according to Elijah, but the one who turns away and thereby leads others to turn away from the commandments of the Lord.

It is right at this point that there takes place the marvelous story of the confrontation between Elijah and the priests of the false god Baal. Here is one man—Elijah—standing before 450 prophets or priests of Baal. What an imbalance in force! The children of Israel gathered around, these who had been led astray by Ahab, their king. "And Elijah came unto all the people, and said, How long halt ye between two opinions? if the Lord be God, follow him: but if Baal, then follow him. And the people answered him not a word" (1 Kings 18:21). Elijah then told the prophets of Baal to make an altar, dress a bullock, and put it on the wood, and then to call upon their god Baal to send fire to burn the sacrifice. He himself would take a second bullock and do the same thing, calling upon the Living God to send down fire. All day long the prophets of Baal called, cried, and shouted to their god, even getting into a frenzy and slashing themselves with knives to make their pleas more effective. Nothing happened. No response came. The air was full of nothing more than their own commotion. Elijah mocked them and told them to cry louder. "Perhaps," he said, "your god is asleep or taking a journey." Their cries and self-injury continued until the evening, but there was no voice—because there was no one to answer and no one to look. Baal is one of the gods who "have eyes, but they see not, ears, but they hear not" (see Psalms 115:5, 6), like Buddha and other such idols. This confrontation—between 450 prophets of a god which is no god, and the one representative of the true and living Creator of the heavens and the earth—is one of the clearest confrontations in history.

Elijah, standing alone, put his bullock upon the wood on the altar,
poured so much water on the altar that the wood was wet and a trench
around the altar was filled with water, and lifted up his heart and said:

> . . . Lord God of Abraham, Isaac, and of Israel, let it be
> known this day that thou art God in Israel, and that I am thy
> servant, and that I have done all these things at thy word. Hear
> me, O Lord, hear me, that this people may know that thou art
> the Lord God, and that thou hast turned their heart back again.
>
> 1 Kings 18:36, 37

Oh, thrilling account! How marvelously kind of God to have given us
this detailed history of such a perfectly clear confrontation—clear to
child and adult, to educated and uneducated alike.

Elijah called in prayer, asking God to let those confused, deceived,
and mixed-up people *know* that God is truly God and that he, Elijah,
had been acting upon God's Word. God answered this prayer. "Then
the fire of the Lord fell, and consumed the burnt sacrifice, and the wood,
and the stones, and the dust, and licked up the water that was in the
trench. And when all the people saw it, they fell on their faces: and they
said, The Lord, he is the God; the Lord, he is the God" (vv. 38, 39). The
fire fell, and the result was what Elijah had prayed for. People were
convinced and bowed before God, as creatures before their Creator.
But—always remember—not all of them bowed, even when they saw
the fire fall. Not all believed, even when they heard speak the Son of
God, Jesus the Messiah Himself. At no point in history when there has
been a confrontation between the prophets of false gods and the
prophets of the true and Living God—not even when the Second
Person of the Trinity worked miracles before people—has the result
been that *everyone* believed.

But on that day, Elijah had his prayer answered and he was vindi-
cated, right after he had been called "the troubler of Israel." God made
it crystal-clear that day that it was not Elijah, who had been pointing out
the seriousness of turning away from God, who was "the troubler," but
that Ahab, who had turned away, had been at fault. The result of God's
making this clear was that many were brought out of the darkness into
which Ahab had led them, and into the light of the truth.

Centuries later, the accusation thrown at Elijah was once more
thrown into the teeth of God's servants, when some men caught Paul
and Silas and brought them into the marketplace unto the rulers. They
said, ". . . These men, being Jews, do exceedingly trouble our city.

And teach customs which are not lawful for us to receive, neither to observe, being Romans" (Acts 16:20, 21). As a result, Paul and Silas were beaten after their clothing was removed and were thrown into prison with many raw wounds on their backs. The jailer was told to be sure to keep them from escaping, so he put their feet in stocks and made them secure. The result of this confrontation—between the determined men who were set on punishing Paul and Silas for preaching the truth of God's Word, and the power of the Living God Himself—was not only the earthquake which freed the men from their stocks and chains, but the "inner earthquake" which freed the guard from his chains of doubting true truth and brought him to a place of asking what he might do to be saved. That night's confrontation was similar to Elijah's in several ways, not the least of which was the accusation with which it started— the claim that Paul and Silas were the troublers of the city.

We need to ask that question today: "Who is the troubler of Israel?" We should ask carefully, as we test ourselves in the light of the following definitions. First, there are the "Jonahs" who are believers, servants of the true and Living God, but are turning away in an opposite direction—geographically, doctrinally, or from some specific message or task—thereby bringing "storms" on innocent "fellow sailors" or depriving whole "cities" of hearing the true truth which they have never heard. Second, there are the "Ahabs" who have turned away from God's Word while in leadership of His people, leading confused people into a variety of false worship, while at the same time accusing the true prophets of disturbing the peace. Third, there are the "Pauls and Silases" who are being persecuted and falsely accused of being "troublers of the city," while they are obediently speaking and teaching the Word of the Lord to all whom the Lord brings to them.

Matthew makes it very clear that it is important to be assured that in God's sight we are among those who are *falsely* accused, rather than in Ahab's or Jonah's place. "Blessed are ye, when men shall revile you, and persecute you, and shall say all manner of evil against you *falsely*, for my sake. Rejoice, and be exceeding glad: for great is your reward in heaven: for so persecuted they the prophets which were before you" (5:11, 12).

54

‿〜‿ ‿〜‿

Wanted Children

And they brought young children to him, that he should
touch them: and his disciples rebuked those that brought
them. But when Jesus saw it, he was much displeased, and said
unto them, Suffer the little children to come unto me, and
forbid them not: for of such is the kingdom of God. Verily I say
unto you, Whosoever shall not receive the kingdom of God as a
little child, he shall not enter therein. And he took them up in
his arms, put his hands upon them, and blessed them.

Mark 10:13–16

"Too young," thought the disciples. "They can't understand, so keep
them away." But Jesus took this opportunity to demonstrate to millions
of yet unborn people, people who would live through all the last two
thousand years, that God wants the children. There is a place for
children. There is no age limit in His invitation—*Come unto Me.* The
promise—*I am the door: by Me if any man enter in, he shall be saved*—
is not limited to those of an important age, any more than to those of an
important position in life. In fact, just as the rich and powerful have a
harder time putting aside hindrances in coming to the Lord, so those
who feel they have reached an age which is worthy of respect have a
harder time putting aside their dogmatic presuppositions and fixed
intellecual positions, as they listen to or study with eagerness and
expectation the Word of God. "It isn't," said Jesus, "a matter of their
being too young and insignificant because of being children, but quite
the opposite. The children can help adults to understand how to receive the Kingdom of God. Anyone who will not receive the Kingdom
of God like a little child will not be saved." Jesus turned the matter in
the opposite direction—not just for the parents of these children, but for
the disciples and then for all of us who have ever lived since.

What is a little child like? All the ones I have known ask questions,
endless questions. A child's questions are asked with the expectancy of

hearing an answer which will be a real answer and will then become the base for a further question. A child wants to make progress in finding out things and is excited about discoveries. A child responds to wonders with enthusiasm, but not without further questions.

> And he spake unto the children of Israel, saying, When your children shall ask their fathers in time to come, saying, What mean these stones? Then ye shall let your children know, saying, Israel came over this Jordan on dry land. For the Lord your God dried up the waters of Jordan from before you, until ye were passed over, as the Lord your God did to the Red sea, which he dried up from before us, until we were gone over: That all the people of the earth might know the hand of the Lord, that it is mighty: that ye might fear the Lord your God for ever.
>
> Joshua 4:21–24

Here Joshua is telling the people of Israel to answer their children's questions about the twelve stones which were taken out of Jordan as a reminder of the waters which had been dried up for the people to cross over. Not only were the children to be told what the stones had been put there to commemorate, but it was to be made clear to them that the purpose of God's drying up the Jordan River was both for the people to cross and so that all the people of the earth might know that God is mighty. Knowing that fact might bring them to worship the Lord forever. Children were to be given the historical story, not just as history, but with an expectation that they could understand and believe that God is compassionate when He performs such miracles and makes sure the account is passed down through the ages. God is compassionate in asking that the *next* generations be informed with clear explanations, showing that He wants the children of the subsequent generations always to be taught in a way that would bring about a result of believing Him and adoring Him.

> Hear, O Israel: the Lord our God is one Lord: And thou shalt love the Lord thy God with all thine heart, and with all thy soul, and with all thy might. And these words, which I command thee this day, shall be in thine heart: And thou shalt teach them diligently unto thy children, and shalt talk of them when thou sittest in thine house, and when thou walkest by the way, and when thou liest down, and when thou risest up.
>
> Deuteronomy 6:4–7

Believing parents are meant to be constantly teaching their children the facts that need to be verbalized, but also the commands of the Lord as demonstrated in life. Within the family there should be a mingling of questions and answers, growing knowledge unfolded from the Word of God, and practical living out of the teaching of the Word. However, there are many people who have no children—single people and childless married couples—and at the same time there are millions of children with no home life at all, let alone a Christian home life. The sharp command—"Go ye into all the world and preach the gospel"—is not fenced in to any one nation nor to any one age group. Children are a portion of this "all the world" and are given a special place in the command in the light of the repeated emphasis on teaching the next generation.

No one is free from influencing children in some way—whether it is the children next door, the children coming into the store or the library, or the children coming to one's class in school. If it is not possible to be with children when they are going to bed, eating breakfast, walking in the park or woods, sitting at meals, or stretched out on a beach or the back lawn, then it *is* possible to gather them together, at least for a Sunday school (which through many years now has become an acceptable place for even the children of agnostics to go), and it is possible to pray or intercede for them.

Just being in the Sunday school of a church or a home class in a Christian's home is not in itself a conclusion. In Matthew, Mark, and Luke, we have the strong warning that anyone who "offends" one of the little ones or causes a child to sin, would be better off with a millstone hung about his neck and being cast into the sea! Quite a vivid picture, and one needing some solemn thought. Yes, today there are little ones being offered drugs, being given dope to smoke or swallow, being led into situations such as the frequent practice in certain clinics of giving contraceptives to girls as young as nine years old in order to "protect them." The just God who is perfect in His holiness has declared that people leading little children into sin—children He has said should be led to know Him—will be punished. Paradise lost? Childhood lost? Innocency so early destroyd as to be almost nonexistent? Trust walked upon? What a horrible fulfillment of what Jesus told the disciples would happen: ". . . It is impossible but that offences will come: but woe unto him, through whom they come!" (Luke 17:1). Woe to all who are hurting and destroying little children today. Jesus says so.

But isn't Sunday school the answer to this? . . . A young man stood looking out over our vegetable garden with me the other day, after I had been remarking on the amazing spiritual lessons to be learned in gardening, and he said with a far-off look in his eyes, "I wish I had been given some answers when I was in Sunday school." He was thinking that some of his past history might have been prevented if he had been given confidence that truth was defendable when he was twelve years old.

"I was twelve when I left Sunday school and gave up all idea of Christianity as being true. You see, I asked questions of my teacher, and the answer was given: 'You can't understand that until you are older. In fact, I don't even understand it myself.' I thought that if that was all he could say, it must all be worthless, and I might as well not bother going any longer."

But what is faith? Isn't a child supposed to have a quick and easy faith? Christian faith is believing truth that is spoken. Abraham *believed* God, and it was "counted unto him for righteousness." God had told Abraham something which he believed. Eve and Adam believed Satan rather than God. There was a definite negative of *not* believing God's Word to them. There has to be something *said* as the Word of God, before it can be believed, and there has to be a verbalized explanation believed before there can be faith. "Faith is the substance of things hoped for . . ." we are told in Hebrews 11:1, and when we are told to comfort one another with this hope, the hope spoken about is faith in the Second Coming of Christ which is a verbalized promise, something specific to believe as true.

A child is being robbed, being offended, or made to stumble, if that child is not given the truth with enough explanation and answers to questions so that there is a measure of understanding. The wonderful faith of a child is the quickness to believe what is told, when the one telling is confident that what is told is accurate. It is sad to have children be told things which are not true, knowing that they will discover the deception later and be disillusioned. It is also sad to have children "ask their fathers" and never get an answer which is an understandable explanation of truth. The Bible is strong about responsibility to the next generation. The millstone is not to be hung about the neck of a child, but of the person harming that child. Physical, moral, psychological, and emotional harm are all bad. But spiritual harm is even more serious. There was a twofold teaching which Jesus was giving in Matthew 18:6, when he spoke of the millstone, because the warning was double. First, there was the warning to anyone who would harm a child, but second, there was the warning that struck in the opposite direction. The disciples were the very ones who had tried to push the children away from Jesus, and now were being brought up short when they asked, "Who is the greatest in the kingdom of heaven?" We are given the answer: "And Jesus called a little child unto him, and set him in the midst of them" (*see* vv. 1, 2).

What a memory for that child through his or her lifetime! This was a flesh-and-blood child, being placed there as an example of the need for being without pride in education, accomplishments, or power, but with the humbleness of being at the *beginning,* looking forward to life, not looking back with pride.

As we are born again into the family of God, we are wanted as children who are eagerly looking forward to life ahead. We are at the beginning, not only in the sense of being brand-new creatures with a new life ahead, but with the expectation and understanding which comes with realizing that the greatest part of life is in the future. We stand at the beginning of eternity, and what is behind us is comparable to the grass in the fields when summer is nearly over. We are not to feel pride or sadness because of the past. These are adult reactions. At this new beginning, we are meant to be filled with excitement about our sure hope. Children—both kinds of children—are wanted by God.

55

∼⍜⍜ ⍜⍜∼

Two Plantings

A friend in a far country—well, to be exact, in America which is far enough from Switzerland—sends us a box of little brown packets of vegetable seeds every year. The harvest's descriptions are tantalizing! "The best of all bush beans. Dark green, round pods, succulent flesh. Tender when cooked a short time—Sweet corn. Supersweet, crunchy, and tender. Stays sweet a long time after picking. Ears 7 to 9 inches long, with 12 to 16 rows of golden-yellow kernels. Yellow, early, extrasweet—One of the sweetest and most delicious first, early, dwarf, wrinkled peas. Vigorous, compact vines. Very productive—Bibb lettuce. Delicious flavor. Small, loosely folded heads." One sits and imagines the harvest, as well as the excitement of watching the plants show the first mist of green lines above the dark soil. One even imagines all the motions of preparing the soil, fertilizing, carefully kneeling to plant the rows of seeds. One thinks of hoeing and watering in the sunset, of admiring the lush growth as time goes on.

Days and weeks go by. A boxful of brown packets of seeds waits on the shelf. Imagination of the whole process of gardening does nothing to produce reality. The seeds have been provided. Sufficient description has been given, not only to give importance to what could be the results of planting, but to indicate what could also bring pleasure and satisfaction to the harvester of these results. The thought of turned-over earth, waiting now in emptiness, begins to gnaw at the inner parts of the diligent gardener. Rain and sun can do no good to seeds that remain in packets in the box in the cupboard! Suddenly there comes a day when all else is put aside to begin the planting. "No seeds can bring forth fruit while they are tightly enclosed in the box, safely kept dry in the packet." This sentence ran over and over in my head and came out in the hearing of those who were helping me to tie string to mark the rows and crumble the earth directly under the string between their fingers—much like crumbling shortening into flour for pie crust. What a vivid place of learning is a garden! What a school—full of unforgettable lessons.

Of course, ground needs preparation. Weeds have tenacious roots, and their seeds are blown by the wind to fill the fields with growth, but not with the crops you want. Of course, the "false plants" need to be weeded out first, and the ground dug up. Empty, prepared ground, however, doesn't remain empty long. If the good seeds stay in packets, false seeds will blow in, creep in from nearby plants, be carried in by gusts of rain. Ground can be prepared and made ready for the planned-for and orderly rows of vegetables which have been plotted out on sheets of poster cardboard and decorated with encouraging embellishments. But the imagination, plans on paper, and even the supply of good seed in brown boxes, plus good intentions are not enough to care for the well-prepared ground. The empty, waiting ground can be so quickly filled up with a heavy crop of weeds.

"Hearken; Behold, there went out a sower to sow" (Mark 4:3). Here Jesus begins His parable with this most important beginning. There would be no lessons to be learned from the parable without the first sentence. This sower took the seeds from their safe, dry place and went out to get them into the ground. There has to be a belief that the seed is valid seed (such as described on the packet), but then there has to come action, based on the choice to do something about the need for getting it into the ground. The moment of sowing has to suddenly become the present tense—an action. Jesus leaves no doubt as to what the seed is: "The sower soweth the word . . . . where the word is sown . . . . when affliction or persecution ariseth for the word's sake . . . . such as hear the word . . . . such as hear the word, and receive it, and bring forth fruit" (*see* vv. 14, 15, 17, 18, 20).

The seed is the Word of God. Jesus says so. We can't be mixed up about what it is we are supposed to sow. It is clear and definite. We have an amazing seed which does not mildew or rot: "The grass withereth, the flower fadeth; but the word of our God shall stand for ever" (Isaiah 40:8). People may be like grass, but the Word of God is not. Strange, but so often the "grass" which withers tries to judge the "seed" which is the Word of God and will keep standing after the grass has withered and faded! Yet, people are given the opportunity of being the sowers of this fantastic, everlasting seed.

This seed is in as good a condition now as it ever was, if it has not been tampered with. As I knelt to plant my beans, I found a few which had been split and torn; only broken halves remained, with no possibility of putting down roots or sending up the first two important leaves. Broken and torn seeds so often have the essential portions removed. The seed must be intact—all there—complete—whole. The Word of God is a complete unit. To put down proper roots and to send up the proper leaves, buds, blossoms, and fruit the whole Word must be planted. Yes, the ground must be good ground, prepared, spaded, and fertilized—but the seed must be intact as it is sown, if there is to be a plant.

The Bible as a marvelous whole, with portions given in the context of the whole, is to be sown as the Word of God. It is this whole Word of God that is spoken of in Isaiah in connection with a harvest of results, here pictured as the moisture which waters the planted earth:

> For as the rain cometh down, and the snow from heaven, and returneth not thither, but watereth the earth, and maketh it bring forth and bud, that it may give seed to the sower, and bread to the eater: So shall my word be that goeth forth out of my mouth: it shall not return unto me void, but it shall accomplish that which I please, and it shall prosper . . . whereto I sent it.
>
> Isaiah 55:10, 11

Oh, marvelous Word of God—it is the seed we are to sow, but it also waters that which falls into the ground! However, what amazing responsibility have we people who have been given this knowledge! We have been given the seed, the Word. Do we "leave it on the shelf in brown paper packages" without putting *first* the need to be very sensitive to the direction of the Master Gardener who has promised to give us directions as to the land, the portions of the earth where we are to do our sowing? There aren't any other sowers—only we people! How tragic to leave the brown earth empty in the season of growth.

It is spring. But is it really spring? Isn't it midsummer? Is it too late? Too early? When to sow?

> I charge thee therefore before God, and the Lord Jesus Christ, who shall judge the quick and the dead at his appearing and his kingdom; Preach the word; be instant in season, out of season; reprove, rebuke, exhort with all longsuffering and doctrine. For the time will come when they will not endure sound doctrine; but after their own lusts shall they heap to themselves teachers, having itching ears; And they shall turn away their ears from the truth, and shall be turned unto fables.
>
> 2 Timothy 4:1–4

What a command! No possible way of wiggling out of it. The season is always *spring* in this command. In case you think not, then the "out of season" applies. And what is to be sown is true truth: "Thy word is true from the beginning . . ." (Psalms 119:160). It is this truth that people are turning their ears away from, in the description in Timothy. What a picture of today! We are being spoken to and we need to get on with our gardening now.

But there is a second planting which is equally important and which must be as frequently considered. I am a seed. You are a seed. How tightly are *we* put away in a box, waiting for the next planting time? "But I was planted ten years ago [or twenty or thirty]"—"It isn't that way with me. I dig myself up too often!" It is an easy rationalization: "Excuse me a minute. I'm not going to be planted right now. I did this bit before." We deceive ourselves into thinking it had to be only once.

"Verily, verily, I say unto you, Except a corn of wheat fall into the ground and die, it abideth alone: but if it die, it bringeth forth much fruit" (John 12:24). Great vividness here. We can't help but understand, if we have planted corn. The two blades coming up, excitingly green and straight, on their way to becoming tall stalks, one day to have ears with kernels on them. Every time it happens, it is exciting to see the brown wrinkled beet seed send up its first dark green shoots. The falling-into-the-ground part has to take place first. There is an order to it which can't be reversed. There is a form given here which is marvelous in its succession.

"What do I do next? I need guidance for *now!*"—"Fall into the ground and die." Romantic? Unrealistic? No—a given order, a given form. Over and over again we need to "die" to self, to ambition, to pride—but also to a humbleness which can suddenly slip into a different kind of pride, to stubbornness in areas which look "more spiritual" to onlookers. The need to fall into the ground and die is the need to *be willing for anything* that is in His plan for us from this moment on. At times it is the willingness to never be seen or heard, to be buried in an African village or an Indiana farmhouse, in a law office or a doctor's consulting room, to be buried as a housewife or a secretary, in a noisy marketplace or on a platform speaking to thousands. The need to be buried to one's own plans or desires—one's own preferences, dreams, or stubbornness—recurs over and over again in life.

The sacrifice can be very real at the point it is made. However, in an unnoticed way, that very same sacrifice can later slip into a kind of fierce pride, and one is in danger of an inner attitude of: "Look how humble I am!" or "Look how well I am suffering." But—glorious truth of reality—we can ourselves be planted over and over again. Alone with the Master Gardener we can say, "Put me into the ground, Lord, now. In this set of circumstances, may I really be a grain of corn. May I be dead to that which would spoil my fruitfulness. *You* bring forth what comes next, Lord." And the sower becomes the seed—so that he or she can go on sowing seed!

56

❧ ☙

Balanced Buckets

Have you ever carried a bucket of water up a hill? Or have you seen someone carrying twin buckets on a fitted wooden yoke which must have two equally filled buckets? Has anyone ever explained to you that the reason your shoulder is getting twisted and pulled out of place (or your back is hurting with a special kind of strain) might be because the weight you are carrying is a one-sided load and wouldn't bother you so much if it were divided into two equal weights? Two buckets—filled with the same amount of water and carried in two hands, giving a balance of weight on each side, or carried on a yoke fitted across your shoulders, pulling with an equal pull—make it possible to carry a weight which would otherwise be *impossible* all on one side. The idea of balanced buckets with a more evenly distributed weight is one to tuck away in your memory for the time it may be urgently needed.

Who knows what primitive situation any one of us may find ourselves in, when knowing a practical way to carry more weight without it "throwing" us might be needed in today's "wars and rumors of wars" and multiplied disasters. We might find ourselves needing to carry buckets of water to our gardens when, for a variety of reasons, the easy sprinkler method is no longer available. When carrying buckets, carry balanced buckets.

Psalms 89:1 is a good song to sing privately to the Lord at the beginning of a day: "I will sing of the mercies of the Lord for ever: with my mouth will I make known thy faithfulness to all generations." There are such a variety of mercies to sing about as we think of the kind thoughtfulness of the Lord in all He has given us. We should make known His faithfulness to *all* generations: our own, our parents' generation if they are living, our grandparents' generation if we are young enough, our children's generation if we have any, our grandchildren's generation if we have reached that age. There are really an amazing number of generations alive at any given moment, and our mouths are supposed to be making known the faithfulness of the Lord to this plural number of generations—whether or not we have children of our own.

One of the central demonstrations of His faithfulness which we need to make known and also to sing privately about is His having given us verbalized communication—His Word, the Bible, preserved from generation to generation so that we don't have to start from scratch, from zero, and discover truth for ourselves in some long trek through fire and flood to a secret hidden cave somewhere. "Thy hands have made me and fashioned me: give me understanding, that I may learn thy commandments" (Psalms 119:73) helps us to recognize that He who has created us has made us in the first place with the capacity to understand what He says, verbalizes, gives us in written form. In the same psalm we find: "Thy word is a lamp unto my feet, and a light unto my path" (v. 105) and verse 148 which speaks of staying awake at night to meditate upon His Word. We continue to realize that His Word to us is meant to be clear, understandable, a day-by-day help in our thinking and meditating, as well as in our walk or our actions—the things we do hour by hour and day by day.

"But," some may wail, "what is there to thank God about in His Word, the Bible, when it mixes me up so much? I can't understand how God can be God and sovereign and yet how I can have choice and not be a computer." This is exactly where the balanced buckets come in! Consider a moment, as if you had never thought of these things before—God *is* God. You and I are finite creatures, created by an infinite, personal, perfect God *who knows all things*. Consider also how hard it sometimes is to explain something you really *know* to a small child who is getting frustrated because he or she cannot understand what you are explaining. I am not talking about explanations in areas where we are not sure or do not understand, but in the very area where our knowledge and talents are at their best.

God is *perfect* in His knowledge, wisdom, understanding, and has always been so. He is infinite, eternal, unlimited, unchangeable. We are finite, had a beginning not long ago, are limited and very changeable in our emotions, attitudes, concentration, interests, and so on. We are made in God's image. We can think and act and feel and communicate and love and have ideas and choices so that we can "bring forth" and make things—be creative in a variety of ways so that other people can "see" what is in our heads as ideas. But we are still very different from God. We cannot ever know or understand all that God knows and understands. The original sin of Adam and Eve was really a demand to know as much as God and to understand as much as God. Satan tempted them at just that point. His denial of the truth of what God had said was couched in a counter promise that if they would do what God had told them not to do, they would know as much as God. This can be both a blatant and subtle temptation.

In our finiteness and nature spoiled by sin, we still can think. God has made us able to read, listen, and come to an understanding, *not ever a perfect understanding,* but some understanding. Knowing us and knowing all truth perfectly, God prepared a communication for us which would give us sufficient knowledge about the universe and Himself, how to come to Him, and how to receive daily strength. This is a communication which is supernaturally balanced.

I think the balanced buckets may help us to recognize something of what we should be doing as we read the Word day by day, ask for His strength to act in accordance with it, and then *do* what He says. He has given us a balance from beginning to end. We are not meant to carry a heavy bucket or burden, full of "choice" or our "significance" or "not being computers," while we tip out all the "water" in the other bucket, which should be full of the balance which the Lord God gave us—the equal teaching that He is sovereign, has chosen us before the foundation of the world, and that nothing hinders His plan.

> *But ye are a chosen generation,* a royal priesthood, an holy nation, a peculiar people; that ye should shew forth the praises of him who hath called you out of darkness into his marvellous light.
>
> 1 Peter 2:9

> . . . *choose you this day* whom ye will serve; whether the gods which your fathers served that were on the other side of the flood, or the gods of the Amorites, in whose land ye dwell: but as for me and my house, we will serve the Lord. And the people answered and said, God forbid that we should forsake the Lord, to serve other gods.
>
> Joshua 24:15, 16

> And one Ananias, a devout man according to the law, having a good report of all the Jews which dwelt there, Came unto me, and stood, and said unto me, Brother Saul, receive thy sight. And the same hour I looked up upon him. And he said, The *God of our fathers hath chosen thee,* that thou shouldest know his will, and see that Just One, and shouldest hear the voice of his mouth.
>
> Acts 22:12–14

For God so loved the world, that he gave his only begotten Son, that whosoever believeth in him should not perish, but have everlasting life.

John 3:16

Then the word of the Lord came unto me, saying, Before I formed thee in the belly I knew thee; and before thou camest forth out of the womb I sanctified thee, and I ordained thee a prophet unto the nations.

Jeremiah 1:4, 5

I Jesus have sent mine angel to testify unto you these things in the churches. I am the root and the offspring of David, and the bright and morning star. And the Spirit and the bride say, Come. And let him that heareth say, Come. And let him that is athirst come. And whosoever will, let him take the water of life freely.

Revelation 22:16, 17

How can it be? How can He choose us *and* call upon us to make a choice? How can we be known before we were born, be chosen for a task before we were born, and yet need to agonize over wanting the Lord's will and the willingness to die to selfishness by putting the Lord first? How can we know without a shadow of a doubt that we have a daily choice to really love the Lord and do His will, to recognize that we are not programmed computers—and yet find joy and comfort in the assurance that He will hold us fast? Jesus has promised this: "My sheep hear my voice, and I know them, and they follow me: And I give unto them eternal life; and they shall never perish, neither shall any man pluck them out of my hand. [That is, any created thing.] My Father, which gave them me, is greater than all; and no man is able to pluck them out of my Father's hand. I and my Father are one" (John 10:27–30).

The Infinite God has given us truth in His Word. He has given us only what we can bear, carry, and handle—and keep our balance. He means for us to carry buckets of truth. We are to carry what He has given us. When we insist on pouring it all into one bucket, we are breaking the balance so thoroughly that we get twisted backs, knobby elbows, hunched-up shoulders on one side! When we insist on changing the balance of what God has given, we ourselves suffer and do not have the comfort we were meant to have.

The truth is what God has given—He *is* sovereign and we *are* true people, not computers or puppets. We have true choice. Both things are true and fit into what *is*. We don't have to be fatalists as are the Mohammedans. We don't have to be determinists. We can know that the reality of that which we live by—in making choices yet recognizing God's providence and planning—is something which *our God is big enough to understand*. We don't have to be God. We can be people. We can be comfortable being people and rejoice in not needing to be God. We can turn Satan away when he tries to make us insist on knowing all that God knows, and we can quote to him one of the last passages in the Bible:

> For I testify unto every man that heareth the words of the prophecy of this book, If any man shall add unto these things, God shall add unto him the plagues that are written in this book: And if any man shall take away from the words of the book of this prophecy, God shall take away his part out of the book of life, and out of the holy city, and from the things which are written in this book.
>
> Revelation 22:18, 19

Balanced buckets—with all the words intact—to be carried with comfort!

57

❦

Comfort's Two Ingredients

"Comfort ye, comfort ye my people, saith your God" (Isaiah 40:1). *When?*

"Wherefore comfort one another with these words" (1 Thessalonians 4:18). *Why?*

"For thus saith the Lord . . . . As one whom his mother comforteth, so will I comfort you; and ye shall be comforted in Jerusalem" (Isaiah 66:12, 13). *Whom? And where?*

Perhaps you cannot taste, measure, or weigh this concept, described in seven letters and arranged in the precise order of the word *comfort*, but it is a word dealing with reality as contrasted to fantasy, a word which gives us the possibility of seeing a transformation taking place in endless incidents in day-by-day life. God has commanded us to *do* many things, and one of them is to be involved in the matter of comfort—as comforter or comforted. There shouldn't be a complete disregard of a direct command such as "comfort one another," or of the willingness to relax into the arms of the Lord and *be comforted*.

Have you a window (in reality or in memory) out of which you can see a small child, eyes shining, hair gleaming in the sun, running in a field of wild flowers or playing in the grass, on sand or among pebbles? Watch while the child laughs and delightedly reaches out an unsuspecting hand to pull some grass or a flower or to pick up sand or a pebble. Suddenly the pure bubble of joy breaks and the shining moment has been shattered by a scream and a doubling-up in pain. A bee has angrily stung the little hand which squeezed it along with the grass, flower, sand, or pebble. A quickly swelling hand indicates physical pain, but the weeping is for more than that. Shock and disappointment have brought a swift change to the smooth freedom of enjoyment of the sunshine and beauty. The dismay, bewilderment, and hurt are deeper than physical, and someone—who is trusted, who has sensitivity, understanding, and concern combined with love—needs to gather up that little person in his or her arms and administer comfort along with whatever first aid must be given. The little one, however, can do one of two things. He can kick and fight the proffered comfort, along with the compress or injection which is being given to take care of the sting—or the sobs can lessen and the child can cuddle up in loving arms, accepting and enjoying the comfort.

The feeling of being comforted flows through the one being comforted. There is no age limit in either direction to being comforted. Comfort can be experienced in infancy before it can be remembered, and comfort can be experienced in old age. There is no cultural boundary to comfort, since it can be experienced in any cultural surrounding, in all strata of society, in any nation, language, tribe, or kindred. The understanding of comfort is open to intellects of varying degrees of brightness or dimness and to minds of the very young or the very old, even if that understanding cannot be clearly verbalized.

God is not talking in riddles or in theological terms that cannot be understood, when He constantly speaks of *comfort* in His Word. First, the ingredients are clear. There must be a comforter and one who needs comfort. However, the comforter cannot comfort someone who does not see the need or who will not accept the comfort. Two personalities are involved. Second, a situation of very real need is involved in the idea of comfort, a recognition of the need for dependence upon someone else. Since the Fall, the succession of such situations has been constant.

Recently, a lovely new friend in Texas busied herself preparing her home for our visit, and as a last touch of "readiness" she stepped out into the garden to turn on a light which would lift the darkness as a drawn-away curtain and make it possible to see the beauty that was there. Humming a song of anticipation, she happily put her hand up to the switch and hit a swarm of hornets which attacked her in concentrated fury. The many stings not only made her arm swell up to double its normal size and other parts of her body swell where the insects' stingers had penetrated, but caused pain coupled with deep disappointment in this hindrance to a long-awaited evening. Her sons were nearby and provided not only a quick drive to the hospital for injections, but comfort in a variety of ways. To have sons and daughters who are sensitive to the need for giving comfort is just as special a reality as that of a mother's or father's comforting of a child. There is no human relationship where the giving and receiving of comfort is not a two-way path, with the urgency of an immediate need and the loving recognition of the need providing the script as to who is to be the comforted one and who is to be the comforter.

The "hornet stings" of physical pain, sudden illness, threat of sudden death, and loss by fire, flood, and hurricane have come in succession through generations of human history since the Fall, when Satan succeeded in separating Adam and Eve from God's presence. We read of "hornet stings" which are a threat in all parts of the world today—war, violence in the midst of so-called peacetime, Communist takeover or coups by various groups, rule by some sort of an elite, economic breakdown, inflation, and the forced sharing of goods—which brings a loss of freedom to use talents to build and create in diverse areas by choice. These are not false alarms but buzzing realities, like a swarm of hornets coming closer and closer. What kind of comfort are we to give and receive, and from whom is it meant to come?

There is a negative aspect to be observed before we can thoroughly understand the positive of anything. For example, Job's comforters

were the wrong kind of comforters. They told Job to examine himself
and see what terrible thing he had done. There was neither real em-
pathy with his suffering, nor understanding of Satan's place in the
attack, nor a reality of hope. Job's word was ". . . miserable comforters
are ye all" (Job 16:2), and it is unhappily a description of some would-
be comforters who really make suffering people more miserable. David
in Psalms 69:20 speaks of his looking for comforters and finding *none*,
and Jesus as He died on the cross had really no one to comfort Him,
since the Father turned His face away from the sight of our sin, which
Jesus bore for us in His own body.

Amazing grace! What amazing grace is the grace of Jesus who went
without comfort, to die so that He could send us *the* Comforter. Did you
ever think of it in this way? The Comforter could not have come, had not
Jesus been willing to suffer *without comfort*. The Holy Spirit, Jesus
said, would come to replace the comfort which He Himself was giving
to the disciples as He spent time with them:

> And I will pray the Father, and he shall give you another
> Comforter, that he may abide with you for ever; Even the
> Spirit of truth; whom the world cannot receive, because it
> seeth him not, neither knoweth him: but ye know him; for he
> dwelleth with you, and shall be in you. I will not leave you
> comfortless: I will come to you.
>
> John 14:16–18

Jesus cares about our being comforted in the land of the living, in this
period of history before He comes back and before we die. But we are
not only to be comforted by the Holy Spirit who dwells in us. We are to
have His help so that we can comfort each other. We need the horizontal comfort of other finite, limited human beings.

Come to Ephesians 6 and listen to Paul as he spoke to the dear people
in that early church and to us today. He had just given a strong teaching
about our battles against the rulers of darkness of this world and
spiritual wickedness in high places (*see* v. 12). He had cautioned us to
take "the whole armour of God" and to stand fast, to be sure to have "the
shield of faith" to quench "the fiery darts" of the wicked one. He had
cautioned us to *pray always* for each other, and he asked for prayer for
himself, that he might speak boldly to make known "the mystery of the
gospel." Yet he tenderly finished his letter with a compassionate promise to send Tychicus, a beloved brother, a flesh-and-blood person who

had to travel to be with them. He did not say simply, "You have the Holy Spirit with you." He said, "I am sending Tychicus to you, that he might comfort your hearts" (*see* vv. 21, 22). They needed comfort and were going to have a person who could look into their eyes, shake their hands, give them a kiss on both cheeks (or however they greeted each other), and listen and speak with what could be described as comforting words—or words with a comforting content.

"The bees are buzzing; the hornets are stinging! I can't stand the pain any longer. I can't stand the pressures another day. I can't live in the body through another siege . . . ." What is the particular cry of our immediate need? And what is the particular cry of need by the one the Lord has put next to us right now?

God says to us: *Comfort ye, comfort ye My people*—now. *Comfort one another with these words*—because Jesus *is* coming again; future history is certain. We look forward to God's comfort for eternity in His own beautiful words of promise: "And God shall wipe away all tears from their eyes . . . ." The day *is* coming when we will be in the midst of the time described here in Revelation 21—when the Lord, the Comforter who is *perfect*, will give His perfect comfort to all who are His people—the comforted. Until then, we are to be conscious of taking an active part in comforting and in accepting comfort—we who have the Comforter living in us.

58

God's Snorkel and Mask

The sky was cloudless and blue; the sea was turquoise and as quiet as a lake. As far as the eye could see, there was an undisturbed surface of water.

"Gorgeous! Sky, sky, sky . . . water, water, water. How marvelous to really see the Florida Keys with our own eyes."

"Oh, but you haven't seen anything yet. Honestly you haven't. Wait until you see what is under the surface."

"Thanks a lot, but I'm satisfied with what I see. It's fantastic, and anyway, I confess that I'm afraid I can't learn to breathe properly under water. That mask affair might be all right, but I can't trust it."

A long discussion took place as to the trustworthiness of an air-producing machine which would take no skill to start out with. Our good friend kept repeating, "All you have to do is put on the mask, jump in, swim under a bit, breathe naturally . . . and look." We examined the mask, politely listened to the explanations of how thoroughly the whole combination could be trusted—the mask, the oxygen, the tubes leading to the source of air supply—but there was a hesitancy, a holding back, a desire to spend time in further examination of the mask. Time was going by. Our precious opportunity to "see" what was being described for us in partial fashion was not for an unlimited length of time. Life—as long as we are here in the land of the living—has no unlimited portions of time. That is all a part of being finite and limited and of being like the grass, which we shiver about as we hear sung in throaty, deep tones: "All flesh is grass."

Suddenly we decided to take the plunge. We really had had all our questions answered. We had accepted the fact that the source of oxygen was a trustworthy machine. We had come to realize that the designer of the mask apparatus had prepared it to open up wonders we could never see otherwise. The next step was to stop wasting time and to get over the side of the boat, into the water with the mask on, and begin to swim and *look*.

One moment before, all we had seen was blue undisturbed surface water as far as the eye could see. Our eyes could not have witnessed to the fact that *anything* was under that surface, except for the occasional fish someone had caught. Now a whole new world opened up, as different from the world above the water as anything one could imagine. Suddenly it was impossible to think of anything but the awesome marvel of purple fanlike plants, gently waving as if in a breeze, light lavender plants with brown markings, pale-beige lace leaves on another plant, and frosty mauve-colored "pine trees" which looked like an artist's design of a purple pine forest. Coral which looked like huge antelope antlers or bare-branched trees was alive with fish, deftly swimming in curves, with all the grace of swooping birds through branches at twilight. Fish swimming in groups looked like a family reunion out for a time of exploring as they darted and then moved slowly between plants and rocks and coral. The variety of striped and spotted and diverse-shaped fish was almost too exciting to stand! The ledges and sudden caverns and the "Grand Canyon" look of certain areas had to be seen to be believed.

There were amazing fish of all sizes and colors, all shapes and shade combinations. Red and orange to bright yellow, green, blue, gray, and purple, they were obviously leading busy lives and having contact with human beings—as a couple of divers with air equipment strapped on their backs sat on the sea bottom feeding them.

It had all been going on before we suddenly saw it—our observations, discovery, and understanding did not make it materialize. We had come to find out the truth about what exists under the surface of the Atlantic Ocean at that location, because we had finally stopped arguing about the reliability of the masks and air supply and had trusted that the source of information was reliable. If we had had to live long enough to invent our own masks and a way of supplying air, our discovery would never have taken place, since our time in that part of the world was only three days long.

People may have longer than three days to live in the world, but comparatively speaking, their time is no longer than this season's grass. A lifetime is not long enough to make the discoveries which would open up the truth of the universe, the truth about the past, present, and future which simply cannot be seen without a "snorkel and mask." As I swam slowly around that day—with my husband and family of six swimming gracefully in a way that seemed more like flying than taking an afternoon "walk"—I couldn't think of any better comparison than the fantastic marvels opened up for us when we look through God's "mask" and breathe the air He supplies for us to stay alive as we make breathtaking discoveries. The Bible, God's Word, is our "breathing mask." Through it we are to see the marvel of His Creation in the past.

> For the Lord is a great God, and a great King above all gods. In his hand are the deep places of the earth: the strength of the hills is his also. The sea is his, and he made it: and his hands formed the dry land. O come, let us worship and bow down: let us kneel before the Lord our maker. For he is our God; and we are the people of his pasture, and the sheep of his hand. *To day* if ye will hear his voice.
>
> Psalms 95:3–7

> O Lord, how manifold are thy works! in wisdom hast thou
> made them all: the earth is full of thy riches. So is this great and
> wide sea, wherein are things creeping innumerable, both
> small and great beasts . . . . The glory of the Lord shall en-
> dure for ever: the Lord shall rejoice in his works . . . . I will
> sing unto the Lord as long as I live: I will sing praise to my God
> while I have my being. My meditation of him shall be sweet: I
> will be glad in the Lord.
>
> Psalms 104:24, 25, 31, 33, 34

As we look through the Word of God, the Bible, as a "mask and
snorkel" we can trust, we also find what we need for the present daily
life in excitingly real glimpses of what He means us to have now,
moment by moment. As we read of increasingly terrible earthquakes,
floods, and disasters and hear from friends in troubled parts of the
world, we are comforted that our "mask" is not too expensive to give to
others and that they do not need membership in a "club" to use it. As we
read and see what God has provided for the immediate moment, we
thank Him that it is there for laborer and president, for queen and
peasant, for anyone who will look and recognize that the One who
prepared this provision for seeing what could otherwise not be seen is
the Creator of all things, God Himself.

So comfort can be found: "[when] Fearfulness and trembling are
come upon me, and horror hath overwhelmed me . . . . Cast thy
burden upon the Lord, and he shall sustain thee: he shall never suffer
the righteous to be moved" (Psalms 55:5, 22). In the same psalm can be
found today's resolve to follow David in the practical act of casting care
upon God: "As for me, I will call upon God; and the Lord shall save me.
Evening, and morning, and at noon, will I pray, and cry aloud: and he
shall hear my voice" (vv. 16, 17).

To whom are we praying when we read in Colossians that we are to
pray with a continuity, for each other as well as for ourselves? It is to the
Creator: "For by him were all things created, that are in heaven, and
that are in earth, visible and invisible . . . And he is before all things,
and by him all things consist" (Colossians 1:16, 17). It is this same One,
our God, our Father, the Creator, who has given us His verbalized Word
which is like a snorkel and mask—to discover things, in whatever area it
speaks, which we could not discover in our own finiteness and limited
nature.

We can trust His Word and look with excitement for the heavenly city described in Revelation 21 and 22. Past, present, and future—we are meant to "see" through His Word. Our excitement is not to be swerved, nor are we to worry that we have the wrong equipment, even when other created people say that we do. Long ago, other people thought the earth was flat, and others today can just as easily put forth theories about Mars which are as frantically derived from mistaken perspectives. We are meant to have confidence in the Creator and in His verbalized truth which was provided for us to look through and discover His explanations, promises, and prophecies.

> For as the heavens are higher than the earth, so are my ways higher than your ways, and my thoughts than your thoughts . . . . So shall my word be that goeth forth out of my mouth: it shall not return unto me void, but it shall accomplish that which I please, and it shall prosper in the thing whereto I sent it.
>
> Isaiah 55:9, 11

The Creator of the universe has created His own verbalized Word to give us a "mask" through which to look with some measure of understanding at the wonders of the past, present, and future. Through His Word we attain the expectancy of one day finding out what eyes have not yet seen or ears heard or the heart of man imagined—someday when He is ready to show us.

59

⌁

Fresh Bread Daily

If you were to fly as a bird to our door, which opens from our little kitchen to the balcony, and peer in on a Sunday morning, you would see me pouring a liter of milk into a pan, putting it on the burner to heat while I put a spoonful of salt, about a half cup of honey, a heaping spoonful of brown sugar, and about three-fourths of a cup of margarine in a large mixing bowl. The tea is being brewed for breakfast (in between tossing these things into the bowl), and a tray is being set. But it doesn't take much extra time to cut a piece of soft, moist yeast and put it in a tiny bowl of lukewarm water (to wait its turn to be added to the other ingredients) and to break and lightly beat three eggs in another bowl. Just before the milk boils, I pull it off the fire and swoosh it over the shortening, honey, salt, and sugar, stir it a bit and leave it to cool. Now other jobs can be done until the just-right moment for adding the eggs and yeast and then the flour—a kilo bag of it, then more and more—stirring and mixing it until it is not too sticky or wet, but just right for kneading!

Fresh bread, fresh rolls—to be formed after church, after the dough has been placed in a clean, buttered bowl to rise, covered with a clean towel during the two or more hours we are to be away at church. Sunday after Sunday, fresh rolls for lunch come steaming to the table to tempt appetites and appease hunger, as well as giving the feeling to guests of having had something especially prepared for them. There is something basic about the word *bread*, whether it conjures up a picture of cracked wheat, whole-grain flour, five-grain flakes, or something made of cornmeal. There is a continuity in history which links us with the past as we understand something about fresh bread—whether it has been baked in an electric oven, a gas range, a wood stove's oven, or an old plaster oven where the coals are raked out to make room for the baking bread.

We are meant to have a background for understanding what Jesus was saying when He declared in John 6:35 that He was the "bread of life." Also, those who stood there that day and heard Him review the Old Testament history for them should have already been taught that there was more than a miracle connected with the manna which their ancestors had enjoyed in the wilderness. These people were speaking of the manna which had miraculously fallen, morning after morning, to be gathered one day a week. They were asking for a sign, a miracle which would be as great as the manna. Jesus was telling them that He Himself was greater than the manna. He—*the* Bread of Life—had come, and those who came to Him would never be hungry.

Back in Deuteronomy, a clarity of explanation as to the double purpose of manna had already been given. The people of God were meant to know and to pass down to their children and their children's children the vividness of this explanation.

> And thou shalt remember all the way which the Lord thy God led thee these forty years in the wilderness, to humble thee, and to prove thee, and to know what was in thine heart, whether thou wouldest keep his commandments, or no. And he humbled thee, and suffered thee to hunger, and fed thee with manna, which thou knewest not, neither did thy fathers know; that he might make thee know that man doth not live by bread only, but by every word that proceedeth out of the mouth of the Lord doth man live.
>
> Deuteronomy 8:2, 3

People were meant to know that, although the physical bread had been given by God to satisfy their physical hunger, God's Word was the more important bread. The day-by-day experience of seeing the difference between hunger and satisfaction, the contrast between starved and well-nourished people, is to be immediately transferred by a child of the Living God into recognizing that there is a spiritual parallel which is vital to eternal life—living which has no sudden death at the end. The life-giving words which Jesus was speaking at the time recorded in John fitted into all that had been taught before.

Here the Messiah, the Second Person of the Trinity, was making it known that He had come to fulfill all the promises and to be the Bread of Life Himself. What He was saying was part of the whole Word of God which was to continue to be daily bread for the spiritually hungry. When we come to *the* Bread of Life, Jesus Himself, we continue to be fed by "every word that proceedeth out of the mouth of the Lord," in His written Word. It is available and has been supernaturally kneaded. The ingredients needed for continued strength and help have been mixed in. It has been prepared. Long ago? Yes, but fresh every day.

Come back to Isaiah 55:2, 3: "Wherefore do ye spend money for that which is not bread? and your labour for that which satisfieth not? hearken diligently unto me, and eat ye that which is good, and let your soul delight itself in fatness. Incline your ear, and come unto me: hear, and your soul shall live . . . ."

What a beautiful way of giving us a sudden jolt! Are we in danger of spending time and money for something which is not only *not* the "bread of life," but is helping to destroy the Word of God in some way, by changing what He has blended into it in His perfect wisdom, knowledge, understanding, and love? He has prepared it for His family and the guests who are invited to "taste and see." Have we labored all our hours of one week, one month, or one year to buy material or intellectual things which will diminish our supply of the true bread and the possibility of sharing it with anyone else? The warning is there, but also the urgent invitation—"eat ye that which is good." The result of this kind of eating is a delight—and, wonder of wonders, it is to be had without money and without price. Why? Because the price has already been paid for this fantastic supply of fresh bread daily, as well as for the offer to come to Him who is *the* Bread of Life.

As Satan tempted Jesus, after Jesus had fasted for forty days and forty nights, he commanded the hungry Jesus to make stones into bread: "If thou be the Son of God" (*see* Matthew 4:3). What a temptation, since Jesus could easily have done this, not only to prove Himself to be God, but to satisfy His hunger. However, it was then that Jesus quoted from Deuteronomy and said, "It is written, Man shall not live by bread alone, but by every word that proceedeth out of the mouth of God." Jesus was not only emphasizing the truth of this Old Testament statement, but was showing that one way the Word of God is to be used is as a weapon against Satan.

Startling, isn't it, to realize that Satan—who tried to make the Bread of Life turn stones into bread so that He could no longer *be* the Bread of Life—is the one who himself turns bread into stones for so many millions of people! It is a sobering thought. Satan's work is turning bread into stones, that people might break their spiritual teeth and have no nourishment in their bodies. He tried to make the Bread of Life turn stones into bread, so that there would be nothing but stones forever. Thank God that Jesus said a forceful *no* and remained in His place as the Bread of Life.

Fran and I had lunch with the late Bishop Pike some years ago in Santa Barbara. After a long conversation, we were standing in the hall ready to say good-bye. Suddenly Bishop Pike got a sad and serious look on his face and began to reminisce: "I remember that when I entered Union Seminary to study theology, it was with a search for truth and for the answers to life. You know, I was really searching for bread. But [and he cupped his hand as if to hold something carefully in it] when I finished my studies, I realized all I had was a handful of pebbles." It was a sad moment, and we often prayed for him as he expected to visit us later. When word came that he had died without water in the desert, our hope was that he had found the Water of Life and the Bread of Life before he died.

> Or what man is there of you, whom if his son ask bread, will he give him a stone? . . . If ye then, being evil, know how to give good gifts unto your children, how much more shall your Father which is in heaven give good things to them that ask him?
>
> Matthew 7:9, 11

The One speaking here is Jesus who Himself is *the* Bread—the true Bread, not stone. He is the same One who, when teaching us to pray, says, "After this manner therefore pray ye: Our Father which art in heaven, Hallowed be thy name. Thy kingdom come. Thy will be done in earth, as it is in heaven. Give us this day our daily bread" (Matthew 6:9–11). He is clearly telling us to pray for our food, our physical bread. Following the Lord's Prayer in the same chapter, Jesus tells us to put first or to seek "first the kingdom of God," and all the material things will be provided for us. Prayer is to include the request for daily physical needs, but clearly it is to ask also for the daily *spiritual* bread from His Word.

> And he took bread, and gave thanks, and brake it, and gave unto them, saying, This is my body which is given for you: this do in remembrance of me.
>
> Luke 22:19

> This is the bread which cometh down from heaven, that a man may eat thereof, and not die. I am the living bread which came down from heaven: if any man eat of this bread, he shall live for ever: and the bread that I will give is my flesh, which I will give for the life of the world.
>
> John 6:50, 51

My Sunday bread has no stones in it. Fresh, wholesome, real bread—nourishing and satisfying. Beware of the enemy who would put stones in place of bread and would try to hide them with a camouflage of crust. The Bread of Life has given us His Word which is trustworthy bread to feed on day by day—always fresh, always complete, always true. Fresh bread daily.

60

❧ ❧

"How Should We Then Live?"

A long dark tunnel of work stretched out with no visible end in view. A tunnel with a rough floor, twists and turns in the dark, and jutting rocks for walls can be a dismal place indeed. The decision to keep on seems impossible at times, although to turn back is a waste and may turn out to be disastrous. A *tunnel of work* may seem only a dramatic choice of descriptive wording, but for any who have been immersed in a project of overwhelming size, involving time which seems to have a boundary line, "tunnel" is a properly chosen description.

My husband, Fran, stood over two tables placed together to give more surface space and worked on manuscripts which were copies of his original, but with handwritten additions and suggestions made by a number of researchers—in varied writing on the wide margins of the pages. Instead of merely reading down one page, Fran had to study several manuscript pages for each sheet of the original. Ideas had to be considered as the handwriting was deciphered, and decisions had to be made. Would the work ever come to an end? Was it right to start it in the first place? What else was having to be put aside in order to do this? Had he understood correctly that which he had taken to be the Lord's leading? Should he continue in this tunnel of work—the writing of the book and the narration of the documentary film—so as to finally produce a film series, book, and study guide on the rise and decline of Western thought and culture, a viable alternative to the humanistic documentaries put out on history, philosophy, science, art, music, law, government, and theology? Or was it all too much? The prayer was: "Show us, Lord. Make it clear to us."

It was before breakfast one morning, with the table full of work waiting silently, and Fran was reading his Bible and I was reading mine. He suddenly said, "Listen, Edith, I've just come to Ezekiel Thirty-three in my reading." And he read the chapter to me. "It seems very clear that the Lord is speaking to me. There is no turning back." We read it and discussed it. We have read this chapter frequently since then. Each time I read it, it seems to speak with fresh strength into our moment of history, this moment in which we have all been placed. The marvel of God's Word is that it was written by the Lord. Oh, yes, it was done through men whom He chose and inspired to write, but it was written to apply to all moments of history in a way which no man could have the wisdom or understanding to do.

"Again the word of the Lord came unto me, saying." This first verse of Ezekiel 33 makes vivid the fact that God is speaking to Ezekiel. In the next verse: "Son of man, speak to the children of thy people, and say unto them . . . ." God is clearly telling Ezekiel to verbalize something clearly so that people can hear with their ears, but also understand with their minds a fact which is to make a difference in their future. What Ezekiel is to say is that when God brings a sword upon the land—or judgment—there is to be a watchman who will stand upon the wall and warn the people in time to do something about the enemy or the coming judgment. That watchman is to blow a trumpet, and that blast is to warn the people *in time.* In fact, the chapter goes on to make it clear that if the person hearing the trumpet is so warned, he will be safe. If not, then he will die. However, if the watchman does not blow the trumpet, the blood of the unwarned people is upon his head.

Here we recognize the compassionate God of the Old Testament. This is a chapter speaking of judgment. Yet it is the place where there is commanded a careful preparation for the warning of the people in time. Actually, there is a strong responsibility placed upon those who are to be watchmen: ". . . if thou dost not speak to warn the wicked from his way, that wicked man shall die in his iniquity; but his blood will I require at thine hand. Nevertheless, if thou warn the wicked of his way to turn from it; if he do not turn from his way, he shall die in his iniquity; but thou hast delivered thy soul" (vv. 8, 9).

"Oh, it doesn't really matter much," you may say. "We'll all be happy in heaven." But the imperative thing for those of us who are believers to notice is that God does not speak to us without meaning. We may not understand the total meaning of his warnings, but they mean *something.* There is meaning to this phrase—*I will require his blood at thine hand*—and to the positive alternative—*but thou hast delivered thy soul.* It is the background for the following verse:

Therefore, O thou son of man, speak unto the house of Israel; Thus ye speak, saying, If our transgressions and our sins be upon us, and we pine away in them, *how should we then live?*
Ezekiel 33:10

It is clear enough. We are meant to verbalize—with understandable content to our words—that which makes it clear that there is a question to be asked. The question for today is—"If humanism has been a failure, if there is no answer to life put forth by men starting with themselves and leaving God out of it all, if the concept of an impersonal, chance universe has brought forth such a chaotic situation as surrounds us today, *how should we then live?* What is the answer to life?" In other words, this question must be asked, to be placed in men's and women's minds to shake them and to make them think. We have a responsibility to do something that will be in the hearing of people, even as a watchman would be out there on the wall where people could see him and hear the warning blast of his trumpet.

The title of my husband's book and film series was chosen from this verse—*How Should We Then Live?* As the documentary traces the periods of Western history and culture from the time of the Romans until now, it becomes clear that humanism has failed. Any daily newspaper you pick up on the stands helps to illustrate the fact that Utopia has not been attained. We pray that every unbeliever, non-Christian, or lost person with no answers for life who sees this film series or reads the book may ask in some way, "How should we then live?"—not as an academic question but as a cry from deep inside where true search dwells.

God's answer in Ezekiel is one of tenderness and compassion. This is the God of the Old Testament who is also the God of the New Testament, and the same—yesterday, today, and forever. "Say unto them, As I live, saith the Lord God, I have no pleasure in the death of the wicked; but that the wicked turn from his way and live: turn ye, turn ye from your evil ways; for why will ye die, O house of Israel?" (v. 11). The trumpet sound, the call to stop and consider the sin and the judgment to come, was a call to turn to God. How? We know that the way has always been the same, always through the Lamb of God. The lambs in the Old Testament worship looked forward to the coming Messiah—the Lamb of God who would take away the sins of the world. Ezekiel 18:31 speaks of the casting away of transgressions and making "a new heart and a new spirit," even as it goes on in the next verse to say the same thing concerning God's lack of pleasure in the death of the wicked. The New Testament tells us that we can be new creatures in Christ Jesus, the Lamb of God, who makes it possible for all things to become new to us. The answer which God gives in Ezekiel's time is also the one we are to speak of in this time. This message He has given us to pass on is to turn

away from evil and turn to God. We know from all of Scripture that the
way is always through the blood of the Lamb.

This is not a time to turn back from the rough sides of our dark tunnel
of work, wherever we are in our lives, in whatever tunnel the Lord has
for us in His plan for us as individuals. Come to the last few verses of
Ezekiel 33:

> Also, thou son of man, the children of thy people still are
> talking against thee by the walls and in the doors of the houses,
> and speak one to another, every one to his brother, saying,
> Come, I pray you, and hear what is the word that cometh forth
> from the Lord. And they come unto thee as the people cometh,
> and they sit before thee as my people, and they hear thy words,
> but they will not do them: for with their mouth they shew
> much love, but their heart goeth after their covetousness. And,
> lo, thou art unto them as a very lovely song of one that hath a
> pleasant voice, and can play well on an instrument: for they
> hear thy words, but they do them not.
>
> Ezekiel 33:30–32

How strong is the Word of God. As sharp as a two-edged sword. Here
we so easily find ourselves at times. It is such a warning to us as God's
people. It is easy to listen to the Word of God through His servants or
directly from the Bible—and to listen as though it were all a symphony
concert. We thrill with the delicate violin notes, shiver with pleasure at
the true tones of the recorder or flute, and feel satisfied with the crash of
cymbals and drums. Then we go out into the night with a sigh and say to
someone, "Wasn't it all lovely? It was marvelously satisfying tonight. I
felt that music all through my body, as if I had been an instrument
myself." Then we go home and go to bed.

But we are told here strongly that covetousness is a barrier, a stopping
place, between *hearing* the Word of God (and even speaking praise
with our mouths full of words of love) and *doing* the Word of God. The
Word of God is not to be heard as lovely ˎ.usic and then walked away
from. Covetousness—of money, material things, time, human honor,
acceptance, success, and a variety of other crass and subtle things—can
become a sudden wall which stops us from being the kind of people
which God means us to be, for our own sakes, for His glory, and for the
needs of the lost people around us. The question *How should we then
live?* needs to be asked by each of us who are Christians, too. *In the
light of all this being true, how should we then live?*